SWORDS INTO PLOWSHARES

SWORDS INTO PLOWSHARES

NONVIOLENT DIRECT ACTION FOR DISARMAMENT

Edited by Arthur J. Laffin and Anne Montgomery

PERENNIAL LIBRARY

Harper & Row, Publishers, San Francisco

Cambridge, Hagerstown, New York, Philadelphia, Washington
London, Mexico City, São Paulo, Singapore, Sydney

Acknowledgment is made for the following: Marcia A. Timmel's essay was awarded first prize in a competition for women sponsored by the Bi-lateral Nuclear Freeze Task Force of the Los Angeles Section, National Council of Jewish Women. Used by permission. "Journey to Missouri" by Martin Holladay was first printed in April/May 1985 *Fellowship* magazine as "Letter from the County Jail." Used by permission of the Fellowship of Reconciliation. "Two Views of United States Federal Spending" is based on information from the pamphlet "Your Income Tax Dollars at Work," published by the War Resisters League, and is used by permission. "International Aggression and Nonmilitary Defense" by Ronald J. Sider and Richard K. Taylor. Copyright 1983 Christian Century Foundation. Reprinted by permission from the 06/6-13/83 issue of *The Christian Century*. "Civil Disobedience as Prayer" by James Douglass, and "Obedience in the Beloved Community" and "Not Guilty" by Shelley Douglass first appeared in *Ground Zero*, and are used by permission.

FIRST EDITION

Library of Congress Cataloging-in-Publication Data

Swords into plowshares.

  Bibliography: p.
  1. Nuclear disarmament.   2. Antinuclear movement—
United States. I. Laffin, Arthur J. II. Montgomery, Anne.
JX1974.7.S97   1987   327.1'74   86-45019
ISBN 0-06-064911-9

87 88 89 90 91 MPC 10 9 8 7 6 5 4 3 2 1

Dedicated to those without names,
  the disappeared, the tortured,
  the forgotten prisoners of conscience,
in gratitude for their gift to us of courage and fidelity,
and the love that unites us on the long road to peace.

Opposite: Banner draped across a Patriot Missile launcher on Easter 1984 during a Plowshares disarmament action at the Martin Marietta plant in Orlando, Florida. The eight participants in this action, known now as the Pershing Plowshares, hammered and poured blood on Pershing II missile components at the plant, as well as this missile launcher. The eight were apprehended an hour later and were eventually convicted of depredation of government property and conspiracy. *Photo from the office of the U.S. Attorney in Orlando, Florida.*

And they shall beat their swords into plowshares,
  and their spears into pruning hooks;
nation shall not lift up sword against nation,
  neither shall they learn war any more.

—Isaiah 2:4 (RSV)

CONTENTS

CONTRIBUTORS

Arthur J. Laffin is a lay Catholic and a member of the Isaiah Peace Ministry and Witness for Disarmament in New Haven, Connecticut, and the east coast-based Atlantic Life Community. He has been actively involved in full-time peace and justice work since 1978, and has focused his efforts on organizing and participating in nonviolent acts opposing the international nuclear weapons buildup, U.S. military intervention in Central America, and U.S. domestic policies that hurt the poor. He has served six months in jail for his involvement in the Trident Nein Plowshares Action. He often speaks and writes on the biblical call to peacemaking and nonviolent resistance, and is coauthor of *The Risk of the Cross*. In the past, he has worked part-time with emotionally disturbed children and has helped to coordinate a housing education program for the homeless.

Anne Montgomery, one of the original Plowshares Eight, is a sister of the Sacred Heart, and a member of the Kairos Peace Community in New York City. She lives and prays with the Aletheia Community on Washington Square, and teaches adults in East Harlem. In the past, she has taught children with learning disabilities. She has served a total of two years and five months in jail for her participation in the Trident Nein Plowshares Action and the Pershing Plowshares Action.

Robert Aldridge was a design engineer for Lockheed Missiles and Space Company for sixteen years, working on the Polaris, Poseidon, and Trident missile systems. When he resigned his job for reasons of conscience, he was group leader responsible for design of the MK 500 MARV, a type of multiple-warhead missile with first-strike military potential. A father and grandfather, he is an outspoken critic of U.S. nuclear policy. An author of numerous articles on the nuclear peril, he has also written several books, including *First Strike*.

John Bach served thirty-five months in prison for draft resistance during the Vietnam War. He is actively involved in disarmament and anti-intervention work as well as the sanctuary movement. He lives in a collective in Hartford, Connecticut, where he is a housepainter.

Agnes Bauerlein is a mother of eleven and grandmother of eight. A Dutch immigrant, she lived during World War II in Nazi-occupied Holland, where her family gave shelter to Jews under persecution. A member of the AVCO Plowshares, she is founder and staff person of the Montgomery County Center for Peace and Justice in Ambler, Pennsylvania.

Judith Beaumont is a Benedictine sister from Chicago and former teacher. A member of the Trident Nein Plowshares action, she is actively involved in disarmament and social justice work. She lives in a religious community in Hartford, Connecticut, where she works at a shelter for homeless women and their children.

Daniel Berrigan is a Jesuit priest, poet, and longtime worker for peace and justice. A member of the Catonsville Nine and Plowshares Eight, he has been arrested and jailed for numerous acts of nonviolent resistance. He has also taught at the college and seminary levels and is actively involved in working with the terminally ill and people afflicted with AIDS. He is the author of over twenty books, including *The Nightmare of God* and *Steadfastness of the Saints*.

Philip Berrigan was the first American Catholic priest imprisoned for opposing the Vietnam War. Arrested and jailed numerous times for acts of resistance to superpower nuclear war preparations, he was part of the Catonsville Nine, a defendant in the Harrisburg conspiracy trial, and a member of the Plowshares Eight. In the early 1970s he and his wife, Elizabeth McAlister, founded Jonah House, a Christian resistance community in Baltimore. A father of three, he is the author of many articles and books, including *Widen the Prison Gates* and *Of Beasts and Beastly Images: Essays Under the Bomb*.

James Douglass is cofounder and a core member of the Ground Zero

Center for Nonviolent Action in Poulsbo, Washington, and longtime disarmament activist. He has been arrested and jailed repeatedly for his nonviolent resistance to the nuclear buildup by the superpowers. A father and writer, he is the author of *The Nonviolent Cross, Resistance and Contemplation,* and *Lightning East to West.*

Shelley Douglass is cofounder and core member of the Ground Zero Center for Nonviolent Action. A mother and writer, she has been arrested and jailed for acts of nonviolent resistance to the nuclear weapons buildup. She is a member and candidate for the ministry of the United Church of Canada.

William Durland is a teacher, lawyer, theologian, author, and peace activist. He is a founder and coordinator of the National Center on Law and Pacifism (now called Center Peace) and presently teaches religious social concerns at Pendle Hill, a Quaker study and contemplation center near Philadelphia.

Russell F. Ford is a former Wesleyan University student and a draft registration resister. He has been actively involved in anti–draft registration work and has participated in many acts of nonviolent resistance to protest U.S. nuclear and intervention policies.

Martin Holladay is a gardener and carpenter from Wheelock, Vermont. On February 19, 1985, he carried out the twelfth Plowshares action, using his hammer on the lid of a Minuteman missile silo near Odessa, Missouri. He was given an eight-year prison sentence for this action, and was sent to the Federal Prison in Danbury, Connecticut. His sentence was reduced in September 1986 to time already served, and he was released.

Carl Kabat is an Oblate priest. From 1965 to 1968 he worked as a missionary in the Philippines and from 1969 to 1973 he worked among the poor in Recife, Brazil. A member of the Plowshares Eight, Plowshares Number Seven, and the Silo Pruning Hooks, he has been arrested and jailed repeatedly for his nonviolent opposition to the nuclear arms race. He is currently serving an eighteen-year prison sentence at the federal prison in Milan, Michigan, for the Silo Pruning Hooks action.

Paul Kabat is an Oblate priest who has been a longtime peace and justice worker in the Midwest. Also a member of the Silo Pruning Hooks, he is currently serving a ten-year prison sentence for this action at Federal Prison in Sandstone, Minnesota.

Sidney Lens, who died on June 18, 1986, was an inspiration to many. He was a labor organizer and veteran civil rights and peace activist. He was senior editor of *The Progressive* magazine and author of numerous articles and over twenty books, including *The Day Before Doomsday.* We, the editors, rejoice in his untiring commitment to justice and peace.

Roger Ludwig, a poet and musician, is former associate pastor for the Framingham Methodist Church. He has been a volunteer worker with the homeless in Washington, D.C., at the Community for Creative Nonviolence. He participated in the Plowshares Number Four and Trident II Pruning Hooks Plowshares actions.

Thomas Lumpkin is a diocesan priest who lives at Day House, a Catholic Worker community in Detroit, Michigan. He is a member of the Detroit Peace Community.

Elmer Maas is a musician and former college professor. A member of the Plowshares Eight and Plowshares Number Four, he has been actively involved in the nonviolent movement for disarmament. He is a member of the Isaiah Peace Ministry in New Haven, Connecticut.

Elizabeth McAlister is a mother of three children and longtime peace and justice worker. Cofounder of the Jonah House Community in Baltimore, she has been arrested and imprisoned for nonviolently resisting nuclear war preparations by the superpowers. A member of the Griffiss Plowshares action, she served a three-year prison sentence at the Alderson Women's Prison in West Virginia.

Stacey Lynn Merkt, a former member of the Koinonia Community in Georgia and Catholic Worker community in Colorado, has been actively involved in working with Central American refugees. She and Jack Elder were the first North Americans to be indicted for transporting "illegal" Central American refugees. She and her husband live in Texas near the Mexican border where they work with Salvadoran and Guatemalan refugees.

Larry Cloud Morgan, a Native American, is a member of the Ojibway Nation. For eighteen years he worked in Chicago at the Native American Outpost, a mental health clinic. He has been actively involved in Indian affairs and in the Minneapolis Catholic Worker. A member of the Silo Pruning Hooks action, he is currently serving an eight-year prison sentence at the federal prison in Terre Haute, Indiana, as a result of this action.

Larry Rosebaugh is an Oblate priest. He worked for six years during the 1970s as a missionary with the poor in Recife, Brazil. He has also lived and worked with the homeless in Chicago and New York. A member of the Milwaukee Fourteen, he has been arrested and served lengthy prison sentences for nonviolent acts of resistance to U.S. nuclear and intervention policies.

Molly Rush is one of the Plowshares Eight. Since 1973 she has been a staff person at the Thomas Merton Center, a ministry for peace and justice in Pittsburgh. She is a mother of six children and grandmother of three.

Ronald Sider is a Mennonite theologian and professor of theology at Eastern Baptist Theological Seminary. He is the author of *Rich Christians in an Age of Hunger,* coauthor of *Nuclear Holocaust and Christian Hope,* and coeditor of *Transformation: An International Dialogue on Evangelical Social Ethics.*

Richard Taylor cofounded the St. Vincent's Peace Center in Philadelphia and works with the Sojourners Peace Ministry in Washington, D.C. He is coauthor of *Nuclear Holocaust and Christian Hope,* and author of *A Peace Ministry in Practice.*

Marcia Timmel lives at the Dorothy Day Catholic Worker House in Washington, D.C., dedicated to providing shelter for homeless families and doing disarmament work. A member of the Plowshares Number Four action, she is married to Paul Magno, who served a three-year prison sentence for his involvement in the Pershing Plowshares action.

Helen Dery Woodson is the mother of eleven children. Of the seven children still at home (ages four to twenty-five), six have mental and physical handicaps. For eighteen years she ran a day-care center, treatment home, and private school. She founded the Gaudete Peace and Justice Center in 1981 in Madison, Wisconsin, and began publishing *Harvest of Justice*. Since 1982 she has been arrested many times for peace actions. A member of the Silo Pruning Hooks action, she is currently serving a twelve-year prison sentence.

INTRODUCTION

This book is a sharing of experience, of "experiments in truth," and of our reflections on both the experiences and the understandings that emerge from them. It is an unfinished book, not only because the experiments must continue, but because we are always groping toward truth, or rather with each tentative step we find its horizons expanding.

Since there is no one "right" way to say no to death and yes to life, we have tried to include a variety of responses to the violent spirit of militarism that affects everyone today. It is violence synthesized in nuclear weapons, since they have become both the chief means of oppression and control and the excuse for it: the rationale for "security" measures that undermine both human rights and any real participation in policy making. In the face of a rapidly expanding nuclear arms race and an unprecedented commitment on the part of world powers, especially the United States, to pursue their ends through the threat of unlimited violence, the very real danger of nuclear war has become a daily fact of life for every human being on the planet. Recognizing the magnitude of this peril, people, now more than at any time since the Nuclear Age began, are working in a variety of ways to avert the prospect of global holocaust.

Drawing on the rich biblical, Gandhian, and American traditions of nonviolent resistance, people in recent years have increasingly recognized the importance of engaging in acts of civil disobedience, which we prefer to call "divine obedience," as a genuine response of faith and conscience to the nuclear threat and to increasing superpower intervention in the Third World. Our contributors, aware of the blocking of the democratic channels for change, have all spoken the truth directly and creatively with their lives. Some have denied the government the means of warmaking: their money, their skills, their very bodies. Others have dismantled weapons or blocked their transport. Still others have protected sisters and brothers fleeing death squads in countries shielded under our nuclear unbrella.

In common, these people responded in faith to the law of love; they acted in divine obedience. Most stepped across the boundary of human law to demonstrate clearly that unless we resist an unjust law, not only are we complicit in its wrong, but we also strengthen its power over us, the power of love's opposite: fear. In common, our contributors acted (and continue to act) conscious of their own weakness and ordinariness, aware too that only in weakness and darkness can hope become a transforming reality.

Why is civil disobedience or divine obedience an imperative for bringing about disarmament? How does one prepare for these nonviolent actions? How does one respond to the charges brought in court? How does one view and cope with the consequence of jail? The primary goal of this book is to provide some initial answers to these and other related questions.

Part I considers how the nuclear arms race presents an immediate threat to our lives and why people, as a matter of conscience, engage in acts of divine obedience. This section includes a full chronology of Plowshares actions—actions in which people have entered nuclear weapons facilties or military bases and literally enacted the biblical prophecy of "beating swords into plowshares" by disarming components of the first-strike nuclear weapons system with hammers and other symbols. Part II addresses the interpretation and meaning of certain recent acts of civil disobedience and divine obedience, especially the Plowshares actions, and offers reflections on the way some people have responded to the consequences of court and jail. Part III describes the variety of nonviolent resistance actions and forms of noncooperation people have undertaken to oppose nuclear war preparations and policies of military intervention. Part IV includes various Appendices on the nuclear arms race, the immorality and illegality of nuclear weapons, the necessity defense, international laws, and developing a nonmilitary defense. Each of these appendices directly complements the first three parts of the book. Finally,

Part V contains a listing of national peace and disarmament groups as well as of local resistance groups. It also includes an extensive bibliography on the arms race and nonviolent resistance.

We hope that this book will help, in some small way, those who are seeking to clarify what civil disobedience/divine obedience involves and assist them in choosing what act of conscience they might undertake at this critical time. We must continue experimenting in truth rather than intellectualizing about it, not basing actions and decisions on our American obsession with efficiency and effectiveness. Faith assures us that the way will grow into the truth, the truth that sets us free from the fears permeating our culture of death. In that spirit we offer a book that its readers must continue writing.

Anne Montgomery, R.S.C.J.
Arthur J. Laffin

ACKNOWLEDGMENTS

We would like to express our gratitude to many special people who helped make this book a reality.

First, we are grateful to each of those whose contributions, encouragement, and support made this book possible.

We feel a special indebtedness to Elmer Maas who offered invaluable insights and suggestions as well as his time and energy in shaping and editing this work.

We are deeply thankful to Julie O'Reilly for her typing assistance and to James Munves for his editorial help during the preparation of the manuscript.

We wish to thank as well the many dear friends in and outside our communities who have offered us strong encouragement and prayerful support, especially Jonah House, the Aletheia Community, the Religious of the Sacred Heart, and the Laffin family.

We are thankful, too, to our editors, John Shopp and Kandace Hawkinson, for their patience and valuable insights.

Finally, we are grateful to all those whose acts of nonviolent resistance made this book possible.

Arthur J. Laffin
Anne Montgomery, R.S.C.J.

PART ONE

Challenge and Response

A two-day vigil outside the Pentagon on December 28 and 29, 1981, commemorating the Feast of the Holy Innocents. This vigil, sponsored by the Atlantic Life Community, drew 120 people. Six participants were arrested, tried and sentenced to prison terms ranging from 30 days to three months. *Photo by Tom Lewis.*

The taproot of violence in our society today is our intent to use nuclear weapons. Once we have agreed to that all other evil is minor in comparison. Until we squarely face the question of our consent to use nuclear weapons, any hope of large scale improvement of public morality is doomed to failure.

Richard T. McSorley, S.J.

In the face of an order to kill from a human person, the law of God must prevail that says "Thou shall not kill." No soldier is obliged to obey a command that goes against the law of God. No one is required to comply with an immoral law. It is time now that you obey your conscience rather than carry out a sinful command.

Salvadoran Archbishop Oscar Romero, one day before his assassination.

You have heard that it was said, "Love your friends, hate your enemies." But now I tell you: "love your enemies."

Matthew 5:43–44

Chapter 1

THE NUCLEAR CHALLENGE

Arthur J. Laffin

The unleashed power of the atom has changed everything save our mode
of thinking and we, thus, drift toward unparalleled catastrophe.

ALBERT EINSTEIN

With the advent of the Nuclear Age in 1945, Einstein,
who had been instrumental in persuading President Roosevelt to build
the atomic bomb, knew history had been radically changed. He realized that, for the first time ever, humans possessed the capability
to destroy the world. He warned that the world would be destroyed
unless we drastically changed our way of thinking and banned nuclear weapons. The superpowers, led by the United States, have ignored his advice (and that of many others) during the last forty years,
and as a result humanity continues to drift toward unparalleled catastrophe.

In our time, the building of nuclear weapons and the intention to
use them have become the central acts of violence to which all other
forms of violence are linked. The violence of oppression, poverty,
and starvation, the violence of racism, the violence against children
and the unborn, the violence committed against women, the violence
of the street, the violence of state torture and imprisonment, the
violence of superpower intervention around the world, and the subtle
violence of our consumeristic life-styles are all drawn together and
reenacted in the intention to use nuclear weapons.[1]

In this chapter, I examine the unprecedented violence the nuclear
arms race poses for our world and show how the U.S. government
has been directly responsible for perpetuating this race of death and
increasing the risk of nuclear war. I also explore the tragic human,
spiritual, and political consequences resulting from our nation's con-

tinued reliance on nuclear weapons for its primary security. Finally, I reflect on the urgent need for people to choose the way of non-violent resistance in response to the ominous challenge before us.

The Nuclear Arms Race and U.S. Involvement

On August 6, 1945, at 8:16 A.M., the U.S. government dropped the first atomic bomb, made of uranium, on the city of Hiroshima, Japan. Nine seconds later, Hiroshima was destroyed, over a hundred thousand civilians were killed, and over a hundred thousand more were maimed and eventually died from the effects of radiation from the bomb. Sixty-five hours later, the U.S. government used a second nuclear weapon, this time a plutonium bomb, on the Japanese city of Nagasaki, which resulted in a similar holocaust. Many *hibaku-sha*—the Japanese term for A-bomb survivors—continue to suffer and die premature deaths from their exposure to the nuclear radiation released by these bombs.

Contrary to statements that the atomic bomb had to be used to save American lives and end World War II, there is now convincing evidence that it was not necessary to use the bomb for these reasons.

Realizing that Japan was on the verge of surrender as early as July 13, 1945, General Dwight D. Eisenhower, along with Admiral William Leahy, head of the Joint Chiefs of Staff, opposed the use of the bomb. They advised President Harry S. Truman that the Japanese would surrender in several months without the use of the bomb and without invasion. In Leahy's own words: "the use of this barbarous weapon on Hiroshima and Nagasaki was of no material assistance in our war against Japan. The Japanese were already defeated and ready to surrender."[2]

Nuclear weapons were used against the Japanese primarily for two reasons: first, the United States wanted to hasten its victory over Japan without the aid of the Russians, who were about to enter the war; second, and most importantly, Truman intended to threaten the Russians and warn them not to challenge United States plans to organize the postwar world.[3]

Through using these genocidal weapons against the Japanese, the United States set the tone for the already emerging cold war with the Soviets and made clear its future intention to use the bomb, if need be, to protect its rapidly expanding worldwide corporate interests and its quest for global empire. It is within this context that the nuclear arms race began.

As the first nation to build and use nuclear weapons, the United States, not the Soviet Union, was responsible for beginning the nuclear arms race. Now both superpowers continue to perpetuate the arms race, each superpower justifying their nuclear buildup by saying the other superpower constitutes a threat.

Historically, the dynamics of the nuclear arms race can be described as an action-reaction cycle between the United States and the Soviet Union. We need only to review briefly the major developments of the nuclear arms race since 1945 to see why this is so. The United States was the first to develop the atomic bomb, the intercontinental bomber, the hydrogen bomb, the submarine launched ballistic missile (SLBM), the multiple independently-targeted re-entry vehicle (MIRV), the maneuverable reentry vehicle (MARV), and the new cruise, Pershing II, MX, and Trident missiles. A few years after each of these developments, the Soviet Union responded with a comparable weapon. In two exceptions to this pattern, the Soviets first developed the intercontinental ballistic missile (ICBM) in 1957 and the antiballistic missile system (ABM) in 1968. In response, the United States developed an ICBM in 1958 and an ABM in 1972.

During the last four decades, the superpowers have amassed an arsenal exceeding 50,000 nuclear weapons. Together these weapons are over one million times more powerful than the Hiroshima bomb. Currently, the United States and Soviet Union add three to ten nuclear warheads to their stockpiles each day. The United States possesses over 30,000 nuclear warheads (10,000 strategic and 20,000 tactical) capable of destroying every major Soviet city forty times over. The Soviets have over 17,400 nuclear warheads (7,400 strategic and 10,000 tactical) capable of destroying every major U.S. city nearly thirty times over.

Since 1945, the announced nuclear policy of the superpowers has been "deterrence." This policy, also described as Mutual Assured Destruction (MAD), is based on the premise that both superpowers will refrain from firing nuclear missiles first because they fear the massive retaliation that would follow. But since the late 1950s, the Pentagon has secretly shifted from this defensive policy to an *offen-*

sive nuclear war strategy of "counterforce" or "first-strike." This strategy is based on the principle of being able to "counter" the enemy's "force" (i.e., strategic weapons and command and control centers) with an initial surprise attack, thereby disabling its capacity to retaliate.

Signs of this strategy first emerged when the secret Single Integrated Operational Plan (SIOP) was approved by the Pentagon in January 1962.[4] This strategy was not announced publicly until May 30, 1975, when Secretary of Defense Schlesinger declared that the United States must have the "flexible option" of targeting "selective" military sites in the Soviet Union. He also said that the United States would consider a "first use" of nuclear weapons to stop a large-scale Communist advance in Western Europe and South Korea.[5] In August 1980, President Carter officially confirmed this strategy upon issuing his Presidential Directive 59.[6] This directive mandates that precision attack missiles be targeted against key Soviet military installations. It also concedes that the United States reserves the right to use nuclear weapons first if its national interests are deemed to be jeopardized, especially in the Persian Gulf. In the case of a perceived attack, this directive clearly authorizes striking *first* at strategic military targets—land-based missiles, airfields, submarines, command centers, and so on.

The Reagan Administration further advanced this counterforce strategy when it issued in 1982 the "Fiscal Year 1984—1988 Defense Guidance." This document calls for U.S. military forces to be prepared to fight and *win* a limited or protracted full-scale nuclear war. To achieve this goal, the document says that American forces must be equipped to "render ineffective the total Soviet (and Soviet allied) military and political power structure."[7] This presupposes the "first use" of nuclear weapons rather than a retaliatory strike.

To reinforce its first-strike posture, the United States, not the Soviet Union, has repeatedly refused to support a "no first use" policy of nuclear weapons. To enable the United States to carry out a successful "first-strike," the Pentagon, the Reagan administration, and Congress have authorized the stepped-up production of a new generation of "first-strike" land-, air-, and sea-based multiple warhead systems that will have unprecedented destructive capability as well as the precision accuracy necessary to destroy specific strategic military targets (i.e., missile silos, airbases, etc.). These weapons include the MX missile, the cruise and Pershing II missiles (now being deployed in Europe), and the Trident D-5 missile. Moreover, to make these and other nuclear weapons systems invulnerable, even invincible, billions of dollars are being poured into the research and development of offensive and defensive laser weapons to be used as part of the new "Star Wars" program (Strategic Defense Initiative).[8] The Soviets have responded by developing similar weapons such as the Typhoon submarine, the Backfire Bomber, and the SS-20 and SSNX-18 missiles.[9]

The development of these first-strike weapons is inherently destabilizing because they serve to create the very condition they are intended to avoid. In the event of a crisis between the superpowers, both sides, each acutely aware of the other's first-strike capability, will now be tempted to use their weapons first for fear of losing them.

Another dangerous dimension of U.S. first-strike posture has been a growing reliance on computers. In recent years, U.S. early warning computers, designed to announce when the United States is under attack, have malfunctioned numerous times. For example, in 1979 and the first part of 1980, there were 3,703 "routine missile display conferences"—low-level, false alerts of nuclear attack. However, several of these alerts were serious enough to come within minutes of launching a nuclear war.[10] Dr. Paul Walker (a national security and nuclear weapons analyst), testifying at the trial of Plowshares activist Martin Holladay in April 1985, stated that, according to congressional testimony by Air Force officials in 1981, there are an average of seven false alerts a day.[11] With both superpowers now developing a sophisticated "launch-on-warning" strategy, which will authorize the firing of endangered missiles at first warning, the risk of nuclear war caused by a computer error greatly increases.[12]

Further compounding the threat of nuclear war is the "deadly connection" between nuclear weapons and military intervention.[13] Ever since the United States used the bomb against the Japanese, it has become the cornerstone of U.S. military and foreign policy. To protect the interests of U.S. multinational corporations and enforce its imperialistic system of dominating smaller nations, the U.S. government has consistently relied on the threat of using nuclear weapons. On at least ten occasions since 1945, U.S. presidents have threatened to use the bomb against other nations. Such threats were made against Iran in 1946, Korea in 1953, Vietnam in 1953 and 1958, and Cuba in 1962.[14] Without a credible nuclear threat, the United States could not carry out its interventionist policies. Nor could the United States, which has only 6 percent of the world's population, continue to control more than 40 percent of the world's resources for its own consumption.[15]

Both superpowers have exercised their superior military strength through direct acts of military intervention and through offering military assistance to numerous countries throughout the world.[16] Today there are some forty wars being waged worldwide in which each superpower has a vested interest. The United States is now employing a strategy of "low intensity warfare" in several Central American countries, causing great instability and human suffering in that region of the world.[17] As the United States and the Soviet Union continue to vie for control of key geopolitical areas (i.e., the Middle East, Central America, Asia, and Africa) and export sophisticated conventional arms and other military aid, especially to some of the most volatile parts of the world, each conflict of our day, however remote or limited, has the potential to spark a nuclear confrontation between the superpowers.[18]

Furthermore, the ability to use nuclear weapons is no longer limited just to the superpowers—at least fifteen additional countries beside the six nations that already have nuclear weapons are rapidly acquiring nuclear technology and the know-how to produce nuclear weapons.

All of these factors increase the probability that somewhere, sometime, nuclear weapons will be used (the nuclear doomsday clock has been placed at three minutes to midnight by the *Bulletin of the Atomic Scientists*). Despite this and despite irrefutable scientific and medical evidence that a nuclear war would kill or seriously injure, at the very least, over two billion people and produce a "nuclear winter" that would drastically alter the earth's atmosphere, thereby endangering all life, the United States continues to escalate the arms race by developing new first strike weapons. Thus the threat of nuclear war is increasingly imminent.

The Human Cost

If the world were a global village of 100 people, one-third of them would be rich or of moderate income, two-thirds would be poor. Of the 100 residents, forty-seven would be unable to read and only one would have a college education. About thirty-five would be suffering from hunger and malnutrition, at least half would be homeless or living in substandard housing.

If the world were a global village of 100 people, six of them would be Americans. These six would have over a third of the village's entire income, and the other 94 could subsist on the other two-thirds. How could the wealthy six live "in peace" with their neighbors? Surely they would be driven to arm themselves against the other ninety-four—perhaps even to spend, as Americans do, about twice as much per person on military defense as the total income of two-thirds of the villagers.[19]

The threat of nuclear violence and the use of military force have clearly become the U.S. government's chief means of maintaining its control over much of the earth's global village and enhancing its worldwide political and economic interests.[20] The end result of this means of control has been exploitation, suffering, and death for countless people worldwide.

The U.S.-led nuclear arms race has claimed and continues to claim a host of innocent victims. In her article "The Early Crimes of World War III," Dr. Rosalie Bertell, an expert on the health effects of nuclear technology, conservatively estimates that the global victims of fallout from nuclear testing number almost 16 million, with genetic damage being passed on from generation to generation until each family dies out. Dr. Bertell also claims that the past forty years of weapons production have caused some 2.3 million radiation victims. Moreover, she contends that between 36,700 and 78,300 new victims are generated each year by nuclear weapons production, by the "routine" pollution of uranium mining, refining and enrichment, by nuclear power plants' reprocessing, transportation, and waste disposal activities.[21]

Nuclear accidents like those that occurred at Three Mile Island in March 1979 and Chernobyl in April 1986 clearly underscore the fallibility of nuclear technology and the great peril nuclear radiation fallout poses for life. And as we know from the Chernobyl accident, radiation fallout knows no territorial boundaries—it can affect people hundreds even thousands of miles away. As long as this lethal nuclear technology exists, accidents like these will inevitably occur and more people will continue to suffer and die.

The human cost of the nuclear arms race, however, is not just limited to the effects of nuclear radiation. The nuclear arms race also has a devastating effect on the poor. Presently the nations of the world, led by the superpowers, spend over $800 billion annually on military purposes, a sum far greater than the total annual income of the poorer half of the world's population. For the two-thirds of the population living in subhuman conditions, this exorbitant military spending means unrelieved poverty and massive suffering.

The United Nations documents that over one billion people in developing countries cannot afford the basic necessities of life. Over 750 million people of the Third World, more than the combined population of the United States and Soviet Union are seriously malnourished. In Ethiopia alone, more than 10 million people now face imminent starvation. And it is estimated that nearly 50,000 children die daily from hunger-related diseases worldwide. The tragic reality of our time is that in pounds per person the world has more explosive power than food! Hence, even if nuclear and conventional weapons are never used, by their cost alone they kill the poor by causing them to starve.

It is not only in Third World countries that the needs of millions are sacrificed at the expense of sustaining the nuclear arms race. In the United States, over 35 million people live below the poverty line, and another 15 to 20 million just barely eke out an existence. Today, one in every four children under six is poor and nearly 10 million children are without adequate medical care. Of the 19 percent of U.S. families headed by women, one-third are poor—and among black and Hispanic families headed by women, the rate is over 50 percent. It is estimated that about 25 million people in the United States are illiterate, between 1 and 3 million are homeless, and almost 10 million are unemployed (during the course of a year almost one in three black workers and one in four Hispanic workers experience some unemployment).[22] The United States also has the fourteenth-highest infant mortality rate in the world.

Meanwhile, the Reagan administration (which has increased the budget deficit to two hundred billion dollars and extended the national debt to over a trillion dollars) has spent over *a trillion dollars* on the military budget since 1981 and will have spent an equal amount by 1988. This excessive military spending only serves to perpetuate a permanent war economy at the expense of great economic deprivation and abject poverty for millions.[23]

In the final analysis, the violence of the nuclear arms race not only threatens the survival of the human family but claims countless lives now.

Idolatry, Nuclearism and the National Security State

There is a general assumption in the United States that, despite the colossal threat nuclear weapons pose, they are still absolutely necessary for maintaining national security. Even the majority of those who oppose further U.S. nuclear war preparations still favor retaining a small nuclear stockpile as a credible deterrent against foreign aggression. Spawned by a deep-seated violence that, since the beginning of recorded history, has possessed the human heart, nuclear weapons have in fact become an idol in which many people place their trust. The words of the prophet Isaiah describe well our present situation:

The people follow foreign customs. Their land is full of silver and gold, and there is no end to their treasures . . . there is no end to their chariots [weapons]. Their land is full of idols and they worship idols made by their own hands.

(Isa. 2:6–8, TEV)

In short, the nuclear idol is a product of a society that has placed its complete trust in military power and material security.

Since the state first developed nuclear weapons, it has consistently fostered the belief that the bomb represents our ultimate security as a nation. This sole dependence on nuclear weapons for our security is what Robert Jay Lifton and Richard Falk describe as "nuclearism." In their book *Indefensible Weapons,* Lifton and Falk define nuclearism as the "psychological, political and military dependence on nuclear weapons, the embrace of the weapons as a solution to a wide variety of human dilemmas, most ironically that of 'security'."[24] For forty-one years the state has instilled nuclearism into the American psyche to such a degree that it has virtually become a national religion.

Contrary to God's commands "Thou shall have no other gods before me," and "Do not bow down to any idol and worship it," (Deut. 5:7, 9, TEV), the state has defied these commands by placing its authority above God's, demanding *absolute* loyalty from its citizens and imposing a religion of nuclearism on the nation. As Elizabeth McAlister has succinctly stated:

There is in the U.S. a fully developed religion that is state-sponsored and initiated. It is a phenomenon that remains unanalyzed. Religious values, along with everything else, are being trammeled by the threat of nuclear annihilation. And it touches the very heart of our faith.

This is a constitutional issue because it violates the First Amendment, which states that no national religion should be established. This state-sponsored religion has many names, but basically it is a religion of national sovereignty or nuclearism. It has its gods, its high priests, its ritual; it is preeminent. And it compels people to acts prohibited by God's law, thus violating our freedom of religion.

This national religion compels a loyalty based on our acceptance of the existence of nuclear weapons as a necessity—they are the source of security. We must—to be good citizens—pay for them, thank God for them. The weapons become sacred objects—a worship forbidden by the first commandment of God.

Moreover, this religion prohibits the acts of justice required by the law of God: to refrain from killing or preparing to kill, to rescue the victims of murder and to intercede on their behalf. It names these acts as crimes.[25]

To pledge our ultimate allegiance to the state and to place our security in idols of death betrays our faith in God and constitutes the ultimate blasphemy.

Despite the Pentagon's attempt to seduce us into accepting the religion of nuclearism, the truth is that the bomb can only destroy life. And deterrence only serves to perpetuate and legitimate the arms race for the government and for those corporations making huge profits from manufacturing these weapons of genocide. However people may try to justify the existence of nuclear weapons, it is *immoral* to build and deploy them.

Increasing numbers of people within the churches and from various faiths and walks of life are coming to the conclusion that to rely on weapons of mass murder for our security is idolatrous and can only lead to the eventual use of these weapons and to the extinction of all life. One noteworthy sign of this changing consciousness is the United Methodist Bishops' peace pastoral letter, "In Defense of Creation," released in June 1986. In their letter the bishops proclaim a "clear and unconditional no" to any use of nuclear weapons and state that "deterrence must no longer receive the churches' blessing, even as a temporary warrant for the maintenance of nuclear weapons." Going beyond the U.S. Catholic bishops stance which offers a "conditional acceptance" of nuclear deterrence as long as active measures for disarmament are pursued, the Methodist bishops further assert that deterrence has become a "dogmatic license for perpetual hostility between the Superpowers" and has "too long been revered as the unquestioned idol of national security." They call for end to the "idolatrous connection between the ideology of deterrence and the existence of the weapons themselves." True security can only be found in that which enhances life, not death.

Blind to this truth, the most powerful political, military, scientific, and business leaders of the nation have consistently invoked "national security" to foster nuclearism. As people have acquiesced to nuclearism, the government has assumed control over every facet of nuclear weapons policy. To "secure" its total control of nuclear weapons, the government has given itself wide-ranging powers, including the right to maintain a high level of secrecy regarding its nuclear policy. From the time of the Manhattan Project in 1942, when the government began serious research on nuclear weapons, U.S. nuclear policy has been veiled in a shroud of secrecy.

What has in fact emerged here is a "national security state," created by a political power elite which uses secrecy, surveillance, economic influence, and military force to fashion a national and global economic and political system for its own ends. The national security state was institutionalized in 1947 when the Truman Administration, seeking to maintain its control over the post-war world and protect growing U.S. economic and military interests around the world, issued the National Security Act, creating the National Security Council (NSC), the Central Intelligence Agency (CIA), and what is now the Department of Defense. The role of the NSC, comprised of the president's top military and political advisers, is to determine for the president all foreign and domestic policies relating to U.S. national security interests. The CIA is responsible for coordinating all governmental intelligence activities. The Department of Defense is responsible for determining U.S. military policy and directing the nation's Armed Forces.

The National Security Act also extended certain emergency powers to the president beyond those given in the U.S. Consitution (the Constitution already gives the president the *exclusive* power to initiate, direct, and enact U.S. military policy). These emergency powers—all pertaining to national security interests—include the prerogative to suspend civil liberties under certain circumstances and to undertake normally illegal covert operations ranging from wiretaps to widespread surveillance. Furthermore, recent presidents, including Reagan, have interpreted these powers so broadly that they have actually authorized military actions to destabilize and overthrow governments whose political or ideological orientations are different from those of the United States (i.e., Vietnam, Chile, Grenada, Nicaragua, and Libya). Such acts of intervention violate the United Nations Charter and are unconstitutional because they interfere with a nation's right to self-determination.

Among other things, the National Security Act gives the president unlimited power to determine when nuclear weapons will be used. There is *no* public participation in any decision to use the bomb. This was made explicit in early 1948 in the NSC's first policy document on nuclear war, NSC-30—"Policy on Atomic Warfare." NSC-30 stated, in part, that the ultimate decision on employment of nuclear weapons in the event of war is entrusted solely to the president.[26] It went on to say that any public debate of the possibility of *not* using nuclear weapons was unacceptable. Furthermore, the document contended that if there was any public dissent about U.S. nuclear policy, it would only encourage the Russians to think that the United States might hesitate to use nuclear weapons and thereby provoke exactly the kind of Soviet aggression the United States seeks to avert. The conclusion of NSC-30 makes this point very clear:

Were the U.S. to decide against or publicly debate the issue of the use of the atomic bomb on moral grounds, this country might gain the praise of the world's radical fringe and would certainly receive applause from the

Soviet bloc, but the U.S. would be thoroughly condemned by every sound citizen in Western Europe, whose enfeebled security this country would obviously be threatening.[27]

Four years after NSC-30, President Truman, in an effort to maintain even greater secrecy surrounding U.S. nuclear/military policy and intelligence activities, issued a seven-page memorandum ordering the establishment of an agency to be known as the National Security Agency (NSA). Classified as top secret, this seven-page order, which has never been made public, remains the "foundation upon which all past and current communication intelligence activities of the U.S. government are based."[28] The NSA, which has been referred to by different political and military officials as the most secretive member of the intelligence community and as more powerful than the CIA, is now the largest U.S. intelligence agency, numbering more than sixty-eight thousand people.[29] No law has ever been enacted prohibiting the NSA from engaging in any activity; it is, in fact, the *only* governmental agency to be exempt from any congressional or legal accountability.

With the NSC, CIA, and NSA firmly in place, government officials during the height of the Cold War and the McCarthy era began to invoke "national security" as a catch-all phrase to justify violating the civil rights of people and lying about or withholding from Congress specific information concerning U.S. military and foreign policy matters. The lies of the "Bomber Gap" in the 1950s and the "Missile Gap" in the 1960s and the lie of using the "Communist threat" and the "domino theory" to justify waging war in Vietnam are poignant examples of this governmental deception.

Despite this behavior by the government, the invocation of "national security" to restrict the release of information about "top secret" military matters is rarely challenged. Current examples of this are the restriction of information on the specific military role of the Space Shuttle Program and the research and development of "Star Wars" weapons.

Although information about nuclear weapons and U.S. military policy has become more readily available, the decision-making process remains essentially removed from the public. We need only to scrutinize the War Powers Resolution (enacted by Congress on November 7, 1973) to underscore this point. According to this resolution, the president can for up to sixty days authorize any military action necessary to protect national security interests. The president is urged to notify Congress before authorizing such action, and required to do so within 48 hours of authorizing such action. For the president to continue authorizing military action beyond the sixty day period, Congress must have approved a declaration of war, approved the president's use of armed forces, or approved an extension of the president's power to authorize such actions for an additional period of time. In light of this, the power of Congress to limit a presidential order authorizing the use of nuclear weapons is remote.

We, therefore, have a situation today where President Reagan (or any president) can not only bomb civilians in Libya, invade Grenada, send troops to and authorize bombing raids in Lebanon and El Salvador, and mine the harbors of Nicaragua without prior congressional approval, but can authorize the use of nuclear weapons if he feels the situation warrants it. The decision to use nuclear weapons would be carried out in essentially the same secretive manner as was the decision to use the bomb against the Japanese.

Congress has done little to challenge this gross abuse of power by the president. Even when the World Court ruled in July 1986 that the Reagan administration violated international law by its military aggression against the people of Nicaragua, Congress failed to take action against the administration's illegal activities. Instead, a majority of both the House of Representatives and the Senate voted to approve one hundred million dollars in military aid to support the terrorist actions of the CIA-backed Contras seeking to overthrow the popularly elected Nicaraguan government. Also Congress has never seriously questioned the high level of secrecy and exclusion of the public surrounding nuclear policy. Its appropriation of money for first-strike weapons and other nuclear war preparations and its support of the War Powers Resolution, indicates that the overwhelming majority of elected officials, both Democrats and Republicans, have succumbed to the interests of the "national security state."

Many people still believe that the president and his advisers, all of whom unequivocally support a first-strike nuclear war–fighting capability, somehow will bring about disarmament. However, after forty-one years of superpower summitry and over six thousand arms talks, the U.S. government has failed to disarm and abandon its nuclear war–fighting policy. Our government talks disarmament in Geneva while deploying first-strike weapons designed to achieve nuclear superiority over the Soviets.

The growth of the "national security state" in the United States is a clear assault on our democratic liberties. And U.S. deployment of nuclear weapons is a clear violation of both U.S. and international law.

International law accords ranging from the Hague conferences in 1899 and 1907 and the Geneva Protocol in 1925 to the Nuremberg Charter of 1945, have prohibited weapons of indiscriminate or mass destruction (nuclear weapons inherently fit this definition). And the U.N. General Assembly in 1961 declared the use of nuclear weapons a direct violation of the U.N. charter and international law. A section of the resolution, which appears in Appendix 3, states: "The use of nuclear and thermonuclear weapons would exceed even the scope of war and cause indiscriminate suffering and destruction to humankind and civilization and, as such, is contrary to the rules of international laws and to the laws of humanity.

The United States, by its own Constitution, is supposed to adhere to these international laws. Article VI, paragraph 2 of the U.S. Constitution provides that:

. . . All treaties made, or which shall be made, under the authority of the United States, shall be the supreme law of the land; and the judges in every state shall be bound thereby, any thing in the Constitution or law of any state to the contrary notwithstanding.

Thus the numerous treaties and laws drawn up after World War II that the United States is a party to have the complete force of law and applicability in any U.S. court. They are "the supreme law of the land." Not to uphold these laws is a direct violation of the U.S. constitution as well as international law.

Despite international laws and U.N. declarations that outlaw the preparations for nuclear war and the use of nuclear weapons and other weapons of mass destruction, despite urgent pleas from millions of people in the United States and worldwide for a freeze and eventual abolition of nuclear weapons, and despite recent appeals from the Soviets to join them in ceasing nuclear testing the U.S. government refuses to begin the process of disarmament. It has proven itself incapable of initiating and producing true disarmament. To place our hope for disarmament in a government that has become morally bankrupt by power and self-interest is an illusion.

The Challenge Before Us

In a nation where state-sanctioned nuclearism endangers all life, where crimes against humanity are daily being prepared for, where the public is excluded from the decision-making process about nuclear policy, and where all conventional political channels have seemingly proved futile for beginning true disarmament, what is the duty of the individual? It is not an overstatement to compare our present nuclear situation with that of the German citizens during the genocidal campaign of the Nazis. In response to that genocide, the Nuremberg War Crimes Tribunal reiterated that "individuals have international duties which transcend the national obligations of obedience imposed by the individual state."[31] The Nuremberg Charter imposes upon citizens the *duty* to violate domestic laws to prevent crimes against peace and humanity from occurring. Furthermore the laws of God mandate us to nonviolently resist unjust laws that sanction killing and other acts of violence.

As the U.S. government and nuclear weapons manufacturers continue to escalate the nuclear arms race through their first-strike nuclear war preparations, it is up to us ordinary people to begin the process of disarmament. History has repeatedly shown that most political change is preceded by direct action and resistance by the populace. To prevent our government from carrying out the ultimate crime of committing global murder, we must engage in direct acts of nonviolent resistance in keeping with our faith and political traditions.

In recent years a growing movement of nonviolent resistance has emerged. Thousands of people across the country, many for the first time, have engaged in acts of nonviolent resistance. They have demanded an end to the arms race, to superpower intervention in the Third World, especially U.S. intervention in Central America, and to U.S. support for the white minority government of South Africa. Nonviolent resistance has also increased dramatically on the international level.

This nonviolent movement is cause for great hope, for it is only through this movement of conscience that true peace and justice will come about. Peace camps, mass demonstrations, vigils, blockades, tax resistance, peace walks, sit-ins, boycotts, fasts, plowshares-disarmament actions, and many other creative nonviolent acts are all powerful expressions of individual commitment to peace and justice.

At this critical moment in history, people of faith and conscience face a moral imperative to translate their beliefs into nonviolent action for life. We all must assume responsibility to avert the destruction of our planet by nuclear war. We must join in solidarity with the growing national and worldwide movement of those of faith and conscience who are working to create a just society and world where the dignity of each person is upheld.

To effect the truly radical change we seek—the eradication of the "national security state," the abolition of war, and the establishment of just political, economic and social order—we must take more frequent direct action on both the local and the national level, and we must take greater risks. We must do more than hold sporadic demonstrations, sign petitions, and vote every four years. When more people participate in nonviolent direct action at places where policy decisions are made and carried out, where weapons systems are researched, built, tested, transported, and stored, and when these actions are sustained over a long period of time, change will occur.

While we all desire a world of peace and justice, we often fear the changes we might have to make in our lives to bring it about. We shudder at the thought of reorienting our careers, relinquishing certain consumeristic addictions, or struggling through a relationship with a loved one with whom we might have moral and political differences. We are overwhelmed by the prospect of prison should we engage in certain acts of resistance. Yet we know that if peace and justice are to become a reality, we have to make some sacrifices in our lives. In his book, *No Bars to Manhood,* written shortly after the Catonsville Nine trial and sentencing in 1970, Daniel Berrigan speaks directly to this point:

We have assumed the name of peacemakers, but we have been, by and large, unwilling to pay any significant price. And because we want peace with half a heart and half a life and will, the war, of course, continues, because the waging of war, by its very nature, is total—but the waging of peace, by our own cowardice, is partial. So a whole will and a whole heart and a whole national life bent toward war prevail over the velleities of peace. . . .

"Of course, let us have the peace," we cry, "but at the same time let us have normalcy, let us lose nothing, let our lives stand intact, let us know neither prison nor ill repute nor disruption of ties."[32]

Dorothy Day once remarked that as we come to know the seriousness of the situation, the war, the racism, the poverty in our world, we come to realize that things will not be changed simply by words or demonstrations. Rather it's a question of living one's life in a drastically different way.

As we seek to respond to the urgency of the nuclear peril, we must be willing to change the very way we think and live. We need to weed out the seeds of violence, fear, selfishness, racism, sexism, and nuclearism from our lives and be converted to the way of unconditional love, sharing, and reconciliation. We need to examine how we can simplify our lives and become nonviolent in our lifestyle and work. We need to learn to resolve conflict on a personal, local and global scale through nonviolent means. We need to join with sisters and brothers to form spiritually based communities of sharing, celebration, and nonviolent resistance.

In our journey to be peacemakers, we must resist all forms of injustice and uphold the sacredness of life whenever and wherever it is threatened. Our resistance should not just be to a particular weapon system, law, or policy but to the web of violence, fear, and greed that underlies our nation's policies and also lies in the very depths of our own hearts. In response to the violence and lies perpetrated by the state, we must learn to incarnate into our resistance the self-emptying love of Christ and the "truth-force" of Gandhi.

In the days ahead, we face many difficult challenges. We face the pervasive militarism and oppressive policies of the national security state, which is increasingly supported by the New Right. We face greater repression of dissenters by the state, as evidenced by the lengthy prison sentences (eight to eighteen years) being handed out to Plowshares activists, the government's infiltration and indictment of Sanctuary workers, and the increased surveillance of groups advocating disarmament or political change. We also face the spectre of growing terrorism—both the terrorism used by powerful nations to dominate smaller nations and the acts of counter-terrorism carried out by various political and religious groups to redress injustice— increasing the risk of nuclear confrontation. Such terrorist acts only create a climate of international hostility which leads to a vicious cycle of violence. The U.S. government recently has begun to invoke the term "terrorist" for others as a pretext for taking pre-emptive action against them (as in the cases of U.S. intervention in Libya and Nicaragua). Despite these and other difficult challenges, we must not succumb to the temptation to despair. We must continue our struggle with hope and courage.

If we as individuals and communities can enflesh more deeply the revolutionary power of nonviolent love in the same way as did Jesus, Francis of Assisi, Gandhi, Martin Luther King Jr., Dorothy Day, Oscar Romero, and countless other women and men throughout history, our hearts can be disarmed of fear and violence, and the powers of this world and the power of the bomb can be overcome. War can be abolished. The miracle of true justice and peace will not emerge through the present political system, dominated as it is by the "national security state." It will come through people committing themselves to resist the evil before them in the same way people of faith and conscience resisted slavery in the nineteenth century and, more recently, racial discrimination and the Vietnam War. It will come when we join together with those people struggling to resist injustice, violence, and war today throughout the world, many at the cost of their freedom and their lives. Such change depends on how much we place our trust in God and in one another and to what degree we choose to open our lives to become channels through which God's healing love and peace can be revealed.

Though the future is filled with great uncertainty the God of history is with us and has, ultimately, overcome the powers and principalities of this world. Believing that "with God all things are possible" (Mark 10:27), let us rejoice in and join with the growing nonviolent movement of faith and conscience working to bring about disarmament and social justice and re-create a new world.

Let us persevere in hope, mindful that if we remain faithful to the truth and seek to do God's will, God will transform our life-affirming acts for disarmament and justice into a harvest of justice, peace, and reconciliation.

NOTES

1. J. Christopher Grannis, Arthur J. Laffin, and Elin Schade, *The Risk of the Cross: Christian Discipleship in the Nuclear Age* (New York: Seabury/Winston, 1981), 20.
2. See Gar Alperovitz, *Atomic Diplomacy: Hiroshima to Potsdam* (New York: Simon and Schuster, 1965), 238.
3. For a more in-depth understanding about the United States decision to use nuclear weapons against the Japanese see Gar Alperovitz, *Atomic Diplomacy* (New York: Viking, Penguin, 1985).
4. Robert Aldridge, *First Strike* (Boston: South End, 1983), 27.
5. Ibid., 33.
6. *New York Times,* August 6, 1980.
7. *New York Times,* May 30, 1982.
8. Aldridge, *First Strike,* 211–226. Also see *Time* magazine, December 12, 1983, pp. 28–31. For a more in-depth understanding of "Star Wars" see Patricia M. Mische, *Star Wars and the State of Our Souls* (Minneapolis, MN: Winston, 1985). Malcolm W. Brown, in his article "The Star Wars Spinoff" (*The New York Times Magazine,* August 24, 1986, p. 69), notes "Both the Union of Concerned Scientists and the Federation of American Scientists have denounced the Strategic Defense Initiative, and some 6,500 scientists and scientific educators have signed petitions pledging not to accept SDI funds. . . . According to a survey conducted last spring by Peter D. Hart, Research Associates Inc., two thirds of 549 American physicists polled expressed doubts that SDI could ever defend the entire population of the nation against ballistic missiles, and sixty-two percent declared themselves opposed to deploying a Star Wars defense."
9. Aldridge, *First Strike,* 255ff.
10. See *The Nuclear Alamanac,* edited by the Faculty Members at the Massachusetts Institute of Technology (Reading, MA: Addison-Wesley, 1984), 175.
11. Taken from the official court transcript of the Plowshares trial of Martin Holladay, U.S. District Court, Kansas City, MO, April 22–23, 1985.
12. Aldridge, *First Strike,* 245–246.
13. See Joseph Gerson, ed., *The Deadly Connection: Nuclear War and U.S. Intervention* (Philadelphia: New Society Publishers, 1986).
14. Jim Wallis, ed. *Waging Peace* (New York: Harper & Row, 1982), 29–30, 44–46.
15. "During the end of World War II, the Council on Foreign Relations and the State Department, in an effort to control U.S. global corporate interests, developed what was called 'Grand Area planning.' The Grand Area was to be a region that was subordinated to the needs of the American economy. As one planner put it, it was to be the region that 'is strategically necessary for world control.' The geopolitical analysis held that the Grand Area had to include at least the Western Hemisphere, the Far East, and the former British Empire, which we were then in the process of dismantling and taking for ourselves. . . . The Area was also to include the Middle East and Latin America" (Noam Chomsky, "Intervention in Vietnam and Central America," published by *Resist,* 38 Union Square, Somerville, MA 01243, May/June, 1985).
16. Since 1900, the United States has directly intervened in the affairs of other countries over twenty times through direct involvement of military forces (*World Alamanac Book of Facts,* [New York: Newspaper Enterprise Inc., 1983], 334–335). Also, from the end of World War II through the mid-1970s the United States, in its Military Assistance Program (MAP), has offered some $55 billion in military

aid to seventy-one countries, many of which have been repressive dictatorships (Howard Zinn, *A People's History of the United States* [Harper & Row, 1980], 558). Also during the last twenty years, the United States and the Soviet Union have been the world's leading arms exporters, spending nearly $200 billion.

17. Borrowed from techniques used during the Vietnam War, low intensity warfare (LIW) uses "active" and "preventative" political, economic, military, and psychological aggression designed to wear down a political opponent. LIW can be directed against a government such as that in Nicaragua, or it can be used against an insurgency such as the Farabundi Marti Liberation Front/Democratic Revolutionary Front (FMLN/FDR) in El Salvador. Governments engaged in LIW may use military might to support a counterinsurgency campaign (as the United States is now doing to support the Contras), or they may conduct attacks on counterinsurgent forces (such as the air strikes against the popular forces in El Salvador directed by the United States). The Reagan Administration has tried to alter public perception and increase acceptance of its LIW involvement by portraying the people opposed ot it as "terrorists" or "communists." The term "Low intensity" comes from a military understanding of conflict and violence as measurable on a spectrum. For further reading on LIW see *Update Central America*, May-June 1986, issued by the Inter-Religious Task Force on Central America.

18. As more countries have acquired conventional arms, military conflicts between nations have drastically increased. In her book *World Military and Social Expenditures, 1982*, Ruth Leger Sivard reports that between 1960 and 1982 there have been sixty-five wars around the world which have resulted in over ten million deaths. With more nations attaining deadly weapons like cluster bombs and "smart" weapons that have a kill probability of nearly 100 percent, conventional warfare is becoming far more destructive than ever before.

19. Simple Living Collective, American Friends Service Committee, San Francisco, *Taking Charge: Personal and Political Change Through Simple Living* (New York: Bantam Books, 1977), 340.

20. For a more comprehensive examination of how U.S. power has been asserted in the world to protect its economic interests, see Noam Chomsky, *Turning the Tide*, (Boston: South End Press, 1985). Noam Chomsky, et al., *The Washington Connection and Third World Fascism* (Boston: South End Press, 1979), Richard Barnet, *Roots of War* (New York: Penguin, 1971), Richard Barnet and Ronald E. Muller, *Global Reach* (New York: Simon & Schuster, 1974), and Zinn, *A People's History*.

21. See Daniel Berrigan, ed., *For Swords into Plowshares, the Hammer Has to Fall* (Highland Park, NJ: Plowshares Press, 1984), 26.

22. Statistics taken from the second draft of the Pastoral Letter on the U.S. Economy, by the National Conference of Catholic Bishops.

23. See Seymour Melman's *The Permanent War Economy* New York: Simon and Schuster, 1974.

24. Richard Falk and Robert J. Lifton, *Indefensible Weapons: The Political and Psychological Case Against Nuclearism* (New York: Basic Books, 1982), ix.

25. Elizabeth McAlister, "Idolatry of the State," *Catholic Agitator* (June 1986), 2.

26. William Arkin and Peter Pringle, *S.I.O.P.: The Secret U.S. Plan for Nuclear War* (New York: Norton, 1983), 50–51.

27. Gregg Herken, *Counsels of War* (New York: Knopf, 1985), 382.

28. James Bamford, *The Puzzle Palace—A Report on the National Security Agency, America's Most Secret Agency* (Boston: Houghton Mifflin, 1982), 1.

29. For a more in-depth understanding of the NSA see Bamford, *The Puzzle Palace*.

30. See War Powers Resolution (Pub. L. 93–148, November 7, 1973, 87 Stat. 555).

31. Telford Taylor (U.S. Chief Counsel at Nuremberg referring to the trial of the Major War criminals before the Military Tribunal there), *Nuremberg and Vietnam: An American Tragedy* (Chicago: Quadrangle Books, Inc., 1970), 84.
32. Daniel Berrigan, *No Bars to Manhood* (New York: Bantam, 1971), 48–49.

Chapter 2

DIVINE OBEDIENCE

Anne Montgomery, R.S.C.J.

Civil disobedience is, traditionally, the breaking of a civil law to obey a higher law, sometimes with the hope of changing the unjust civil law. For example, the lunch counter sit-ins in the 1950s challenged the validity of segregation laws in the South. But we should speak of such actions as divine obedience, rather than as civil disobedience.

The term "disobedience" is not appropriate because any law that does not protect and enchance human life is no real law. In particular, both divine and international law tell us that weapons of mass destruction are a crime against humanity and it is the duty of the ordinary citizen to actively oppose them. Richard Falk points out that "the international law of war has been at all stages an outgrowth of moral convictions that rested on some sense of underlying reality; a foundation for international law is often associated in the West with 'natural law.'" This natural law framework of international law "is radically inconsistent with the current postulate of strategic nuclear doctrine," and therefore "a grave continuing series of violations of international law are taking place, causing peril to world peace and human destiny."[1]

The term "civil" has also lost its meaning since it implies faith in the system's openness to change. In reality the forces of violence are entrenched in the powers that control our "democracy," among them the Pentagon, the CIA, and large corporations.[2] "Our struggle is not against flesh and blood but the principalities and powers of this world" (Eph. 6:12). On this deeper level we need, as Jim Douglass says, much more than civility "in an act of disobedience to the coming murder of the human race. Love, the Love of God—not civility—is the power to overcome evil."[3]

And so we practice divine obedience.

Gandhi has shown us that divine obedience draws its power and, indeed, is inseparable from a nonviolent way of life, an integral living out of the loving truth that grasps us. Like divine obedience, nonviolence is an active force against rather than a passive acceptance of evil; nonviolence cannot be confused with refusing to act to change an unjust situation. Gandhi was strong on this point, adopting the term satyagraha, "truth-force," to describe an attitude and a style of action that is more than just a strategy to obtain a political goal. We must first open ourselves to the truth—a truth synonomous with love, a truth that is more than just an accurate judgment of an unjust situation. We must respond to the touch of God, to the inspiration that is our very strength. We speak the truth against injustice and, in our vulnerability to the very violence we oppose, hope to transform it through the greater spiritual force of love. This is the "law" of the cross, of "dying daily." Such nonviolent acts of resistance can be literally "disarming."

Therefore, in redefining terms the emphasis is on a life empowered by truth and love as opposed to a passivity that shares in the violence of injustice by acquiescing to it. The emphasis is on obedience to the law of love and on the call to uphold it in the face of systematized divisions, enmity, and violence. To be consistent, such a life and the action flowing from it must be marked by characteristics that may appear foolish to the "wisdom belonging to this passing age" and "its governing powers" (1 Cor. 2:6, NEB).

First and foremost, rather than the "order" fashioned by creating and then defeating enemies, peace is the work of unity, of breaking down those barriers, literal and symbolic, created by injustice and fear. It is the work Jesus offered as a sign of his authenticity and promised that anyone "who has faith in me will do . . . and will do greater things still . . ." (John 14:12, NEB). This unity is both source and goal of divine obedience and should, therefore, characterize its whole process, however imperfectly. The small community, be it a live-in community or one meeting at regular intervals for reflection, prayer, and action, is an effort to enflesh the command to be one, to be true to our common humanity as well as the covenant written in our hearts.

Many prospective peacemakers, feeling helpless, ask where to begin. Simple first steps to empowerment include meeting with a few others to share tensions, fears, and hopes, to reflect on Scripture and other readings on nonviolence, and to let prayer flow from this sharing and reflection. These meetings can be a focus for research and action on a local arms industry or military base. This whole meeting process requires working through layers of personal differences, inhibitions, and fears to reach a deeper level of support and strength that cannot be cheaply bought. We first begin to be peacemakers among ourselves in our local group.

Our struggles as a group remind us of our implication in the power plays and greed at the source of the violence in the larger society from which we cannot isolate ourselves. Abraham Heschel points out that, although we may claim not to be guilty of the corruption in that society, we are all responsible.[4] This sense of common responsibility not only drives us to speak out with our bodies as well as our words as did the prophets; it also enables us to see our action as a work of reconciliation rather than of conflict. The promise of Jesus to be present where two or three are gathered in his name is thus more than a summons to liturgical prayer. The truth of our nature requires a community that, while respecting religious differences, lives a practical spirituality. It is a reflection of the Trinitarian life built into our existence: we must be emptied if we are to discover a source of life real enough to dispel our fear of losing our own lives, in however small or great a way, for sisters and brothers. We must enflesh this life in all its poverty and power and, in so doing, discover a community of suffering and love that knows no boundaries.

Therefore, when we plan acts of divine obedience, we begin our process with community prayer, reflection, and decision making; we try to reach a harmony, deeper than differences in philosophy and style, that will maintain our spirit through the trial and prison processes, which often require reaching consensus under difficult conditions. To make our prayer and action one, to reach out to the "other" in a personal way, requires that we emphasize depth and relationship rather than numbers and high-powered organization. The power of forms of resistance like massive blockades stems from the strength of their "affinity groups"—small communities woven into a larger one. In such communities we can learn the true meaning of "conspiracy": "breathing together" the Spirit of life and being formed by it into people faithful to the covenant of love—the law written in our hearts.

In community we also examine our attitudes toward the arms workers, military personnel, police, and court officers we will encounter, reminding ourselves that we are bound together by our responsibility for violence as well as our desire that life be protected. We pray that in any confrontation the surfacing of fears and hopes on both sides may result in greater mutual healing and understanding. Often the anger of a guard or worker has proved to be but the "first line of defense," the wall that, broken down, opens the way to communication and the beginnings of a wider community. We need to trust without compromise. Otherwise we limit the human possibilities for conversion and growth in others as well as in ourselves.

Regarding the question of our effectiveness we have to "think small." In a real sense, our weakness *is* our strength, for it leaves us trusting in the power of God rather than in media power, vote power, or numbers power, however desirable these may be. Second, we believe with Gandhi that means and end are contained together in the seed our witness plants. If it is a community action, there is already more community in the world; if it is a repentant action, there is already more reconciliation; if it is a loving action, there is already more love casting out its opposite, fear. We can only open ourselves to the free intervention of mercy in the history we live. So the real question becomes: "By whose standards are we judging effectiveness—or can we judge it at all?" The Gospel promise of "greater works" is to those who believe. We must be responsible and do our homework, research and choose our site with care, reflect and pray over the pros and cons of the action and symbols, and open up channels of support and communication. But in the end there is always a gap between faith and feasibility, and the moment of speaking the truth becomes a leap of faith that opens us to the power of that truth.

Finally, actions inspired by the "truth-force" are creative, marked by a certain empowerment and freedom. There is no one "approved" way to resist the mechanics of death that have invaded our multiple social and political structures, although some forms of noncooperation, such as draft and tax resistance, are obviously crucial. Between the lone witness, whom we hope is supported by community, and the mass blockade are a wide range of the smaller, community-inspired actions requiring various degrees of commitment and risk. Groups have climbed over or cut through fences to expose the weapons built or stored behind them and the hypocrisy of such "security." They have sat in front of trains carrying death to our new Auschwitz in Puget Sound. Some have renamed the Pentagon, White House, and arms factories, as well as the weapons produced, with death symbols and have blocked entrances by symbolically "dying." Other small groups have carried out Plowshares actions, obeying the biblical command to us, the people, "to beat swords into plowshares."

These are all experiments in truth, the learning with our whole selves of what our minds can grasp only partially, what is required to be peacemakers, and the sharing not just of ideas, but something of that experience. This sharing can take the form of banners, leaflets, songs, and liturgy, as well as dialogue with military personnel, workers, police, and onlookers. Such efforts at communication before, during, and following acts of divine obedience are crucial to the ongoing effort to transform conflict into something closer to communion.

Because of the growing gap between those who really make policy decisions and ordinary citizens, symbolic actions like marking weapons with blood have grown in importance. It is almost impossible today to find a direct action like the lunch-counter sit-ins of the 1950s that directly touches those in power; for example, it is hard to break a law legitimizing a weapon except in a symbolic way. For this reason, symbolic direct action has become increasingly important. We can take symbolic direct action by blocking the doors of the factories that produce arms or the trains that transport them. We can dismantle one or two nuclear weapons as a symbol of our deeper responsibility to disarm the violence that created such weapons.

Symbols have a condensed, almost physical power and are especially important in an age when the inundation of words makes us nonlisteners. Symbols touch us on a deep, subconscious level and release memories and fears, aspirations and energies. The weapons themselves, like the ancient idols demanding the sacrifice of children, have become false symbols of protection from the very fear they inspire.

On the political level, as E. P. Thompson points out, weapons are symbols to hold our power structures together, structures that have suppressed and replaced politics with an ideology supported by the security services and the media.[5] We can go further and say that these weapons are the inevitable expressions of the violence central to the ideology of power. Because the gods of violence demand service as the price of "security," we adopt the repressive structures and strategies we condemn in others. But from our own hearts and traditions we are able to bring forth symbols that, like the two-edged sword of Scripture, divide truth from falsehood and the living from the dead.

Much of our creativity focuses on the choice of those symbols that will become our action or accompany it. Some have aroused emotions and raised serious questions of propriety, such as the pouring of blood on doors or weapons. The very "offensiveness" of bloodiness is part of the message. War is not polite; dismembered bodies are messy and nauseating. But symbols can point in many directions. Blood also speaks of human unity and of the offering of oneself, in however small a way, in a new liturgy of life and hope. Hammers, too, are a powerful and controversial symbol. We think of carpenters' hammers as creative, forgetting sometimes that building a new dwelling can require the dismantling of a dangerous structure first. When the dwelling is our unique planet and the danger both actualized and symbolized by life-threatening weapons, the "beating of swords into plowshares" becomes an urgent responsibility. Such an action is both symbolic and direct, since it carries out in a carefully defined scenario a small but real disarmament that thousands of treaties and conferences have yet to accomplish. It is a reenactment of the scriptural prophecy and serves to remind us all that the "days" referred to by Isaiah and Micah are not a future idealized time, but now.

An act of divine obedience such as entering an arms factory or military base and hammering on a missile cone or launcher is not taken lightly but requires that the process followed for other resistance actions be more intense and prolonged. In solitary and communal prayer we discern possibilities and the relationship between faith and feasibility. We examine obstacles and risks not only in the action itself, but possibly in long prison sentences and their effect on other relationships and responsibilities. We must work through our convictions and feelings concerning court and jail procedures. We must, too, face realistically the possiblity of physical harm to one of us and we must do all we can to avoid what might be more hurtful to the guard responsible than to ourselves.

Finally, when research and reasoning have reached a certain point before an action that seems "right," there is usually a moment or a series of moments, hard to describe, of "coming together": of community and action, of time and place—a moment of "seeing through a glass darkly," yet with the sureness of faith. We are not sure everything will turn out perfectly, but we are sure that it is right to go ahead. We will stop if violence threatens, but we are sure, too, that the doors meant to open will do so. Whether or not the physical ones do so, the community action itself is the opening of a door, a step into freedom, and a prayer for the intervention of mercy in history, for we refuse to believe that we are walled into fatalistic cycles of war and oppression or destined for holocaust. Above all, we are certain that the whole point of the process is our obedience and that the results are in the hands of God.

Divine obedience, then, calls us not to answer threat, real or imaginary, with counterthreat, force with counterforce, but rather to break through this cycle by entering a new one on a deeper level. It is the Trinitarian life-cycle of descent into our own insecurity and emptiness, of being empowered by the Word of truth, of being freed yet bound to one another—to all our sisters and brothers—in the loving breath of the Spirit rising in us in the name of Life. It is the call to believe, in very real and desperate circumstances, here and now, that faith "gives substance to our hopes" (Heb. 11:1, NEB). Our response, therefore, becomes a message of hope.

NOTES

1. Richard Falk, Lee Meyrowitz, Jack Sanderson, "Nuclear Weapons and International Law," 1980. Typescript, 1, 2.
2. Elizabeth McAlister, "A Community of Sanity," *Sojourners*, May 1983, 28.
3. James Douglass, "Loving Disobedience," *Ground Zero*, May–June 1982, 6.
4. Abraham J. Heschel, *The Prophets* (New York: Harper Torchbooks, 1969), 16.
5. E. P. Thompson, "On Peace, Power and Parochialism", *Nation*, September 24, 1983, 244.

Chapter 3

A CHRONOLOGY OF THE PLOWSHARES DISARMAMENT ACTIONS: SEPTEMBER 1980–SEPTEMBER 1986

Arthur J. Laffin

On September 9, 1980, eight people entered a General Electric plant in King of Prussia, Pennsylvania, where the nose cones for the Mark 12A nuclear warheads were manufactured. There they enacted the biblical prophecies of Isaiah 2:4 and Micah 4:3 to "beat swords into plowshares" by hammering on two of the nose cones and pouring blood on documents. Theirs was the first of what have come to be known as "Plowshares" disarmament actions. The eight participants—known now as the "Plowshares Eight"—were subsequently arrested, tried, convicted, and sentenced.

Other communities and individuals since then, after recognizing and reflecting on the imminent peril nuclear weapons pose for all life, have symbolically yet concretely disarmed various components of the strategic nuclear triad of land-, sea-, and air-based weapons: the first-strike MX, Pershing II, cruise, Minuteman ICBMs and Trident II missiles as well as the Trident submarine. Accepting full responsibility for their actions, the people involved have always peacefully awaited arrest following each act.

Resonating closely with these Plowshares actions are the nonviolent direct disarmament actions of others who do not see their action arising specifically out of the biblical prophesy of Isaiah and Micah, but from their consciences. Through their disarmament actions they have extended the community of individuals who are prepared to take serious personal risks to say that we must disarm now.

As of September 1986, there had been seventeen Plowshares and related disarmament actions. There had also been one action (the Martin Marietta MX Witness) where people intended to disarm some missile components but they were unable to do so due to heavy security. Twenty people who had participated in these disarmament actions were serving prison sentences ranging from one year to eighteen years, while several others were on probation or on parole.

During these trials most of the defendants have represented themselves and have been assisted by legal advisers. In their defense many have attempted to show, through personal and expert testimony, that their actions were morally and legally justified and that their intent was to protect life, not commit a crime. Eight of these cases have been tried in federal court, while the other nine have been tried in state court. The following chronology briefly describes the various disarmament actions and trials and states the sentence each person received.

Plowshares Eight

On September 9, 1980, Daniel Berrigan, Jesuit priest, author, and poet from New York City; Philip Berrigan, father and cofounder of Jonah House in Baltimore; Dean Hammer, member of the Covenant Peace Community in New Haven, Connecticut; Elmer Maas, musician and former college teacher from New York City; Carl Kabat, Oblate priest and missionary; Anne Montgomery, Religious of the Sacred Heart sister and teacher from New York City; Molly Rush, mother and founder of the Thomas Merton Center in Pittsburgh; and John Schuchardt, ex-marine, lawyer, father, and member of Jonah House, entered the General Electric Nuclear Missile Reentry Division in King of Prussia, Pennsylvania, where nose cones for the Mark 12A warheads were made. They hammered on two nose cones, poured blood on documents, and offered prayers for peace. They were arrested shortly thereafter and initially charged with over ten different felony and misdemeanor counts.

In February 1981, they underwent a jury trial in Norristown, Pennsylvania. During their trial they were denied use of the defense that their actions were legally justified due to the threat posed by nuclear weapons, and they were not allowed to present expert testimony.

Due to the court's suppression of individual testimony about the Mark 12A and U.S. nuclear war–fighting policies, four left the trial and returned to witness at GE. They were rearrested and returned to court. They were convicted by a jury of burglary, conspiracy, and criminal mischief and sentenced to prison terms of five to ten years. They appealed and the Pennsylvania Superior Court reversed their conviction in February 1984. The State of Pennsylvania then appealed that decision. Following a ruling in the fall of 1985 by the Pennsylvania Supreme Court in favor of the state on certain issues (including the exclusion of the justification defense), the case has been returned to the Superior Court Appeals Panel. As of September 1986, their case remained in the Pennsylvania courts.

Plowshares Number Two

On December 13, 1980, Peter DeMott, former seminarian and Vietnam veteran from Jonah House, entered the General Dynamics Electric Boat (EB) shipyard in Groton, Connecticut, during the launch ceremony for the "U.S.S. Baltimore" fast-attack submarine. Noticing an empty EB security van with keys in it, he got into the van and repeatedly rammed the Trident "U.S.S. Florida," in dry dock, denting the rudder. Security guards then broke into the van and arrested him. Conducting his own defense during a week-long jury trial, he was convincted of criminal mischief and criminal trespass and sentenced to one year in jail.

Trident Nein

On Independence Day, 1982, Judy Beaumont, Benedictine sister and teacher from Chicago; Anne Montgomery, of the Plowshares Eight; James Cunningham, ex-lawyer from Jonah House; George Veasey, Vietnam veteran also from Jonah House; Tim Quinn, expectant father and housepainter from Hartford, Connecticut; Anne Bennis, teacher and child-care worker from Philadelphia; Bill Hartman, full-time peace worker from Philadelphia; Vincent Kay, housepainter and poet from New Haven, Connecticut; and Art Laffin, member of the Covenant Peace Community in New Haven, entered EB in Groton, Connecticut to issue a "declaration of independence" from the Trident submarine and all nuclear weapons. (*Nein* is the German word for "no.") Four boarded the Trident "U.S.S. Florida" by canoe, hammered on several missile hatches, poured blood, and with spray paint renamed the submarine "U.S.S. Auschwitz." They were arrested within half an hour. Meanwhile, five others entered EB's south storage yard and hammered and poured blood on two Trident sonar spheres. They were apprehended after three hours. During their two-week jury trial, they were disallowed a justification defense and expert witnesses were prohibited from testifying about the dangers and illegality of the first-strike Trident. They were convicted of criminal mischief, conspiracy, and criminal trespass and ordered to pay $1386.67 in restitution to the Navy. They were sentenced to jail for up to one year.

Plowshares Number Four

On November 14, 1982—five days after the Trident Nein sentencing—John Grady, auto mechanic and pizza deliverer from Ithaca, New York; Ellen Grady, aide to an elderly woman and peace worker, also from Ithaca; Peter DeMott, of Plowshares Number Two; Jean Holladay, grandmother and nurse from Massachusetts; Roger Ludwig, poet and musician involved in work with the poor in Washington, D.C.; Elmer Maas, of the Plowshares Eight; and Marcia Timmel, from the Dorothy Day Catholic Worker in Washington, D.C., entered EB. Three boarded the Trident "U.S.S. Georgia" and hammered and poured blood on several missile hatches. Four others entered the south storage yard and poured blood and hammered on Trident components before being quickly apprehended. Like those in the Trident Nein action, they underwent a jury trial and were denied a justification defense. They were convicted of criminal mischief, conspiracy, and criminal trespass. They received prison sentences ranging from two months to one year.

AVCO Plowshares

On July 14, 1983, Agnes Bauerlein, mother and grandmother from Ambler, Pennsylvania; Macy Morse, mother and grandmother from Nashua, New Hampshire; Mary Lyons, mother, grandmother and teacher from Hartford; Frank Panopoulos, member of the Cor Jesu community from New York City; Jean Holladay, of Plowshares Number Four; John Pendleton, member of Jonah House; and John Schuchardt, of the Plowshares Eight, entered the AVCO Systems Division in Wilmington, Massachusetts, where MX and Pershing II nuclear weapons components are produced. They hammered on computer equipment related to these weapons systems and poured blood on blueprints labeled MX-"Peacekeeper." They also issued a written indictment against AVCO and its co-conspirators, including the "national security state" and the armed forces, for committing crimes against God and humanity by manufacturing for profit weapons of genocide. They were apprehended within an hour. During their jury trial they were able to present a justification defense, but this defense and expert testimony were disallowed by the judge prior to jury deliberation. They were convicted of wanton destruction and trespass. They were sentenced to jail for up to three and a half months. A decision on their appeal is still pending at the time of this writing.

Griffiss Plowshares

On Thanksgiving Day, November 24, 1983, Jackie Allen, nursery school teacher from Hartford; Clare Grady, artist and potter from Ithaca; Dean Hammer, father and member of the Plowshares Eight; Elizabeth McAlister, mother and cofounder of Jonah House; Vern Rossman, minister, father, and grandfather from Boston; Kathleen Rumpf, a Catholic Worker from Marlboro, New York; and Karl Smith, member of Jonah House, entered Griffiss Air Force Base in Rome, New York. They hammered and poured blood on a B-52 bomber converted to carry cruise missiles as well as on B-52 engines. They also left at the site of their witness a written indictment of Griffiss Air Force Base and the U.S. government pointing to the war crimes of preparing for nuclear war and depicting how the new state religion of "nuclearism" denies constitutional rights and punishes acts of conscience. Unnoticed for several hours, they finally approached security guards and were arrested.

In this, the first Plowshares case to be tried in federal court, their justification defense was denied and expert testimony was disallowed in the presence of the jury. They were acquitted by a jury of sabotage, but they were convicted of conspiracy and destruction of government property. They received prison sentences ranging from two to three years. Their appeal was denied in federal court in March 1985. They have all served their sentences—ranging from sixteen to twenty-four months.

Plowshares Number Seven

On December 4, 1983, Carl Kabat, of the Plowshares Eight, and three West Germans—Herwig Jantschik, Dr. Wolfgang Sternstein, and Karin Vix—entered a U.S. Army base in Schwabisch-Gmund, West Germany, and carried out the first Plowshares action in Europe. They publicly announced their action in advance but did not disclose the exact date or place.

Early in the morning on December 4, they entered the base and, with hammers and bolt cutters, disarmed a Pershing II missile launcher. They were soon apprehended by U.S. soldiers. Following their arrest, they were all released on their own recognizance. Carl returned to the United States and did not attend the trial. During the first week of February 1985, Herwig, Wolfgang, and Karin were tried before three judges and two lay judges and convicted on charges of trespass, attempted sabotage, and destruction of property. Herwig and Wolfgang were sentenced to 1800 DM ($900) or ninety days in jail while Karin was sentenced to 450 DM ($225) or sixty days in jail. Karin and Herwig chose to serve the prison sentence while Wolfgang elected to pay the fine.

Pershing Plowshares

In the season of Passover, on Easter Morning, April 22, 1984, Per Herngren, student and peace worker from Sweden; Paul Magno, from the Dorothy Day Catholic Worker in Washington, D.C.; Todd Kaplan, involved in work with the poor in Washington, D.C.; Tim Lietzke, member of Jeremiah House in Richmond, Virginia; Anne Montgomery, of the Plowshares Eight and Trident Nein; Patrick O'Neill, university student and peace worker from Greenville, North Carolina; Jim Perkins, teacher, father, and member of Jonah House; and Christin Schmidt, university student and peace worker from

Rhode Island, entered Martin Marietta in Orlando, Florida. Once inside, they hammered and poured blood on Pershing II missile components and on a Patriot missile launcher. They also served Martin Marietta with an indictment for engaging in the criminal activity of building nuclear weapons in violation of divine, international, and national law. They also displayed a banner that said: "Violence Ends Where Love Begins." They were apprehended after several hours. During their jury trial in federal court they were denied a justification defense. They were convicted of depredation of government property and conspiracy. They were sentenced to three years in federal prison, given five-year suspended sentences with probation, and each ordered to pay $2900 in restitution. Both their appeal and motion for reduction of sentence have been denied in federal court. Herngren, a Swedish national, was deported on August 27, 1985, after serving over a year of his sentence. They have all served their sentences—ranging from one to two years and remain on probation through 1991.

Sperry Software Pair

On August 10, 1984, John LaForge and Barbara Katt, housepainters and peace workers from Bemidji, Minnesota, dressed as quality control inspectors, entered Sperry Corporation in Eagan, Minnesota. Once inside, they poured blood and hammered on two prototype computers designed to provide guidance and navigation information for Trident submarines and F4G fighter bombers. They also served Sperry with a citizens' indictment declaring that Sperry was committing war crimes in violation of national and international law. After a two-day jury trial in federal court in which they were allowed to present a justification defense, they were convicted of destruction of government property. Judge Miles Lord imposed a six-month sentence, then suspended that sentence on condition of six months of probation.

Trident II Plowshares

On October 1, 1984, William Boston, housepainter and peace worker from New Haven; Jean Holladay, of the Plowshares Number Four and AVCO Plowshares; Frank Panopoulos, of the AVCO Plowshares; Leo Schiff, draft registration resister and natural foods chef from Vermont; and John Pendleton, of the AVCO Plowshares, entered the EB Quonset Point facility in North Kingston, Rhode Island. They hammered and poured blood on six Trident II missile tubes and unfurled a banner that said: "Harvest of Hope—Swords into Plowshares." They also placed a pumpkin at the site and posted a written "Call to Conscience" on the missile tubes condemning these weapons under international and religious law and calling on those responsible to cease their crimes against humanity. They were arrested within half an hour and charged with possession of burglary tools, malicious damage to property, and criminal trespass.

During their jury trial, expert witnesses were allowed to be qualified in the presence of the jury. However the judge ruled this and other expert testimony irrelevant and denied a justification defense.

After the state's case, the judge dismissed the trespass charge. At the end of their two-week-long trial, the prosecution dropped the burglary tools charge (a felony carrying ten years) as the defendants pled guilty to the malicious damage to property charge. After two days of prayer, the five had concluded that pleading guilty was the most nonviolent course to take. On October 18, 1985, the five were sentenced to one year and fined $500. Jean was granted parole in April 1986 after serving six months of her sentence. While the three others were released in August 1986, Frank was given an additional two months for a contempt charge relating to his refusal to disclose to the judge who drove the group to EB. He was released in October 1986.

Silo Pruning Hooks

On November 12, 1984, Carl Kabat, of the Plowshares Eight and Plowshares Number Seven; Paul Kabat, an Oblate priest from Minnesota; Larry Cloud Morgan, Native American and mental health care worker from Minneapolis; Helen Woodson, mother of eleven children and founder of the Gaudete Peace and Justice Center from Madison, Wisconsin, entered a Minuteman II missile silo controlled by Whiteman Air Force Base in Knob Noster, Missouri. Once inside the silo area, they used a jackhammer and air compressor to damage the silo cover lid. They then offered a Eucharist and left at the silo a biblical and Native American indictment of the U.S. government and the institutional church for their complicity in the pending omnicide of nuclear holocaust. They were arrested close to an hour after their action by armed military guards authorized to use "deadly force" against intruders. (As has been the case in each of the Plowshares actions nobody was harmed.) Following their arrest, they were declared by the court to be a "threat to the community" and were thus held on "preventive detention" and denied bond.

They underwent a jury trial in federal court in February 1985 in Kansas City, Missouri. They were convicted of destruction of government property, conspiracy, intent to damage the national defense, and trespass. On March 27, 1985, they received the most severe prison sentences to date of any Plowshares group: Larry—eight years; Paul—ten years; and Carl and Helen—eighteen years. They were also given three to five years probation and ordered to pay $2932.80 each in restitution. On November 1, 1985, U.S. District Judge D. Brook Bartlett, their trial judge, reduced Helen's sentence from eighteen to twelve years. All but Helen appealed their case, and these appeals were denied in October 1986.

Plowshares Number Twelve

On February 19, 1985, Martin Holladay, a carpenter from Wheelock, Vermont, entered another Minuteman II missile silo of Whiteman Air Force Base near Odessa, Missouri. He damaged the lid of the silo and some electrical boxes with a hammer and chisel. He also poured blood on the silo and spray-painted "No More Hiroshimas" on it. He left at the site an indictment charging the U.S. government with committing crimes against God and international law by its nuclear war preparations. After his arrest, he was denied bond and held until trial. During his four-day jury trial, he was denied the opportunity to present a justification defense. On April 25, 1985, he was convicted of destruction of government property and destruction of national defense material. He was sentenced on May 16, 1985, to eight years in federal prison and five years probation. He was also fined $1000 and ordered to pay $2242 in restitution. His appeal was denied in federal court in July 1986. In September 1986, his sentence was reduced to the time he had already served—nineteen months—and he was released.

Trident II Pruning Hooks

On April 18, 1985, Greg Boertje, ex–army officer and peace organizer from Louisiana; John Heid, former Franciscan seminarian and social worker from Ithaca; Roger Ludwig, of the Plowshares Number Four; Sheila Parks, former college teacher from Medford, Massachusetts; Suzanne Schmidt, mother, grandmother, worker with the disabled, and member of Jonah House; and George Veasey, of the Trident Nein, entered the EB Quonset Point facility in North Kingston, Rhode Island—the same site where the Trident II Plowshares action had occurred seven months earlier. They poured blood and hammered on three Trident II missile tubes and spray-painted "Dachau" on them. They left there a "Call to Conscience" indicting General Dynamics for war crimes and preparing for a war of aggression in violation of international, constitutional, and spiritual law. They were also able to celebrate a Jewish-Christian ceremony of faith and hope. Arrested after a short time, they were charged with possession of burglary tools, malicious damage to property, and criminal trespass and held on $18,000 bond. While Sheila and Suzanne were released nearly a month after the action on a "Promise to Appear" (PTA) and John after five months, Greg, George, and Roger remained in jail for nearly nine months, refusing to accept a PTA for reasons of conscience. Shortly before their trial date, the judge released the three unconditionally from prison. During their two-week jury trial, the judge denied their justification defense, insisting that their motives were irrelevant to the case. They were convicted of all three charges. On March 31, 1986, they were sentenced to three years, then were given a one year suspended sentence (with credit for time served) and two years probation. Greg, Suzanne, and Sheila are appealing their case. George, Roger, John and Greg were released during the summer of 1986, and Suzanne and Sheila by January 1987.

Michigan ELF Disarmament Action

On May 28, 1985, Tom Hastings, peace activist involved in radio work from Wisconsin, entered a wooded area in Michigan's upper peninsula and sawed down one of the poles carrying the Navy's "Extremely Low Frequency" (ELF) transmitter antennas, which are used to coordinate the communications, command, and control process of all nuclear submarines in the United States. He remained at the site for forty-five minutes, praying, singing, and planting a circle of corn around the pole. The next morning, he gave a part of the pole to Congressman Bob Davis's office and turned himself in to the local sheriff. Held for forty-eight hours, he was released on personal recognizance. He underwent a jury trial and was convicted of malicious destruction of property. On September 27, 1985, he was sentenced to fifteen days and two years probation.

Pantex Disarmament Action

On July 16, 1985, Richard Miller, involved in work with the poor in Des Moines, Iowa, began dismantling a section of railroad track from the railroad spur leading from the U.S. Department of Energy's Pantex Nuclear Weapons Assembly Plant in Amarillo, Texas, to a main line of the Topeka and Santa Fe Railroad. After first taking extensive precautions to prevent accidental derailment and avoid personal injury, he labored with railroad tools for seven hours, removing a thirty-nine foot section of rail. Pointing out the comparison between the Nazi extermination camp at Auschwitz and the Pantex factory, which is the final assembly point for *every* nuclear weapon made in the United States, he put up a banner that read: "Pantex = Auschwitz. Stop the Trains." He further stated: "At Auschwitz the trains carried the people to the crematoria; at Pantex the trains carry the crematoria to the people." Charged with "wrecking trains" and destruction of national defense materials, he underwent a jury trial in federal court and was convicted. On November 8, 1985, he was sentenced to two four-year sentences to run concurrently. He is now serving his sentence and has chosen not to appeal his case.

Wisconsin ELF Disarmament Action

On August 14, 1985, Jeff Leys, draft registration resister and peace worker from St. Paul, Minnesota, continued the process of disarming ELF (*see* Michigan ELF Disarmament Action) by sawing two deep notches in an ELF pole, hoping to weaken it and leaving the rest to natural forces. (Unlike the Michigan ELF still under construction, the 56-mile Wisconsin ELF system is fully operational, with 1.5 million watts flowing through it). In a statement he carried with him to the site he explained: "I act today in accordance with the teachings of Gandhi, Christ, and the Indians—and in accordance with the basic underpinnings of humanity, as expressed in the various world religions . . . and international laws." After an hour, Jeff walked to a transmitter site to turn himself in. Jailed after his arrest, he was tried by a jury on September 30, 1985, and was convicted of criminal damage to property. On October 29, 1985, Jeff was sentenced to five months in jail and given a three-year suspended sentence with three years probation. He was also ordered to pay $4775 in restitution. In April of 1986 Jeff began serving his three-year sentence because he refused to pay restitution for reasons of conscience. He is due to be released in August 1987. His appeal was denied in September 1986.

Martin Marietta MX Witness

On September 27, 1985, Al Zook, from Denver, Colorado; Mary Sprunger-Froese, from Colorado Springs; and Sister Marie Nord, from Minnesota, entered Martin Marietta's Denver plant. (Martin Marietta has a $2 billion contract for building and testing the MX missile). With the intent of disarming components of the MX missile, they carried blood and hammers into the MX work area. Finding the area highly secured by employees wearing "Peacekeeper" security badges, the three were not able to enter areas where MX work is done and directly disarm any MX components. They were, however, able to pour blood on large interior windows overlooking the work areas and unfurl their banner: "Swords into Plowshares." They were quickly arrested and each charged with felony burglary and criminal mischief. The burglary charge was eventually dropped; however, the criminal mischief charge was changed from a misdemeanor to a felony. They were imprisoned for one month before they were released on their own recognizance. On March 5, 1986, they were found guilty by a jury of criminal mischief exceeding $300. During their trial the judge refused to hear their justification defense. On May 1,

1986, they were sentenced to two months in prison with credit for one month of time already served.

Silo Plowshares

On Good Friday, March 28, 1986, Darla Bradley and Larry Morlan of the Davenport Catholic Worker in Iowa; Jean Gump, mother of twelve and grandmother from Morton Grove, Illinois; Ken Rippetoe, member of the Catholic Worker in Rock Island, Illinois; and John Volpe, father, former employee at the Rock Island Arsenal, and member of the Davenport Catholic Worker, entered two Minuteman missile silos controlled by Whiteman Air Force Base near Holden, Missouri. Dividing into two groups, the first group of three went to Silo M10 while the second group went to Silo M6. Hanging banners on the silo fences, one of which read "Disarmament—An Act of Healing," they employed sledgehammers to split and disarm the geared central track used to move the 120-ton missile silo cover at the time of launch. They also cut circuits and used masonry hammers to damage electrical sensor equipment. They then poured blood on the silo covers in the form of a cross and spray-painted "Disarm and Live" and "For the Children" on the silo pad. They left at the site an indictment charging the U.S. government with committing crimes against the laws of God and humanity and indicting as well the institutional Christian church for its complicity in the arms race. They were arrested nearly forty minutes after their action by heavily armed military police. Following their arrest they were taken into custody and then released on their own recognizance.

On June 27, 1986, they were convicted of destruction of government property and conspiracy. In addition, Jean, Larry, and Darla were cited for contempt for refusing to answer questions about where they met prior to their action, who drove them to the silo, and who contacted the CBS "60 minutes" film crew to film the action. They served seven days in jail following the trial. John and Ken were also briefly imprisoned for refusing to cooperate with the conditions of their release so long as the others were imprisoned for contempt. On August 22, 1986, Larry, Jean, Darla and Ken were each sentenced to eight years in prison and five years on probation, while John was sentenced to seven years in prison and five years on probation. John and Darla were ordered to pay $1680 in restitution while Larry, Jean and Ken were ordered to pay $424. They were each fined $100. As of November 1986, all but Jean were appealing their case.

PART TWO

Truth and Consequences

Participants in the Trident Nein plowshares disarmament action during their September 1982 trial in a New London (Connecticut) Superior Court. They are (from left to right) George Veasey, Judith Beaumont, Anne Montgomery, Arthur J. Laffin, Anne T. Bennis, Vincent Kay, James Cunningham, Timothy Quinn, and William Hartman. They were eventually convicted of criminal mischief, conspiracy and criminal trespass for having boarded a Trident submarine on Independence Day, hammering on its missile hatches, pouring blood on it, and renaming it the "USS Auschwitz" with spray paint. They had also hammered and poured blood on two Trident sonar spheres nearby. *Photo by Gordon Alexander of* The Day *in New London, Connecticut.*

One who breaks an unjust law must do so openly, lovingly, and with a willingness to accept the penalty. I submit that an individual who breaks a law that conscience tells him or her is unjust, and who willingly accepts the penalty of imprisonment in order to arouse the conscience of the community over its injustice, is in reality expressing the highest respect for the law.

Martin Luther King, Jr., "Letter From Birmingham City Jail"

We must widen the prison gates, and we must enter them as a bridegroom enters the bride's chamber. Freedom is to be wooed only inside prison walls and sometimes on gallows, never in the council chambers, courts, or the schoolroom.

Gandhi

If you obey my teaching, you are really my disciples; you will know the truth and the truth will set you free.

John 8:31–32

Chapter 4

ON BLINDNESS AND HEALING

Philip Berrigan

If justice comes by means of the law, Christ died in vain.

Galatians 2:21, NAB

Several years ago, a few of us were discussing, with some wonderment and pain, the slow public awakening to the mounting peril of nuclear war. Even then, politicians were insanely truculent, weapons threatening from their lairs overkill on overkill, provocations constant from the superpowers, especially from the United States. Then my brother Dan brought the conversation up short with, "Well, you know, the bomb covers its tracks."

Yes, I've thought many times since, the bomb does indeed cover its tracks. As early as Hanford and Los Alamos, when scientists were laboring to make it "work," the bomb was setting up a deadly mutuality between itself and the human spirit, as though to say, "Look here! There's me and there's me in you. Let's make it fully unanimous!"

Consequently, what was horrifyingly obvious to a few—the high crime in building atomic bombs, deploying them, and going to the brink with them repeatedly—was not generally obvious. The bomb had covered its tracks—it had seduced us into complicity. It had no life apart from the human spirit, where it held its "high ground." Finding a welcome, it enervated, stunted, sometimes crippled the spiritual sight called understanding and the spiritual resolve called fortitude.

Very much to the point is the gospel story of Christ curing the man born blind. That stalwart man knew and accepted certain undeniable facts: he had in fact been blind from birth and he was now in fact healed and had received sight from Jesus, despite the prior fact that "it is unheard of that anyone ever gave sight to a person blind from birth" (John 9:32, NAB). In contrast, the rulers of the day reacted to the cure of blindness with a blindness of their own; they resisted the man's cure because to do otherwise would be to accept *their* cure—cure of their lust for privilege and power, cure for their fear of losing *control*. They saw but one thing clearly, and it was this: acccepting the cure of the man born blind was tantamount to accepting Jesus. And accepting him meant an end to their hypocrisy, cruelty, and the patronage by the Romans.

There is a splendid pedagogy on blindness in Luke 11, a teaching on three levels moving from the mundane to the physical to the spiritual. If practical people don't hide lamps in their cellars or under bushel baskets, if they treasure eyesight to remain functional, so much more should they nourish their sight by God's truth and by truthful lives. "Take care, then, that your light is not darkness" (Luke 11:35, NAB). What an anomaly to encounter those who prudently light up their houses, prudently care for their eyesight, yet remain conscious of the most grievous blindness of all—the darkness of a pinched and hateful spirit?

To be sure, the bomb "covers its tracks." It embodies technological genius along with immeasurable threat and destructiveness. These combine to bludgeon and numb the spirit—why think about the unthinkable, why imagine the unimaginable, why ponder "the day after"? For our part, we cover its tracks by spoon-feeding and petting our idols. In Luke 14 Jesus expounds on three idols—family, possessions, and self, all mutually reinforcing, all obstacles to the cross which is "salvation and life." These three have innumerable progeny. Family has bloodline, ethnicity, class or caste, race (color), religious ideology, nation-state, and empire. Possessions have titles, deeds, stocks, bonds, bank accounts, wills, insurance, a wife or husband, children, and country. Self has ambition, narcissism, careerism, megalomania, prejudice, cruelty, and indifference, to mention but a few.

Idols suppress the truth; their life and livelihood is illusion, indulgence, division, violence—various faces of the lie. The bomb, being a gross, ominous, technological lie ("Peacekeeper," to use Reagan's term?), employs satellite lies to cover its tracks. These lies, our spiritual garbage, work in resonance to the Big Lie of the bomb, creating a mutuality, a *cor ad cor,* a receptive solidarity. The bomb covers its tracks, but our idols/lies also reciprocate and brush them out. And tragic numbers remain accomplices and victims, remain in the strict sense "bombed out."

The bomb has as well one last powerful ally, one usually unmentioned. It has the law.

(I write this as the Reagan administration is in its second term. "You ain't seen nothin' yet!" Well, we're seeing it. Plans for unprecedented military appropriations for the Strategic Defense Initiative ("Star Wars"), for sending military aid to intensify the invasion of Nicaragua, for approval of MX, for an escalation even of its previous orgy of lawlessness and terrorism. Meanwhile, the warheads pour out of Pantex in Amarillo, Texas, and more and more first-strike weapons take their awful stations. Such mad irresponsibility curses divine law and prostitutes human law, whether international or constitutional. Indeed, nuclear lunacy is the law; the "wisdom" of nuclear fang and claw is the law; three minutes to nuclear midnight is the law.)

One must not think, as most legal scholars do, that the law has fallen victim to superpower belligerence or that law has merely fallen into disrepute. The Bible offers a radically different view, exposing human law as pretender to divine law and therefore as counter to the law of love, justice, and peace.

The old civil rights ballad used to ask, "Which side are you on, girl/boy? Which side are you on?" For our purposes, the question could go, "Whose law do you keep, girl/boy?"

The Word of God holds under judgment all social arrangements not in accord with the law of love and strict, definitive justice—the civil religious establishment, corporate or state capitalism, political parties and pacts, the military and police, corporate media and education, cities, nation-states, empires (all the "civilized" foundations for competition, exploitation, and war). It holds them under judgment as disobedient, unjust, and violent. Human law provides undergirding for this rebellion against God and human meaning; it is the code of the counter-Kingdom, of the old order, of a time and history terminated by Christ's incarnation. As such it enforces sanction for social (dis)order, for the bureaucratizing of sin, death, and injustice, offering an indispensable metaphysic and ethic, plus the illusion of equality through impartial treatment under the law.

The state itself, an absurd and pretentious imposter of divine sovereignty, cannot be thought of, cannot exist without law. Biblically and practically, the state and the law are one.

Paul, a Pharisee and legal scholar, converted from the "law" when he realized that officialdom, under legal fiction, has murdered the Lord of Life. Paul said of the "justice" of the law: "It crucified the only person who knew no sin" (2 Cor. 5:21 NAB). Furthermore, Paul understood that his early persecution of Christians, all legal, continued the harassment and killing of Christ. ("Saul, Saul, why do you persecute me?" Acts 9:4, NAB). These terrible truths led Paul to other conclusions about the law: "You have broken with Christ if you look for justice in the law; you have fallen from grace" (Gal. 5:4, NAB). "It is through the law that sin became sinful to the fullest extent" (Rom. 7:13, NAB).

When law does not uncompromisingly uphold human life as sacred, when it makes no provision for conscience and love of enemies, when it does not protect and rescue the weak and helpless (the state would evaporate if it did, so would the state's law), then it is social and political sin, a subtle and deviant curse, deserving only to be resisted and broken.

No crime can compare with official or legal crime, not even the most perverted, grisly, psychopathic assaults upon human life. No private crime can compare with the state's patronage of profitmongering and the destruction ensuing from that, or its identification with the rich and ostracism of the poor, or its military adventures with their inevitable perversion of spirit, waste, and slaughter, or its assumption of godlike qualities in the execution of alleged or real malefactors. All legal! "It is through the law that sin became sinful to the fullest extent."

No crime can compare with official or legal crime—political, corporate, systemic, and now global in threat and destructiveness. The nuclear strike forces of both superpowers are on legal hair trigger; humankind is on legal countdown. The Cold War face-off, with nuclear or interventionist flashpoints in Central Europe, the Middle

East, Central America, and Korea, propels humanity to a nuclear Calvary, one just as legal as the first.

Some say, with a kind of desperate hope, that God has yet to be heard from. The statement itself is vague and slightly presumptuous. God has been heard from—in the person of Christ, and in the resisters of Greenham Common in England, of Mutlangen in West Germany, of Offut Air Force Base, Electric Boat Company, and the Pentagon.

God continues to be heard from as well in the resistance of various Plowshares witnesses. Participants in these actions have been imprisoned and those still awaiting sentencing face virtually certain conviction and jail. In every case, their obedient and lawful acts have encountered a welcome of sorts at the corporate and military hellholes—security scarce, deadly force restrained, ample time to begin conversion of the lethal hardware from its perverted and slavish state. In every case, it was as though creation "groaning in travail, awaited the salvation [justice] of God's children" (Rom. 8:22–23, NAB).

In every case, their testimony, whether stated at the nuclear Dachaus or in court, was a simple prayer that all might see the "tracks" and the bomb lurching on ahead. Theirs is the prayer of Bartimaeus, the blind man: "He threw aside his cloak, and jumped up and came to Jesus. Jesus asked him 'What do you want me to do for you?' 'Rabboni,' the blind man said, 'I want to see!' " (Mark 10:50–51, NAB).

Chapter 5

SWORDS INTO PLOWSHARES

Daniel Berrigan

Seeptember 27, 1980, marked my first visit to the monastery at Gethsemani, Kentucky, since the death of Thomas Merton in 1968. I was asked to offer the homily at morning Mass; the text was from Matthew 11:25–30 (JB), for the feast of St. Vincent de Paul:

I bless you, Father of heaven and earth, for hiding these things from the learned and clever, and revealing them to the children . . .

And Matthew continues, with unexampled solemnity more typical of John:

. . . No one knows the Son except the Father, just as no one knows the Father except the Son—and those to whom the Son chooses to reveal Him.

Then a glance descends; face to human face, he takes us in:

Come to me all you who labor and are over burdened, and I will give you rest. Shoulder my yoke, learn from me; for I am qentle and humble in heart and you will find rest for your souls. Yes, my yoke is easy and my burden light.

In Jesus we learn of the modesty of God.

I set this down in a time of promethean muscle building, muscling in, a time of no limits, a time when literally everything is allowed: genetic splicing, abortions on demand, nuclear warheads pocking the landscape. We learn too well the sad litany of human excess; a na-

---

Editors' Note: On September 9, 1980, the "Plowshares Eight" entered a General Electric nuclear missile plant in King of Prussia, Pennsylvania, and disarmed two nose cones of the Mark 12A reentry vehicle. Daniel Berrigan, one of the participants in this action, writes here of his reflections. These reflections first appeared in slightly different form in the October–November 1980 issue of *The Catholic Worker*.

tional political campaign, for example, in which the nuclear arms race is simply not an issue, the only question being, how much more how quickly. Death always inflicted elsewhere, the artificers of death presumably safe and sound in a nuclear free fire zone? We are gently driven mad.

To be alive to the future, one had best poke about in the past, at least now and then. I went to the monastery to seek a measure of light on why I had gone, some weeks before, to King of Prussia, Pennsylvania. And there, in the words of our statement,

. . . beat swords into plowshares . . . exposed the criminality of nuclear weaponry and corporate piracy. . . . We commit civil disobedience at General Electric because this genocidal entity is the fifth leading producer of weaponry in the U.S. To maintain this position, GE drains $3 million a day from the public treasury, an enormous larceny against the poor.

We wish also to challenge the lethal lie spun by GE through its motto, "We bring good things to life." As manufacturers of the Mark 12A reentry vehicle, GE actually prepares to bring good things to death. Through the Mark 12A, the threat of first-strike nuclear war grows more imminent. Thus GE advances the possible destruction of millions of innocent lives.

If a plumb line could lie horizontal, in time rather than space, then the line, tight as a bowstring, would lie between the monastery and General Electric. I do not know how to put matters more simply. Somewhere along that line we stand (if we are lucky, it is literally a lifeline). We touch it; the line is not dead at all, inert. It vibrates with the message of a living universe. At one end, a monastery, a hive of stillness and listening and strength. And at the other, an unspeakable horror, a factory of genocide.

To taste death and life, you go to headquarters; you listen and learn from the experts.

No sylvan setting for General Electric, no fooling around. Austerity, efficiency, cost value, big bang for big buck. You drive into an industrial park, down a broad macadam highway; building after building, anonymous, walleyed, abstract. A campus of world experts in the science and practice of abstract death.

September 9, 1980. We rose at dawn after (to speak for myself) a mostly sleepless night. In and out of dream, in and out of nightmare. The refrain was part nuptial chant, part dirge; the latter theme dominant, the former a minor key indeed. Brasses, kettle drums, and now and again, the plaintive flute in obligato, the cry of an infant in the river reeds . . .

We had passed several days in prayer together, an old custom indeed, as old as our first arrests in the late sixties. We were mostly vets of those years, survivors too, survivors of the culture and its pseudos and counters, survivors of courts and jails, of the American flare of conscience and its long hibernation, survivors in our religious communities, in our families (they have survived us!). By an act of God and nothing of our own, survivors of America—its mimes, grimaces, enticements, abhorrences, shifts and feints, masks, countermasks. Survivors (barely) of the demons who, challenged, shouted their name—Legion!

We knew for a fact (the fact was there for anyone who bothered to investigate) that General Electric in King of Prussia manufactures the reentry cones of Mark 12A missiles. We learned that Mark 12A is a warhead that will carry an H-bomb of 335 kilotrons to its target. That three of these weapons are being attached to each of three hundred Minuteman III missiles. That because of Mark 12A accuracy and explosive power, it will be used to implement U.S. counterforce or first-strike policy.

We knew these hideous cones ("shrouds" is the GE word) were concocted in a certain building of the General Electric complex. The building is huge: we had no idea exactly where the cones could be found.

Of one thing we were sure. If we were to reach the highly classified area of shipping and delivery and were to do there what we purposed, Someone must intervene, give us a lead.

After our deed, a clamor arose among the FBI and state and county and GE (and God knows what other) police who swarmed into the building. "Did they have inside information? Was there a leak?" Our answer: of course we had Inside Information, of course there had been a Leak. Our Informant is otherwise known in the New Testament as Advocate, Friend, Spirit. We had been at prayer for days.

And the deed was done. We eight looked at one another, exhausted, bedazzled with the ease of it all. We had been led in about two minutes, and with no interference to speak of, to the heart of the labyrinth.

They rounded us up, trundled us out in closed vans. We spent the day uncommonly cheerful in that place of penitence, in various cells of police headquarters. We underwent what I came to think of as a "forced fast," the opposite of forced feeding and undoubtedly less perilous to life and limb. Around the corridors of the spiffy new building (we were in GE country, the local economy is 40 percent GE, GE brings good things to life) the atmosphere was one of hit and miss, cross-purpose, barely concealed panic. How the hell did they get into the building so easily? How about the jobs of those of us who were purportedly guarding the nuclear brews and potions?

Lines to Justice Department, Pentagon, FBI were red hot. Why can't you get your act together up there? And what are we to do with these religious doomsayers? Let them go, let them off light, let them off never? Please advise!

About noon another ploy got underway. They loaded us in vans again; back to the scene of the crime. It was like a Mack Sennett film played backward; first you were sped away in Black Maria, then you were backed freakishly into the same doorway. (It devolved later they wanted identification by the employees.)

But they wouldn't talk, so we wouldn't walk.

They carried four of five of us out of the van into that big warehouse room with the bloody floor, the bloody torn blueprints stamped "Top Secret." And then the missile cones, broken, bloodied, useless. No more genocide in our name! And the wall of faces, police, employees, silent as the grave, furious, bewildered, a captive nation.

Under shrill orders from somewhere, the charade was halted. The procedure was illegal. A District Attorney said it might endanger their whole case. Indeed.

So back to durance vile. They locked us up, they kept saying: "Sure we'll feed you, presently we'll charge you." And nothing happened.

By 5 P.M. the more inventive among us were ready to close their eyes, strip their shoelaces, and pretend we were eating spaghetti Rossi in the West Village.

Then something happened. One by one we were led out. Take off your shoes. And (to the six males) take off your pants.

It appeared that, these objects being stained with our blood, they were severely required as evidence.

So, like the bad little boys in the fairy tale, supperless and shoeless, we were led off to our destiny by Stepmother State.

An intuition that we and others have been pondering for a long time grows on us, presses closer.

To wit: in a time of truly massive irrationality, one had best stop playing the old academic-ecclesial game of scrabble, as though merely putting words together could make sense of moral incoherence, treachery, and meandering apathy, could break that spell.

Rationality? Reason? If these were ever in command, they had certainly fled the scene during the Vietnam War. I would be willing to venture that sanity and reason have never sat in the catbird seat again.

In the saddle of power and decision we have instead a kind of "Eichmania" analyzed by Merton, a tightly hierarchical, spiritually captivated, ideologically closed insanity. In it are caught the multi-corporations and their squads of engineers and planners, on and up to the highest responsible chairs of command—the Pentagon and White House. All so to speak (so to doublespeak) to "bring good things to life."

And then outward into society the malaise touches all with a leprous finger; meandering apathy, at least as complex an illness as rotten power. Apathy, the natural outcome of such authority so used.

We have evidence of such indifference to moral and physical disaster in other modern societies, societies whose citizens, under whip and lash, or under a rain of bread and a politics of the circus, stood helpless to win the nod of blind, deaf fate, to speak up, to force a hearing.

Such apathy shows face today in our inability to summon resistance against nuclear annihilation. Screen out the horror; a shutter comes down. Best not to imagine what might be, best to act as though the worst could not be.

The phenomenon before the catastrophe is remarkably like the phenomenon after the catastrophe. Many of the survivors of Hiroshima, afflicted with radiation sickness, conceal their illness as long as possible, "act as though" they are not stricken. They go so far as to falsify family history, conceal the fact that they were in the orbit of death on the day of the bomb.

No wonder that today Americans find it more plausible, more conducive to sanity to ignore our nuclear plight, to fight survival in areas where the facts are less horrid, the cards less stacked. Economic woes, job layoffs, inflation—we have enough trouble drawing the next breath. And you with your little hammers and bottles of blood go out against Goliath? Thanks. Good luck. But no thank you.

Blood and hammers. The symbolic aspect of our GE action appealed to some and appalled others. But almost no one who has heard of the action lacks an opinion about it, usually a passionately stated one.

In pondering these passions, so long dormant, newly released, one learns a great deal—not about passions in a void, but about vital capacities for survival, sociability, spirituality.

Some who hear grow furious; some of the furious are Catholics; Catholics also guard us, judge us, prosecute us. This is an old story that need not long detain us.

What is of peculiar and serious interest here is the use and misuse of symbols, their seizure by secular power; then the struggle to keep the symbols in focus, to enable them to be seen, heard, tasted, smelled, lived and died for, in all their integrity, first intent.

Their misuse. How they are leveled off, made consistent with the credo of the state. Thus, to speak of King of Prussia and our symbol there: blood. Its outpouring in the death of Christ announced a gift and, by implication, set a strict boundary, a taboo. No shedding of blood, by anyone, under any circumstances, since this, my blood, is given for you. Blood as gift.

Hence the command: no killing, no war. Which is to say, above all, no nuclear weapons. And thence the imperative; resist those who research, deploy, or justify on whatever grounds such weaponry.

Thus the drama; the symbol outpoured implies a command. Do this; so live, so die. Clear lines are drawn for public as well as personal conduct. Church and state, the "twin powers," always in danger of becoming Siamese twins, are in fact kept from a mutually destructive symbiosis by imperative and taboo. More, they are revealed for what they in fact are—radically opposed spiritual powers, as in Revelation 13. Church can never be state; state is forbidden to ape or absorb church. And this mutual opposition, this nonalignment, this friction and fraying, erupts from time to time in tragic and bloody struggle. The church resists being recast as Caesarian icon. The state, robust, in firm possession, demands that the church knuckle under, bend knee, bless war, pay taxes, shut up. Church, thy name is trouble.

The choices are not large. Toil and trouble or—capitulation. In the latter case all is lost. The symbols are seized at the altar and borne away. Now the blood of Christ, the blood of humans, is cheap indeed; for what could be cheaper than blood the church itself has declared expendable? That blood is now a commodity, a waste. When Caesar speaks, blood may be shed at will, by Christians or others, it makes no difference. Which is also to say: there exists no longer any distinction in fact between armed combatants and citizens, between soldiers and little children. Killing has become the ordinary civil method of furthering civic ends. The sacred symbol of blood, whose gift urged the command "Thou shalt not kill"—that blood is admixed, diluted, poisoned. It is lost in a secular vortex, immensely vigorous and seductive, urging a different vision. Labor is commodity, the flag is a sacred vexillum, humans are productive integers, triage rules the outcome. Finally, a peremptory secular command: "Thou shalt kill when so ordered—or else."

It seems to me that since Hiroshima, to set an arbitrary moment, this debasing of the sacred symbols into secular use and misuse has proceeded space.

To undo the blasphemy, what a labor.

We have been at this for years—dramatic events, deliberately orchestrated, arbitrary but intensely traditional, liturgical, illegal, in every case wrenching the actors out of routine and community life to face the music, face the public, face the jury.

Is it all worth it? In measure the eight who acted at King of Prussia have already answered the question. At least for themselves, and for one another. One of them said in the course of our discussion, "Even if the action went nowhere, if no one understood or followed through on it, I would still go ahead."

Worth it for ourselves. Each of us had, before the act, to plumb our motives, consult loved ones, care for the future of children, arrange professional and community responsibilities, measure in fact all good things against this "one necessary thing." And decide.

The eight so decided—yes. Such an act must be taken, even though it disrupt almost everything else, call many things in question, inflict suffering on others. The value of the act is thus measured by the sacrifice required to do it; an old and honored Christian idea, if I am not mistaken.

(For us, going as we did in fear and trembling from the Eucharist to General Electric had the feel of the last hours of Jesus, his journey from the upper room to death. We held our liturgy the night before, broke the bread, passed the cup. Light of head, heavy of heart, we nonetheless celebrated by anticipation the chancy event of the following day; and the trial to come; and the penalty. Our logic? the body was "broken for you," the cup "poured out for all."

The logic was not only our own. At one court hearing the prosecutor asked, with more than a show of contempt, under prodding from his chief, who referred to me as "this so-called priest" and "this wandering Gypsy" (sic), "And when did you last celebrate Mass?" I was obviously to be shown up as not only rootless but faithless as well.)

But what of the larger meaning of the action, its value for the church and the public?

Here one must go slow. The value of the act for those who propose it, sweat it out, do it—this is more easily determined. Value is created, so to speak, in the breach, in a decision to gather, unite voices in an outcry, to precipitate a crisis that, at least for a time, will strip away the mask of evil.

But I know of no sure way of predicting where things will go from there, whether others will hear and respond, or how quickly or slowly. Or whether the act will fail to vitalize others, will come to a grinding halt then and there, its actors stigmatized or dismissed as fools. One swallows dry and takes a chance.

There was one sign that our action touched a nerve. A hasty attempt was made on the day of the action itself to discredit us through a dizzying list of charges. Ideology, panic, and special interests combined to barrage the media and the public with a verdict before the verdict—more violent crazies had gone on a rampage. The charges included assault, false imprisonment, reckless endangerment, criminal mischief, terroristic threats, harassment, criminal coercion, unlawful restraint. Talk about overkill! We sat in court, transfixed, gazing on our images in the crazy mirrors of the state fun house.

It takes a large measure of good sense to stand firm at such moments. People gifted with our nefarious history must remind themselves that at King of Prussia, hammers and blood in hand, we set in motion a lengthy and complex drama. One should speak perhaps of three acts.

The first act belonged in the main to us, an early morning curtain raiser, the action underway. In a sense the adversaries have not yet appeared; only a few subalterns act on their behalf, in their name: the guards and police and employees. But GE has not yet turned on its voltage. No official appears in justifying garb to bespeak the ancient myths, to invoke sacro-secular outrage at the violation of a holy place, property off bounds, the shrine accessible only to initiates. (Antigone has buried her brother's body, but Creon has not yet flogged his way to condemn her.)

Then a second act opens. It marks the marshalling of forces of law and order, the invoking of daemons of natural law, secular karma.

Anger, retaliation are in the air, the gods of property buzz furiously overhead. The actors all but tear up the script of act one; and assault is mounted on the earlier reliance on "higher law" or "con-science." Behold true conscience, behold the highest law of all, the law by which all citizens must live, the law that is our common safeguard against anarchy!

So in the manner of Shakespeare or Pirandello or Sophocles, act two is a kind of play within the play. The audience is bewildered, thrown off guard. It had read a certain kind of admirable moral truth in the face of the young woman Antigone (in the faces of a nun, of a mother of six, of a lawyer, a professor, a seminary graduate—

faces like the credentials of moral worth)—now it hears another kind of truth. This is not the truth of "symbolic action," which from a legal point of view is always murky, easily discredited, and reaching troublesomely as it does into dark existence (the forbidden burial of a brother, the breaking and bloodying of icons) must be exorcised, discredited—by measured, relentless argument.

The argument, of devastating force, in ancient Greece as today, I call that of the Great If.

The example of Antigone, the example of the eight, is deliberately magnified, made stark. Behold their act, performed under clerical guise, under the guise of virtue. Behold their act, as viewed by the state, the guardian and interpreter of public morality. (What an unconscious and ironic tribute is paid the defendants here, as though in the court itself, the state were erecting stone by stone a monument to the conscience it so fears—and so magnifies.)

In any case, citizens and believers, whatever divagations of spirit they were beckoned toward by the conduct of the protagonists, by their age or condition or credentials (above all, by their dark probing symbols)—all this is brought up short and abrupt. You are in court, this audience, as extensions of the jury, who are in effect extensions of the judge. You are not here to indulge in murky existential probings, but to consider the letter of the law and in your hearts to approach a verdict . . .

Finally, act three. Many scenes and changes; the great world, a time between events (action/trial), the agora, a courtroom, the many places where people discuss, argue, make up their minds and unmake them again, slowly or with speed come to a conclusion, the knotting of the action.

In court, the argument of the Great If is relentlessly pursued. The crime of the eight is segregated from the world, the faces of the defendants, mirrors of conscience, are hooded. The inert symbols, hammers, empty bloodied bottles, lie there, tagged, soulless, mere items of evidence. They are relics of moral defeat, emblems of legal punishment; as such, the prosecutor will refer to them with disdain and handle them with distaste. They will be compared, subtly or openly, to the tools of safecrackers, to bloodied knives and guns. What If such implements became the common tools of so-called conscience? What If all citizens, under whatever itch of notoriety, took up such tools (like the soiled hands of Antigone, heaping foul dust on her brother's body) against the law of the state? How sordid a venture!

In the course of this act, the classic Greek formula is verified; the purging of pity and fear.

These must be purged, for pity and terror get in the way of spiritual change. They are obstructive emotions; to be taken seriously, no doubt, but strictly as preliminary to the main event.

That event, in a large sense, is destined to occur neither on stage nor in the court. It is rather the unending passionate pursuit of moral good, the righting of injustice, the ousting of death; the reordering of an ethical universe and of its social and political forms.

But in order to be purged, pity and fear have first to be aroused.

How acute the Greeks were! In the first days following our action, friends invariably spoke of their forebodings, their dread of the harsh sentences that undoubtedly would befall us, their fear that our action would be ignored or misconstrued.

Pity and fear. The pity narrows emotional largesse, the fear spreads out inordinately, claims all minds. Fear of the future, fear for children bereft of parents, fear of the state and its legal savageries . . .

One emotion is too narrow, the other too diffused. Neither finally is useful; that is to say, neither serves to heighten the truth of the universal predicament (which is not defined by prison sentences, but by nuclear annihilation)—or to grant hints and leads as to a way out.

I must inject here a message from the jails of Pennsylvania. If the eight have insisted on anything, it is that their trial and imprisonment are not the issue at stake. Pity for them gains nothing. Neither does fear for them or for their children and spouses. The eight go their way, a way meticulously chosen and after much prayer. But the issues they raise will continue to shadow their lives and vex their hearts. It is the corporate crimes of General Electric, the race toward oblivion that this monstrous entity both fuels and illustrates.

Finally, what drove us to "such extremes"?

To reach the truth, one must turn from Creon to Antigone; from the prosecutor, in our case, to the gospel.

In America, in 1980, it could hardly be called useful to the common weal or a mitigation of the common woe that a group of religious folk enter a megadeath factory—in vain proof that they are in possession of some kind of magical counterforce.

Why then?

Let us say merely because they hungered for the truth, for its embodiment, longed to offer a response to its claim on us. That even through us, an all but submerged voice might be heard, the voice of "God not of the dead, but of the living."

From our statement: "In confronting GE, we choose to obey God's law of life, rather than a corporate summons to death. Our beating of swords into plowshares is a way to enflesh this biblical call. In our action, we draw on a deep-rooted faith in Christ, who changed the course of history through his willingness to suffer rather than to kill. We are filled with hope for our world and for our children as we join this act of resistance."

Chapter 6

DISARMAMENT ON TRIAL

Elmer Maas

When we are brought to trial for Plowshares and disarmament actions, we try to speak about what we have done and why, focusing attention upon the urgent need for people to take personal responsibility for the disarmament of nuclear weapons, the swords of our time. Yet we are indicted by the court with criminal charges including trespass, destruction to property, and damage to the national defense. How do we answer these charges and, at the same time, speak clearly about the real issues?

The courts have consistently disallowed explanations of motive and purpose during trial and have closed their doors to nearly all efforts to raise defenses that would address matters most relevant to the Plowshares actions.[1] Relying on legal precedents or citing the lack of any legal precedent at all, judges have restricted testimony to facts that would substantiate criminal charges, and they have threatened defendants with contempt of court and immediate imprisonment for speaking about nuclear weapons, the peril that the weapons pose, and other facts that might communicate to juries the true motive for and purpose of the actions.

Despite this repressive atmosphere, those on trial try to say as much as they can: in taking the witness stand they speak very simply of their own lives and of what has brought them to a decision to enact the biblical imperative of the Old Testament prophet Isaiah, "to beat swords into plowshares." Beginning a step-by-step narrative of the action itself, they tell of entering factories where nuclear weapons are made, silo launching pads where the Minuteman II missiles are housed, Air Force bases where cruise missiles are being retrofitted into B-52 bombers, and shipbuilding factories where Trident submarines are docked. They speak of how they carried hammers and their own blood to these places and describe beating upon the weapons and pouring their own blood to symbolically and directly disarm components of the first-strike nuclear arsenal.

The defendants explain that they have acted to save and protect human life, that in this time of nuclear peril the saving and protecting of life has two distinct parts: the sounding of a warning and the direct destruction of the instruments of violence that threaten all lives on earth. As in the story of the shepherd in the book of Ezekiel, those who have knowledge of a danger or threat to the lives of others are culpable if they do not make that danger known; the blood of the victims is on the hands of those who fail to sound the alarm.

The destruction of the weapons, in turn, becomes a direct fulfillment and personal enactment of the biblical imperative: "They shall beat their swords into plowshares and their spears into pruning hooks; nation shall not lift up sword against nation, neither shall they study war any more" (Isa. 2:4). The particular swords of our time addressed in the Plowshares actions are the components of the first-strike nuclear arsenal. Far from serving as a deterrent to war, this war-initiating system, now moving toward a launch-on-warning status, makes every moment of our lives a potential flashpoint of nuclear incineration.

The victimization brought about by the bomb is all-pervasive, therefore the "beating of swords into plowshares" considers as well the growing number of present victims of cancer, leukemia, and other diseases whose sufferings have been traced to nuclear radiation caused by weapons testing, nuclear reactors, and various parts of the cycle of uranium mining and processing. The total number of deaths to date caused by nuclear testing alone has been estimated at sixteen million.

Also among the nuclear victims are the poor. As human services are reduced, as increasing numbers of people throughout the world live in conditions of poverty and repression, and as an increasing portion of the human family endures hunger and starvation, the Pentagon has asked for and budgeted two trillion dollars for a five-year nuclear build-up, including the Strategic Defense Initiative and a functional capability for winning a protracted nuclear war.

Juries, of course, rarely hear very much, if anything at all, about nuclear weapons during the personal testimony of defendants. Any mention of the weapons or the first-strike system usually brings immediate objections from the prosecution that are sustained by the judge. The judge often explains that "nuclear weapons are not on trial" and that the "courtroom is not a forum for political debate." The judge then tells the jury to disregard anything that might be interpreted as motive or purpose. Judges have even gone so far as to instruct the jury shortly before time of deliberation that any consideration on their part of motive or purpose would be in violation of their sworn oath as jurors. There is no hint made by the court of the jury's power as the conscience of the community to render an independent verdict based upon its own assessment of the merits of the case.

Yet speaking the truth about the weapons is an important part of the act of "beating swords into plowshares." It is an important part of the action statement and of one's statement at trial. So that some of the facts and issues regarding details of the nuclear peril can be placed before the court and so that jurors might be able to deliberate on matters more closely attuned to the real facts and circumstances of the case than otherwise made available to them, defendants often prepare and present what are called affirmative legal defenses.

A defense of necessity or justification, for example, is available when one performs an action that under ordinary circumstances would be illegal, but under special emergency conditions is justified. (An example would be breaking into a burning building to save a child.) For the defense of necessity to be raised one must usually show that the danger is imminent, that there are no legal alternatives available, and that a causal relation exists between the action one undertakes and the abatement of the harm one seeks to avoid.

Through their own testimony and through the testimony of invited witnesses with expertise in nuclear weapons, nuclear physics, medicine, history, and other fields, evidence has been presented in a number of Plowshares trials exposing the immediate and omnipresent danger of nuclear war and its potential catastrophic consequences. Testimony has been offered explaining why legal alternatives to the course of action undertaken by the defendants are not available. Recognized historians have testified that acts of conscience such as those undertaken by the defendants are necessary to abate the threat of nuclear war.

While some judges preclude the availability of the justification defense before the defense case begins and others hear testimony with the jury excluded from the courtroom, much testimony regarding the nature of the first-strike weapons system and the immediate peril of nuclear war has been presented before some juries. However, most judges in Plowshares and disarmament trials have instructed jurors that they may not consider justification or other affirmative defenses in their deliberations.[2] Judges have taken it upon themselves to decide that insufficient evidence is presented to enable the jury to make up its own mind with regard to necessity. One judge in particular ruled that he could not conceive of any evidence that the defendants might present through expert witnesses that would meet the burden of the justification defense.[3] In light of such comments, at least one appellate panel has ruled that the matter of justification should be a jury question.[4] This ruling, however, was appealed by the prosecution and overturned in a recent State Supreme Court decision.

In addition to raising the defense of necessity, defendants often point out that under principles established by the Nuremberg tribunal following World War II, individual citizens are responsible for crimes of war undertaken in their name by their governments, and that citizens not only have a right but an obligation to interfere with and stop these crimes. With special reference to National Security Decision Document #13 of the Reagan administration authorizing a five-year plan to adapt the U.S. strategic nuclear arsenal to a capability for fighting and winning a protracted nuclear war, defendants have presented briefs based on the Nuremberg principles and other principles of international law. They have attempted to raise defenses that would enumerate before the court and jury the defendants' rights and obligations in the face of these and other developments in U.S. nuclear planning, including the Strategic Defense Initiative. Defendants have been denied the opportunity to even raise this defense or present witnesses.

Defendants at trial have attempted to raise closely related issues by addressing the matter of criminal intent. Recognizing that the prosecution must prove criminal intent, defendants have often argued that evidence should be presented showing that their actions were not based on criminal intentions, that indeed they acted to save life in the face of preparations for nuclear war, such preparations themselves being crimes of unprecedented magnitude. But, once again, the courts have denied such efforts, ruling that criminal intent be narrowly defined and reducible to only whether or not the defendants intended to enter the missile factory in question and hammer on the weapons, knowing that they would be in violation of specific state or national laws.

Some Plowshares defendants, in reflecting upon the court's systematic denial of efforts to speak about nuclear weapons and to raise affirmative defenses that would attempt to keep the focus on the real issues, have seen this pattern of denials as symptomatic of a larger denial within our society. It is specifically the denial of one's personal responsibility for questioning what has become the absolute authority of the bomb, of nuclear weapons. They see the unquestioned authority of the weapons as part of what is clearly a growing state religion, a state religion of nuclearism. The weapons have become gods of metal, and the state acts to punish those who would disarm or damage these idols with charges of trespass, damage to property, or damage to the national defense. A number of Plowshares groups have raised this issue in a pretrial brief elaborating upon the unconstitutionally established state religion of nuclearism.[5] They have moved for dismissal of all charges inasmuch as the laws, as applied in these cases, are used to protect this unconstitutional state religion. These motions have been denied.

Consistent with the pattern of denials that have suppressed defendants' efforts to speak to the real issues during trial, the judges' instructions to juries have limited jurors to considering only evidence that would substantiate specific charges of trespass, damage to property, and so on. Defendants try nevertheless to remind jurors that as the conscience of the community they have the power to act on their conscience, even independently of the instructions of the judge. After all, they need be answerable to no one for their verdict. Such suggestions to juries by defendants, however, elicit sharp reprimands to defendants by the judge, who often threatens defendants with contempt of court when they continue to inform the jury of its power. On occasion defendants do continue to speak, not only to inform the jury of what it is in fact able to do, but as a nonviolent protest of the court's consistent effort to suppress the truth.

At other times as well, defendants nonviolently witness to the illegality of court proceedings by continuing to speak truths that should be heard, and these defendants have been immediately jailed for contempt of court. (Some defendants have also received contempt of court charges and additional jail sentences for not answering questions put by the prosecution that might implicate others.) Other defendants have chosen not to participate in the proceedings at all and, with the exception of a short statement before the jury or at time of sentencing, allow their silence and noncooperation to witness to the absence of legitimacy within the court process. Others, having attempted to testify and raise what issues they can, choose a point when the court has definitively refused to deal with the real issues and stand quietly with their backs to the court as a public witness to the absence of truth and justice in the halls of justice. Some have left the court during trial or on the day of sentencing to return to the location where their action originally occurred, to say that "here" is where and how the truth can be spoken.

In each of the Plowshares and disarmament trials to date, juries have returned verdicts of guilty and prison sentences have become increasingly harsh. But the community of disarmament continues to expand in the spirit of Isaiah and Micah as the enactment of their ancient prophecies becomes a source of light and hope for our times.

NOTES

1. The generalities and observations in this chapter are based on experiences of Plowshares defendants on trial. In each case groups or individuals have been brought to trial for beating swords into plowshares, for symbolically destroying weapons, and in each case charges of damage to property have been brought against the defendants. While there are similar patterns in court rulings on admissible evidence for jury consideration in Plowshares trials and trials for nonviolent resistance that have not involved property damage, the patterns have not been identical.

2. The exception in this case is the judge in the trial of the Sperry Software Pair, Judge Miles Lord. Even though the jury returned a guilty verdict, Judge Lord, in his instructions to the jury, outlined the elements of the justification defense and granted its availability to the jury in their deliberations. See Appendix II for excerpts of Judge Lord's instructions to the jury and comments at time of sentencing.

3. In the Plowshares Eight trial in Norristown, Pennsylvania, in 1981, Judge Samuel Salus precluded the testimony of Robert Aldridge and other experts on nuclear weapons on the grounds that none of the evidence these witnesses might offer would be relevant to a justification defense. A short excerpt from the trial transcripts might be helpful:

THE COURT (Judge Salus): I will allow to be put on the record the name of the witness that you called, Mr. Aldridge. And I said his testimony is not relevant to the issues at hand.

MR. SCHUCHARDT: You don't know what his testimony is.

MR. PHILIP BERRIGAN: I thought the jury was to decide the facts.

THE COURT: The jury does decide the facts. I decide the law and relevance. And that is a matter of law.
(Transcript of Notes of Testimony, Comm. of Penna. vs. Daniel Berrigan et al., March 4, 1981, 132.

Similar rulings preventing jurors from hearing any expert testimony at all on nuclear weapons have been made during Plowshares trials in Connecticut, Florida, and Rhode Island.

4. When the Plowshares Eight conviction was appealed and overturned by an appellate panel, Judge Spaeth, in writing a concurring opinion, observed:

Nor is the [nuclear] peril confined to those who will be "irradiated, burned, and blasted." It extends much farther, to our survival as a species. If only a small fraction of the nuclear missiles now able to be fired, either by us or the Soviet Union, are fired, a "dark nuclear winter" will occur: a cloud of debris will block off our sunlight; temperatures will plunge; and our death by freezing or starvation will follow. Scientists have identified a 100 megaton explosion as the "nuclear war threshold" that once crossed will lead to such a global catastrophe. See "After Atomic War: Doom in the Dark," *Philadelphia Inquirer,* November 1, 1983, at 1. It is in the light of this peril that the reasonableness of appellants' belief must be judged.

Perhaps a jury will discount evidence that our situation is as desperate as the authorities I have alluded to believe. Or perhaps a jury will regard appellants' conduct as mere bravado. On either of these views, appellants' plea of justification will fail. But we must leave such appraisals to a jury. For we are not entitled to hold, "as a matter of law," as the dissent would, that a jury could not find that our situation is as desperate as appellants offered to prove, and then, proceeding from that finding, could not go on to decide that appellants' conduct, however unlikely of success, represented a reasonable response. I admit that for my part—and here at least I suppose that the dissenters and I are not far apart—I am skeptical of the appellants' conduct. I believe there are better ways, the bishops' among them. But that is what trial by jury is all about: to ensure that the defendant is not judged by a skeptical judge but by his peers.

(Comm. of Pa. v. Rev. Daniel Berrigan et al., Appeal from the Judgment of Sentence in the Court of Common Pleas of Montgomery County, Criminal, No. 2647-80, Concurring opinion by Judge Spaeth, February 17, 1984.)

This appellate panel ruling was overturned by the Pennsylvania Supreme Court in the fall of 1985 and the Plowshares Eight appeal is at the time of writing still under review in the Pennsylvania courts.

5. See Appendix 2 for the text of the brief on nuclearism filed by the Griffiss Plowshares.

Chapter 7

SPIRITUAL POWER BEHIND BARS

Anne Montgomery, R.S.C.J.

A time to plant and a time to uproot . . .
A time to seek and a time to lose . . .

Ecclesiastes 3:2,6, NEB

Many people understand political action, public demonstration, even "civil disobedience"—what we would name "divine obedience"—but consider the consequences of such action—jail—to be a stumbling block, a waste of time when they might otherwise be continuing their work for peace and the poor on the streets. Paradoxically, just as crossing the line in action clarifies one's vision, so the experience of the nonaction, the seemingly useless life of prison, reveals a level of truth-force difficult to perceive from the "outside." There is a good reason for this difficulty. The center of power that can be reached in any imprisoned life is as hidden as the buried seed. "For you have died, and your life is hidden with Christ in God" (Col. 3:3, RSV).

This is not to say that prison is a good place. It is not the desert of the hermits who fled a corrupt Roman Empire. Rather, this "desert" encapsulates some of the most dehumanizing and debilitating aspects of our modern "empire." Prison is a repression of the freedom and creativity crucial to productive life and action. It is an expression of the fear and violence that undermine our "free" institutions, the fear and violence that seek to secure weapons, to control and punish, and it concretizes that violence in a way that we who accept the consequences of our actions cannot avoid. We do not choose prison. We choose, rather, to resist the forces of death within and without and to entrust the fruits of our truth telling to God. But here there is an opportunity to live out the essence of our action: to meet violence in its petty, institutionalized forms outside ourselves, to meet it again in our own reactions, and in both situations to allow the transforming power of love to work in and around us.

Most obvious at first, however, is the helplessness, the loss of control, the reinforcement of all that is degrading to human dignity and self-respect. We come with a sense of peace, of celebration even, buoyed by our recent act of resistance. But then we find ourselves instant criminals—we are strip-searched, fingerprinted, numbered. Worse, we meet and compare experiences with those for whom prison is not the result of an act of resistance but of its opposite— a further rejection by a society that provides little help or sympathy for the marginalized, whether the problem stems from drugs, economic need, or abuse. Our own "ineffectiveness" to change anything is all too obvious—a seeming confirmation of the words of mainstream critics.

It is in this most adverse situation, however, that the power of God can be released, because any illusions we might have had about "justice" are shattered and our hands are sometimes literally bound. The promise stands that "God works for good with those who love him" (Rom. 8:28) in all things—not just in the good situations but also in the midst of evil ones, the mistakes and the results of our sin. This is our faith.

Jim Douglass has called prisons the "monasteries of the future" because of this emptying process and the need to depend entirely on God. This prediction has been criticized because prison is an environment so inimical to the human development that is the foundation of a healthy contemplative life. But is this criticism valid in the world as we know it, where the majority of its population lives in scarcely human conditions or under repressive governments? If the contemplative spirit flows from the Spirit of Christ, it can only be strengthened by identification with the poor, the oppressed, and the marginalized. We who can never lose the privilege of our education, inner resources, or the free act that landed us in prison in the first place can still become more grounded in reality by touching the lives of so many unfortunate sisters and brothers, by experiencing something of their inability to choose the next meal or to find a measure of silence and solitude, something seemingly so essential to contemplation. Prayer must be as simple as breathing—not as an exercise or a method, but as the movement of the Spirit breathing within the whole of creation.

Life in prison is part of a continuing "experiment in truth." Actions of divine obedience are moments in this continuum of prayer and community building, of witness and of its deepening in the life that follows. This is a truly creative process, never perfected but always full of new possibilities.

Chapter 8

LIBERATION IN CAPTIVITY: A FABLE

John Bach

There was once a prison that ran pretty well. It encircled the lives of some eight hundred men, all of whom would have preferred being someplace else. It ran as well as it did because it employed the carrot and the stick, the iron fist and velvet glove, and a Skinnerian method of behavior reinforcement. It managed somehow to keep the eight hundred men emotionally apart in spite of the fact that they lived on top of each other. It succeeded in large measure because it succeeded in instilling the following lessons: do your own time; go along and get along; don't make waves; look out for number one; don't get involved; make acquaintances not friends; and so forth. Since these were the same lessons that the men had been taught all their lives, they were easily applied here and were not questioned for the most part. The men became suspicious, macho, abusive, lustful, envious, and thus they kept each other in line.

The prison ran pretty well because it not only kept the inmates apart; it kept them at each other's throats. Favoritism was bestowed; racism was practiced and provoked; classism was reinforced; big and small manipulations took place; inalienable rights were doled out to the well-heeled as privileges. Prisoners were encouraged to become like the prison that enslaved them. Violence among inmates was, according to the situation, either punished, overlooked, or rewarded. The prison figured that everyone had his price, and for the most part the price was shamefully crumb-sized.

The prison ran pretty well, like the larger society it reflected—there was more emphasis on proper working order than on people. Yet, sometimes in fables, as well as in real life, goodness happens for no apparent reason—at least not for reasons that most people understand or accept. And such was the case in this prison, which had always run pretty well.

Things began to happen, things not unlike the occasional weedy flowers that grew out of cracks in the concrete walls. It happened that a handful of prisoners recognized each other as brothers, and they organized to stop rape within the prison. This was not as hard as they had thought. They went further. They encouraged others to share, not horde, to open up, not close off or shut down. They read books together and discussed them; they shared their life histories. Slowly walls came tumbling down as they began to trust each other. They did favors for each other without thought of recompense. Birthdays were celebrated; contraband cakes were baked; musical reviews were written and performed. An underground paper (*The Shit-House Press*) was published and circulated. "Stay strong" was a common parting. Smiles and grins, like the weedy flowers, began splitting the concrete. The oasis began crowding out the desert.

The men looked out for each other, stood up for each other, occasionally went on hunger strikes and work strikes, were transferred across the country, were put in the hole, lost good time and parole dates. It didn't matter. A sense of responsibility and resistance evolved and as long as that endured and prevailed it gave the men a sense of freedom that mere physical imprisonment could not take away. It no longer mattered so much to the men which side of the wall they were on. Their sentences were not just so much time *out* of their lives, but time *of* their lives that could be just as worthy a period of growing and living as any other. People who had never cottoned much to the notion of miracles (like the person who is writing this) had to rethink their beliefs on the subject. It was all a dream and it was real.

All of this was like sand in the grinding cogs, and the prison, which was no longer running pretty well, responded, as one might suppose, with small-mindedness and brutality. It went too far though and did not discover until too late that it was no longer dealing with eight hundred self-serving individuals, but with a community of related people who had tasted a better way of life and who were not willing to wipe that out of their lives.

A strike was organized. Black, Hispanic, and white inmates worked together. This was a rare occurrence indeed, and the prison was horrified. It pressured some men, bribed others, but nothing worked; it was like threatening Br'er Rabbit with the briarpatch.

One Monday morning, the prison that for years and years had run pretty well didn't run at all. A nonviolent work strike surrounded the prison which surrounded the eight hundred lives. Thousands of dollars of revenue were lost as the prison industry shut down its defense department, war profiteering work. Inmates took control of their lives, had meetings, discussed central issues, took risks. Even during the next tense nine days there was still no violence, no destruction of property, no abusive language, no vamping or exploitation, which in the past had pretty much been the order of the day. What there was was a truly human community in the face of great adversity.

The prison that wasn't running at all eventually got back to running pretty well. The prison broke the strike, and to its way of thinking it had been a decisive victory for the bleak forces of lock and key. But all the inmates knew, and the prison knew too, in the lifeless marrow of its bones, that what had happened was not something the prison could ever take away or deny or belittle or disrespect or not live in fear of, for it was the life force moving toward liberation, which is the working of goodness among people. It was a remarkable progression of consciousness: it was liberation because of and in spite of jail.

This fable really happened at the federal prison in Danbury, Connecticut, in the spring of 1972, and I was there. Since then I've returned there and other places like it that run pretty well, and the scene has changed a lot. Like community, this sense of liberation in captivity is a gift, and sometimes you just can't make it happen beyond an individual level. But in every case the victory *is* in the struggle, and as long as the flame of resistance remains unextinguished, there is no defeat or dishonor or even imprisonment of the spirit.

Other examples of this abound in the ongoing examples of witness around us. It surfaces in the dozens of origami paper cranes strung from the bars of a jail cell and in the look of joy and freedom on a grandmother's face as she is led to a police van after her first arrest. It is reflected in the small acts of daily heroism done in anonymity and most clearly (and joyfully) in the continuing Plowshares actions in spite of long prison terms. This notion of liberation in captivity comes alive in the willingness of people to take risks and suffer to turn the consequences into positive experiences as they endeavor to build a better world. Just that. Life itself, to the fullest.

Chapter 9

PRISON WITNESS: EXPOSING THE INJUSTICE

Judith Beaumont

The spirit of the Lord has been given to me,
for he has anointed me.
He has sent me to bring the good news to the poor,
to proclaim liberty to captives
and to the blind new sight,
to set the downtrodden free,
to proclaim the Lord's year of favor.

Luke 4:18

Reflection on this passage in which Jesus identifies himself with the mission of the prophet in Isaiah 61 has inspired countless responses by the Christian community over the centuries. In a small way the passage has been fulfilled once again by a community in Connecticut—primarily women and not all Christian—who confronted the unjust conditions in the Connecticut Correctional Institution for Women in Niantic.

Following the Trident *Nein* Plowshares action at Electric Boat Company in Groton, Connecticut, on July 5, 1982, Anne Montgomery, Anne Bennis, and I were held on bond for about seven weeks in the pretrial unit of the only women's prison in the state. Convinced in our hearts that Trident must be disarmed, we knew when we chose to act that we would have to spend time in prison. Prison is not a good place to be, but the opportunities for ministry are abundant, as we were to find out.

Although the facility as a whole was considered minimum security, the pretrial unit where we were held was at least medium security. Our first days were spent rejoicing in our symbolic act of disarming the *U.S.S. Florida* Trident submarine and two sonar spheres for other beasts of mass destruction. Messages of support from friends and strangers began arriving and even some of our sister inmates could appreciate what we had done. As we settled in to the daily routine of inactivity, we began to be aware of conditions at the prison. Gradually we got to know other women and heard about the situations that angered them and the conditions that violated their own ethic of fairness.

The absence of planned activities—no classes, no craft projects, little outdoor recreation—was perhaps the worst circumstance we identified. Personally I didn't mind so much at first because I welcomed the time to pray, read, and answer letters. But for most women the time hung heavy. There were few books available and no magazines or newspapers. The color TV in the dayroom and the radio in the laundry were the only media available. We longed to get out in the small yard but all of us were cooped up inside for days. Summer was given as the excuse for school not being in session.

The facility was quite dirty and poorly lit—terrible light for reading. The overall sanitation was awful—there were moldy shower curtains, broken plumbing, and the usual cockroaches in the toaster. Inmates were locked in rooms without toilets at night. To use the facilities we had to bang hard on the bedroom door or shout to be heard by a correctional officer who might be downstairs and out of earshot. This was especially hard on the pregnant women, who also suffered from inadequate diet. Some women resorted to "piss cans"—one pound coffee cans they had confiscated from the kitchen garbage.

One of the more disturbing policies of the prison was the one allowing male officers to be assigned to the sleeping areas. They could lock and unlock the doors of bedrooms and bathrooms at any time of the day or night, peering through them at the times the women were most likely to be dressing or undressing.

There were frequent complaints about the quality of medical attention and length of time it took to see a doctor. We heard the cries and moans of the drug addicts detoxing "cold turkey" without medication or supervision.

As we listened to the complaints and saw this dehumanization for ourselves, we began to realize our need to liberate these women and ourselves from these oppressive conditions. We began by telling our friends who came to visit about them. Some of them encouraged us to write about what we had experienced. Letters were sent to friends and former co-workers, who in turn sent the letters to others who might share our concerns. Letters were written to the prison ombudsman, who came to listen to our concerns.

As time went on our increasing awareness of the problems led us to realize the institutional violence of the criminal justice system. Most of the women I met were primarily victims rather than criminals. They had been abused and victimized by racism, poverty, poor education, male violence and sexual exploitation. They were not bad people. They were the victims of a society that idolizes nuclear weapons as its human-made god of safety and that pours billions of dollars into coffers for their continued production.

For their "crimes" these women were warehoused in overcrowded facilities where only a very few were given the opportunity to change their lives. It is only fair to say also that there were good people working in corrections and the occasional exposure to their genuine concern was a treasured moment.

Each time we went to court it was a joy to get outside the prison and to be with the six Trident *Nein* men and our growing support group. But upon returning to Niantic, like all the other women, we were subjected to a vaginal search for contraband. Our legal advisor appealed to the judge to sign an order prohibiting these searches. Predictably he refused so the searches continued.

About two weeks before trial we were released rather unexpectedly and once on the outside had even more opportunities to relate our experiences to others who shared our concern. During the weeks we were on trial two women from among our supporters also acted at Electric Boat and were held at Niantic as "Jane Does." As part of their noncooperation they refused the vaginal search upon return from court and were placed in the detention unit, which also houses the mentally ill inmates and those who are suicidal. They were able to gather information about that unit and the absence of treatment and care for those with the most severe problems.

As soon as our trial ended a meeting was called to hear about Niantic and to decide if something could be done to remedy the unacceptable conditions. Social workers, educators, lawyers, and community activists came to listen and decided that something must be done. After further meetings the Connecticut Coalition for Women in Prison was formed to address the problems we had identified. Three tactics were selected: negotiation, legislation, and litigation. The work was parceled out to different groups and individuals. Over a period of several months research was done and new groups and individuals including former inmates were contacted. Members of the Coalition met with prison officials and were given a tour. Finding that not much could be accomplished by negotiation, legislation and litigation became the focus of Coalition activity. One bill to fund the mental health unit was introduced through the efforts of a Coalition member. Some of us testified at committee hearings. This bill did get passed.

Preparation began for the filing of a class action suit on behalf of all the Niantic inmates and their children. Anne Montgomery was in Niantic at the time for her part in Trident *Nein,* as were the women from Plowshares Number Four. They all were talking with other inmates about conditions and about the need for plaintiffs.

In the midst of all this I returned to Niantic myself. Having refused to pay restitution to Electric Boat, I was sentenced to one year. Knowing that much work needed to be done inside, I went with some eagerness. I hoped to confront the body cavity search regulation. My opportunity came when I went to court for a sentence reduction hearing. It was denied as expected, but I returned from court determined to resist the search we all found to be so offensive, humiliating, and painful. When I refused to submit to it I was taken to the locked unit and placed in a room with only an iron bed with a thin mattress, toilet, and sink. I would be locked up for twenty-three hours a day until I submitted to the search.

I was allowed a phone call to the Coalition attorneys, who were prepared to act. The next morning a call came from the lawyer informing me that she was hand-delivering a letter to the Assistant Attorney General asking for a change in the search regulation and my release. By lunchtime I was back in the general population and the word was out that there would be no more body cavity searches for court returnees unless probable cause could be shown. The news was received by the inmates with disbelief and rejoicing. The timing could not have been better. This was just the encouragement the women needed to continue working on the lawsuit.

Several inmates had agreed to meet with the lawyers and law students. After a number of interviews, the named plaintiffs were selected and the suit was filed in federal court. After many hearings the Department of Correction agreed to a settlement without going to trial. On most counts the plaintiffs can claim victory. However, it remains to be seen whether the Department of Correction will comply as they have agreed. It will be necessary for inmates to keep close watch on conditions and to speak up when they find themselves unfairly treated. Let us hope that the prison resistance can be maintained and that periodic visits by civil disobedients (divine obedients) will be occasions not only to resist the war preparations going on in Connecticut but also to gather information about current conditions and the identity of inmates willing to challenge the unjust conditions found.

Prison conditions cannot be changed by resisters alone, but with a hard-working support community on the outside the "system" can be challenged and made to conform to what is more right and just and liberating.

Resisters blessed with different gifts have engaged in other forms of witness in prison. Some have been teachers or tutors; others have done counseling or led Bible study groups. Some have chosen to carry on their resistance by refusing to do any prison jobs. While in prison, resisters have come to know sisters and brothers, learn of their struggles, and share their dreams and hopes for a better life.

All of us have received a great deal from those we have met in prison. In our times of loneliness and frustration there have been sisters and brothers there who understood, who cracked a joke at the right moment, who shared the little they had: tea bags, pencils, crochet hooks—little things on the outside but so much more on the inside.

Many acts of resistance have grown out of works for justice. In prison we become intimately connected to the work for justice as we live and work with those people who are the victims of the arms race. We learn compassion, work for small changes, struggle in ways we've never dreamed of, and long for a world in which liberty is proclaimed and prisons will be no more.

Chapter 10

I AM SO SMALL: ONE WOMAN RESPONDS TO NUCLEAR WAR

Marcia A. Timmel

The threat of nuclear war enshrouds me like a darkening cloud. I am only one woman. One very ordinary woman. What can I do?

I am in Ohio, working with ordinary women, poor women. I watch their children, babies I helped bring into the world. I feel the children's hunger, the pain in their chilled bodies under thin gowns. I see them sleeping in cardboard boxes. Their mothers' anguish becomes mine.

Why is there no money for milk, heat, cribs? It has all gone for weapons—bombs that one day will incinerate these precious babies if poverty does not kill them first.

What can one woman do?

I can say yes to life with my life.

I kneel on the steps of the Pentagon on Good Friday and pray for the grace to say yes to God. I pour my own blood onto the pillars from a baby bottle—my blood offered as a plea that the children might live.

I am imprisoned for a month. Have I accomplished anything? I am only one little woman.

Remaining in Washington, I meet the man who will become my husband. Together we live in community, offering shelter to the homeless and food to the hungry.

Yet we live at Ground Zero, in the slums only blocks from the White House. How can we offer the poor shelter from the cold if we do not try as well to shelter them from the bomb?

I stand on the deck of a nearly finished Trident submarine, a household hammer in my hand. I tremble, my knees weaken. What am I doing here? This is the most deadly weapon in the world; more than 2000 Hiroshimas are under my feet. I feel weak, powerless. What can I do?

With my sisters and brothers I, an ordinary woman, can hammer this nuclear sword into a biblical plowshare. In faith I hammer.

I am arrested. Two weeks after my wedding I am sentenced to four months in jail.

Now I am home, working at the shelter and soup kitchen. Now my husband is imprisoned for a Plowshares action and is serving a three-year sentence. Once again we are separated by prison, by the bomb, and I must carry on alone.

The arms race grows. I struggle with loneliness, fear, despair. I search for hope and find none. Where, oh God, are you?

I am so small, and the darkness is so great.

I pray and find peace. If there is no hope, I must become hope, hope for the world, for even ordinary women are greater than the bomb. We need not submit. We can hammer swords into plowshares and demand that our nations make war no more.

I am only one woman, but I can be faithful.

And I will.

Chapter 11

PRISON POEMS

FROM ALDERSON: LENT, 1985
Anne Montgomery, R.S.C.J.

I walk the road,
  one mile, more or less,
up the hill to view
  Outside
these sun-tipped hills,
  mocking? hollowed to hold death?
  or are they cradles of spring's
    birth, echoing our longing?

and Inside:
  A distorted mirror of worldwide
    pain:
    hospital—
    razor-wired detention—
    drug unit—
  then downhill to the valley of our
    ordinary,
    mind-numbing
    daily
    come and go.

and yet Inward
  to face another mirror—darkened—
    someone walking long ago
      in small space
        and time
      but made a difference—
        how?

The "how" our hope
  not big numbers
    big names
    big news
  but its very substance-self
    discounted
    forgotten
    discontinued
    lost and buried
  and, behold,
    alive:
the Oneness
—we can name the Name—
  good news for all,
    breathed deep
  into the soil of our
    here
      and
        now

(Written in Alderson Federal Correctional Institution, spring 1985)

THIS PARADISE EARTH
Roger Ludwig

This paradise earth
  we turn into a wasteland
    of trivial pursuit,
battlefield of petty differences,
  prison of dire necessity
    devoid of meaning and miracle.

O come recover
  paradise with me,
    with any sister, any brother
in the love of the Risen One
  who joins us in our hands joined.

O come and wed
  this wealth in poverty,
    this patience so full of promise.

O come and die
and live in this constant
ending and beginning again.

(Written in the Adult Correctional Institution, Cranston, Rhode Island, spring 1985)

THOUGHTS ON DETERRENCE
(In Season and out of Season)
Anne Montgomery, R.S.C.J.

The leaves are past their turning,
like the road that curves between the trees
and stops,
dead at this door,
deterred perhaps
but only from going back—
denying or forgetting
that it must lose its boundaries,
all signs secure in shape and color,
and tunnel deep.

And so the leaves,
dropping now,
their last clinging to color and form
cut short by an arbitrary wind.
They fall—
a platitudinous lesson for slow learners:
all about dying to live,
losing to find—
the fallow season of creation
when seeds, in the darkness of this rotting place,
gather strength from broken soil,
drink deep from hidden springs,
turn upwards,
and
in that push towards light,
resist.

(Written in Connecticut Correctional Institution for Women, Niantic, fall 1982)

PART THREE

Living Tradition and Living Hope

Eight people praying on the tracks of the Nuclear Train on February 24, 1984, just prior to the train's delivery of approximately 120 hydrogen bombs to a Trident submarine base in Bangor, Washington. These eight people knelt in the train's path while 200 other vigilers stood alongside the tracks holding candles. The eight were arrested by local police, but were not charged for their actions. The nationwide tracks campaign, organized by the Ground Zero Center for Nonviolent Action and the Agape Community, has participants in over 300 U.S. towns and cities, who are committed to tracking, vigiling beside, and blocking deliveries of the Nuclear Train and the Trident Missile Motor Trains. *Photo by Dick Doughty.*

What we do is very little, but it is like the little boy with a few loaves and fishes. Christ took that little and increased it. He will do the rest. What we do is so little we may seem to be constantly failing. But so did he fail. He met with apparent failure on the Cross. But unless the seed fall into the earth and die, there is no harvest. And why must we see results? Our work is to sow. Another generation will be reaping the harvest.

Dorothy Day

What the world expects of Christians is that Christians should speak out, loud and clear, and that they should voice their condemnation in such a way that never a doubt, never the slightest doubt, could arise in the heart of the simplest person. That they should get away from abstraction and confront the blood-stained face history has taken on today.

Albert Camus, on the lack of church resistance to the rise of Nazism

Because everything we do and everything we are is in jeopardy, and because the peril is immediate and unremitting, every person is the right person to act, and every moment is the right moment to begin, starting with the present moment.

Jonathan Schell

Chapter 12

CIVIL DISOBEDIENCE AS PRAYER

James Douglass

One way of seeing jail today is to regard it as the new monastery. In a society preparing for nuclear war and ignoring its poor, jail is an appropriate setting in which to give one's life to prayer. In a nation that has legalized preparations for the destruction of all life on earth, going to jail for peace—through nonviolent civil disobedience—can be seen as a prayer. In reflecting today on the Lord's Prayer, I think that going to jail as a way of saying "thy kingdom come, thy will be done" may be the most basic prayer we can offer in the "nuclear security state." Because we have accepted the greatest evil conceivable as a substitute for divine security, we have become a nation of atheists and blasphemers. The nuclear security state, United States or Soviet Union, is blasphemous by definition. As members of such a nation, we need to pray for the freedom to do God's will by noncooperating with the ultimate evil it is preparing. Civil disobedience done in a loving spirit is itself that kind of prayer.

On the other hand, civil disobedience can be done in a way that, while it is apparently not cooperating with nuclear war, it still ends up cooperating with an illusion that underlies nuclear war. In any attitude of resistance to the state there is a kind of demonic underside, a power turned upside down that wishes to gain the upper hand. Civil disobedience that is not done as prayer is especially vulnerable to its underside.

A simple truth at the root of nonviolence is that we can't change an evil or an injustice from the outside. Thomas Merton states this truth at the conclusion of one of his last books, *Mystics and Zen Masters,* as a critique of "nonviolence" as it is understood by its proponents in the Western world. Merton questions "the Western acceptance of a 'will to transform others' in terms of one's own prophetic insight accepted as a norm of pure justice." He asks:

Is there not an "optical illusion" in an eschatological spirit which, however much it may appeal to agape, seeks only to transform persons and social structures *from the outside?* Here we arrive at a basic principle, one might almost say an ontology of nonviolence, which requires further investigation.[1]

Nonviolent noncooperation with the greatest evil in history is still, according to Merton's insight, a possible way into illusion, a more subtle form of the same illusion that we encounter behind the nuclear buildup. Even in nonviolent resistance, unless we accept deeply the spirit of nonviolence, we can end up waging our own form of war and contributing to the conclusion we seek to overcome. Because the evil we resist is so great, we are inclined to overlook an illusion inherent in our own position, the will to transform others from the outside.

If one understands civil disobedience as an assertion of individual conscience over against the evil or injustice of the state, the temptation to seek an "outside solution" is already present. Conscience against the state sounds like a spiritually based or "inside solution." We are, after all, stating our willingness in conscience to go to jail at the hands of the state that threatens an unparalleled evil. But our conscience set off against the nuclear state takes an external view of people acting on behalf of the state. And ultimately such a view externalizes our own conscience.

In the acts of civil disobedience I have done, I have never met "the state." As far as my own ambition goes, that has been disappointing. I have met only people such as police, judges, and jail guards who cooperate (and sometimes noncooperate) with the evil of nuclear war in complex and often puzzling ways. I have never met a person who embodies the state or nuclear war. In their nuances of character, police, judges, and guards come from the same stew of humanity as do people who perform acts of civil disobedience.

A spiritually based nonviolence, one that truly seeks change from within, has to engage deeply the spirits of both sides of a conflict. Civil disobedience as an act of conscience against the state tends to focus exclusively on our own conscience as a source of change. Yet in the act of civil disobedience we meet particular people like ourselves, not "the state," and the most enduring thing we can achieve through such an act is, in the end, our relationship to the people we touch and who touch us. Our hope should not be for any strategic victories over such representatives of the state but rather loving, non-violent relationships with them in the midst of our arrests, trials, and prison sentences. The danger of seeing civil disobedience as an assertion of conscience over against the evil of the state is that it may get confused into an assertion against these particular people, so that we may never really see our relationship to them as primary. In making friends with our opponents—in the police, in the Pentagon, or in the Soviet Union—lies our greatest hope of overcoming nuclear war.

A more fundamental question suggested by Merton is: who is this "I," this self, that is doing the act of conscience in civil disobedience? If civil disobedience accentuates or heightens this sense of self—if it gives it a sense of power—is that necessarily a good thing? Civil disobedience is often referred to today as a way of empowering its participants. For socially powerless people nonviolent civil disobedience can be a profoundly liberating way out of bondage, as one part of a larger revolution. But empowerment can also be used to cover a heightened sense of an individual self that may be a step into further bondage.

We who see ourselves as peacemakers—and don't we all?—would be deeply shocked if we could see the extent to which we act personally for war, not only in our more obvious faults, but even in our very peacemaking. Our intentions and actions for peace lead to war if they are based on a false self and its illusions. If the purpose of civil disobedience is to "empower" such a self, it is a personal act of war.

The nuclear arms race summarizes the history of a false, violent self—of many such false selves magnified in national egos—in an inconceivable evil. What the nuclear crisis says to us, as nothing else in history could, is that the empowering of a false self creates a crisis that has no solution, only transformation. We can't *solve* an arms race based on enormous national illusions, illusions that both exploit and protect an emptiness at the center of millions of lives. Those illusions can only be cracked open to the truth and fear and emptiness at the core of each national pride, then revealed as truly reconcilable with their apparent opposites in the consciousness of another people.

Civil disobedience for the sake of empowering a false self serves as the warring nation-state on a smaller scale. Civil disobedience as that kind of empowerment is an attempt to solve one's problems and frustations by externalizing them in a theater in which innocence confronts the evil of the nuclear state. But we are not innocent.

The greatest treason, as T. S. Eliot points out in *Murder in the Cathedral,* is to do the right deed for the wrong reason. Civil disobedience in response to the greatest evil in history, done to empower a self that can't face its own emptiness, is the right deed for the wrong reason. Because of its motivation, it may also twist itself into the wrong deed. An ego-empowering act of civil disobedience will in the end empower both the self and the nuclear state, which while tactically at odds are spiritually in agreement. Such resistance, like the state itself, asserts power to cover a void. Civil disobedience, like war, can be used to mask the emptiness of a false self.

Civil disobedience as prayer is not an assertion of individual conscience over against the evil of the state. Protesting against something for which we ourselves are profoundly responsible is a futile exercise in hypocrisy. The evil of nuclear war is not external to us, so that it can be isolated in the state or in the Nuclear Train loaded with hydrogen bombs.[2] The nature of the evil lies in our cooperation with it. What Merton is suggesting is that as we cease cooperating in one way with that evil, our well-hidden tendency is to begin cooperating with it more intensely and more blindly in another way, defining the evil in a way external to us a way that only deepens and hardens its actual presence in ourselves.

The power of the evil of nuclear war is nothing more than the power of our cooperation with it. There is no evil exclusively out there, over against us. The evil is much more subtle than that. This is why it continues to exist. When we cease cooperating with evil at its source in ourselves, it ceases to exist. When we accept responsibility for nuclear war in the hidden dimensions of our own complicity, we will experience the miracle of seeing the Nuclear Train stop and the arms race end. To paraphrase Harry Truman, the bomb stops here.

Civil disobedience as prayer is not an assertion of self over against an illusion but an acceptance of God's loving will because of our responsibility for evil: "Not my will but thine be done." The prayer of the Gospels, like the prayer of Gandhi, is at its heart an acceptance of what we don't want: the acceptance of our suffering out of love.

Jesus and Gandhi are precise about what is meant by God's will in a world of suffering. Gandhi in summing up Jesus' life said, "Living Christ is a living cross; without it life is a living death."

To be nonviolent means to accept our suffering out of love. The evil that causes suffering is an evil whose source is more deeply interior to ourselves than we have begun to understand. The prayer of civil disobedience that says, "Not my will but thine be done"— by sending us to death or to that sign of death that is jail—is a recognition that in truth we belong there, and that we will in any event ultimately find ourselves there.

Civil disobedience as prayer is not an act of defiance but an act of obedience to a deeper, interior will within us and within the world that is capable of transforming the world. "Thy kingdom come, thy will be done." To live out the kingdom of God through such an action is to live in a loving relationship to our brothers and sisters in the police force, in courts, and in jails, recognizing God's presence in each of us. It is also to accept responsibility for an evil that is ours: as we are, so is the nuclear state.

The two most violent places I've ever been in my life have been the Strategic Weapons Facility Pacific (SWFPAC), where nuclear weapons are stored at the heart of the Trident base, and the Los Angeles County Jail, where people are stored. I went to SWFPAC to pray for peace and forgiveness in front of enormous concrete bunkers, the tombs of humankind, a prayer that took me in turn to the L.A. county jail (on the way to a more permanent prison) where ten thousand people are kept in tombs. The deepest experiences of peace that I have had have been in these same terrible places.

I believe that a suffering God continually calls us to be in such places for the sake of peace and justice. I believe that the kingdom of God is realized there. Civil disobedience as prayer is a way into that kingdom.

NOTES

1. Thomas Merton, *Mystics and Zen Masters* (New York: Dell, 1967), 287–288.
2. The nuclear train carries hydrogen bombs from the Pantex Plant in Amarillo, Texas, to the Trident submarine base in Bangor, Washington, and to the Charleston Naval Weapons Station in Charleston, South Carolina. The train will eventually transport nuclear warheads to the new Trident base being built in King's Bay, Georgia.

Chapter 13

OBEDIENCE IN THE BELOVED COMMUNITY

Shelley Douglass

The trees outside my window are covered and weighed down with snow. The evergreens bear huge loads of it, the white contrasting with their dark green; the leafless alders are outlined in white, their branches making a delicate pattern against the darker green. I've been out in the cold to feed the rabbit and the wild birds and to make sure that the rabbit has unfrozen water to drink. The dogs, Loki and Sam, have been playing in the snow all morning, cavorting and raising great showers of the white stuff. Today is December 30, 1984—almost a new year. This was the year of my fortieth birthday, the year that our oldest child started college, the year that our youngest became a teenager. This has been a year of reckoning, of trying to understand where I've been and how my life is being drawn into the future.

Next year will be 1965. Twenty years ago, in 1965, I took the first steps on a path that led here, to this room surrounded by snow-covered trees, this room at the world's end. Those first steps were steps on a march, the march from Selma to Montgomery, Alabama. At the time it seemed that such a march must bring a dismantling of the structures of racism. I felt that the change must indeed have already come, a feeling that grew out of the experience of that day's walk and out of my own shallow understanding of the problem.

The experience of the walk was true. My understanding of the problem was not. Together they led me to a feeling that has remained with me: that the problems we face are urgent, must be solved yesterday—and that they have already been solved, if we could only see it. The day we marched in Montgomery became for me one-half of a paradigm of nonviolence.

My experience of Montgomery began with a forty-eight-hour bus ride from Madison, Wisconsin, down to Alabama. There were thirty-odd students on the bus, which was chartered by the University of Wisconsin Newman Club. We were going to Montgomery because a call had been given asking people who believed in the human family to come and march for equal voting rights. The call had followed days and weeks of violent repression of blacks who were trying to register to vote. Martin Luther King, Jr., had invited us to come and show our support; we felt it was the least that we could do. As we journeyed through the South we became more and more frightened. Transistor radios brought us news reports of the violence ahead of us: police dogs and horses, fire hoses and billy clubs, and vigilante violence by the Klan and the White Citizens' Councils. Our marathon bus ride ended in the parking lot of a black Catholic church; its windows were blacked out as though in war. We found that the church had been threatened with retaliation if it hosted marchers. The black-out curtains were a prudent gesture to confuse any watchers. Curled up on the floor in our sleeping bags, we dozed uneasily through what was left of the night.

The next day, a sunny bright one, we joined a never-ending stream of people marching through downtown Montgomery. It seemed that the whole world was there—all shades and colors and shapes and sizes of people, representatives of all religious beliefs. We knew no one in that crowd, but we observed the care that was taken of each of us. If we were hungry, a stale doughnut would appear from somewhere. If we were too hot, there was someone nearby who would be grateful for the loan of a sweater. People held hands and helped each other over curbs and up hills. When we arrived at the Alabama state capitol and gathered under the Confederate flag flying there, we knew that we were the reality and that that flag and what it stood for were passing. Martin Luther King, Jr., spoke often of the beloved community. The day we marched in Montgomery brought me a taste of that community, a community at risk, a community of courage and caring, a sharing community.

Three years later the death of Martin Luther King, Jr., finished the picture for me. It was spring, near Easter. The United States had involved itself in Vietnam; now our marches were housing marches in Milwaukee, peace marches in Washington and New York. We had begun to see that racism and war had corporate roots, and students at the university were protesting recruitment on campus by corporations and organizations that profited from the war: Dow Chemical, maker of napalm, Honeywell, Rockwell, the CIA . . . an endless list. The violence on our campus had escalated. It wasn't unusual to get a whiff of tear gas between classes. Talk among student groups had turned to the question of violence versus nonviolence. We had tried nonviolence and it hadn't worked; many people in despair and anger were considering terrorism as a tactic.

A gunshot shattered what little peace existed that spring: Martin Luther King, Jr., was dead, shot outside a Memphis motel. His assassination came just as he was publicly linking racism and the Vietnam War. It seemed no accident. King's death swept us into depths of depression. He was our leader; we had never met him but we honored him; we loved what he symbolized: the beloved community. It seemed to me at least that the community had died on that Memphis balcony.

On the day of King's funeral I sat in our kitchen peeling onions and listening to the radio broadcast of the services. Paul, who was two, and Mark, who was one, were playing around my feet as I worked and cried. Mark, our adopted interracial child, seemed especially at risk that day: what future was his now? The mourners at the funeral sang "We Shall Overcome" but I couldn't sing along with them; instead I looked around for the boys, who had suddenly become unnaturally silent. It was then that I saw the beloved community. The two boys, one dark-skinned with brown eyes and curly hair, one white-skinned with blue eyes and straight hair, stood together in the kitchen holding hands and singing along. They sang "We Shall Overcome" because that's what you do—you hold hands and sing along. It was then that I knew the other side of the beloved community: the suffering, grieving community that is united in its love and joyful because out of its suffering comes its triumph. Thank you, Martin Luther King, Jr.

Seventeen years after King's death I sit here in my corner of our room and look around me at the signs of the beloved community: seashells from the people of Belau, carved "peace chickens" from Salt Lake City, wall hangings from Central America, calligraphy from Japan, photographs of people from all over the world, part of our community. But I wonder: Paul, who was born in Madison, began college himself this year. We were concerned about the arms race, the Vietnam War, the draft, racism. He is concerned about the arms race, the Central American war, the draft, racism. For twenty years I've been following this path that began in Montgomery, and what has really changed?

I believe that a lot of things have changed, but I can be sure of one thing: I have changed. Twenty years ago I marched to change other people, and when I committed civil disobedience it was to modify the injustices in an otherwise just system. Many of us went out to march or to act to correct others' mistakes, and then we returned to our own lives preparing for our futures as part of this society. What I have come gradually to understand since then is that such activity will not produce change. I do not believe that we have failed—we shortened the war in Vietnam, we did achieve some change for black people, we have raised awareness of oppression in many countries and of the part we play in it. We have, I believe, been largely responsible for the prevention of nuclear war so far. But we are only beginning to look at the roots of the problem and to see how deep and embedded they are.

There is a counterpart to King's beloved community, a dark side. We could call it the uncaring community or perhaps the community of hatred. The bonds of this community are bonds of greed and oppression, and they hold the world together in an embrace of suffering and despair. The difference between the two communites lies in our acceptance or rejection of the ties that bind us, our love for or apathy toward one another. Through the civil rights movement and the Vietnam War I began to understand that the whole system was at fault; through the women's movement and the nuclear disarmament movement I have come to see that the deepest roots of the evil are in me.

It was very easy to leave my life for a while to go and change somebody else; it was a bit harder to change my life-style and begin to confront my own complicity in an exploitative system. It is harder still to change my attitudes: my laziness, my willingness to do the easy thing, my reluctance to be open to others, my reliance on the comfortable rut. What I've come to realize is that unless I can make that inner change—and unless we all can—the outer change I achieve will be only an adjustment in the same machine of uncaring. Somehow I have to learn to live the beloved community that exists, and as I do that it will become more visible.

What I've come to believe is that there is no separation between "actions" and the rest of life. All of my life must be an action, an opening for that community to take form. If I can live with the vision of that community, some of my actions will be disobedient to the civil laws of any country I may live in. If I see the beloved community, for example, I will probably refuse to pay income tax because my money would be used to harm my brothers and sisters; if I see a train full of hydrogen bombs going by, the beloved community calls to me to stop it. Being obedient to the vision of the community of love will necessarily involve disobedience to laws that embody our division.

There is a further dimension. If I truly see the beloved community, then even those whose actions I oppose are a part of that community, and my resistance to their violation of community must simultaneously remind them that they are also part of us and invite them into the community. Only with all of us present will we be a full community, and only with all of us present can we find solutions to the injustices that beset us. The great temptation is to set up another boundary, a boundary around those of us who have a commitment to peace and justice, and to deny our community with those who run nuclear trains or serve on Trident submarines. If we succumb to that temptation then I believe we are creating the same shadow community that we attempt to resist. We have to address the denial of community in our own hearts, wherever we find it. In addressing this denial of community by our community we will find ourselves doing civil disobedience again: to be obedient to the vision of community we must be disobedient to our movement's tendency to judge and draw easy lines. We will be doubly disobedient: first, to state laws that protect instruments of death and, second, to mores and assumptions within ourselves that disunite us from those whom we resist.

Twenty years after Martin Luther King's life began to teach me about nonviolence, I return in a deeper way to his truth and vision. I understand that we can exclude no one, not Sheriff Pritchard, not Ronald Reagan—no one can be left out of our vision of community.

I understand that we must invite ourselves and our adversaries into the loving and suffering community, and that to the extent we accept our own invitation, we will become disobedient to laws and roles that sunder us. Our disobedience will grow out of a deeper obedience, and we will become one.

Chapter 14

FAITH, HOPE, AND A NONVIOLENT CAMPAIGN

Molly Rush

Imagine a world without nuclear weapons. It's difficult. Nuclear bombs exist and are *real;* the threat of extinction is *real*. This reality, which seems to cancel out any future, is so overwhelming that it forces us into passive resignation—call it psychic numbing, a sense of helplessness, or despair. We put the blame on God, saying, "It's all in Revelation." Or we hope that God won't let it finally happen. In any case, we feel that nothing can be done. Even some resistance efforts suggest an attitude of righteous futility instead of Christian hope grounded in a loving but tough-minded realism.

Could anything be changed? We knew we had already been changed—by having to confront the reality of the bomb in our lives. Fear, conscience, imagination, hope—these all cause us to make new decisions and to change. Could we entertain the audacious idea that acts of nonviolent resistance at two local producers of components for first-strike nuclear weapons, Rockwell International and Westinghouse, could change anything?

About four years ago a small group in Pittsburgh began meeting to pray about and discuss the nuclear threat, a threat that seemed— and often still seems—overwhelming, remote, and beyond our grasp. We couldn't see the weapons; they were built in plants in Ohio, Maryland, and California as a result of the decisions made at the corporate headquarters in Pittsburgh. The assembly process took place mysteriously, out of sight, if not entirely out of mind.

Our months of thought and prayer led to a written proposal that formed the basis for the River City Nonviolent Resistance Campaign. We sent copies of the proposal to both Rockwell and Westinghouse, informing them that we would leaflet weekly, alternating from one company to the other. We would from time to time engage in "graduated provocations," by which we meant civil disobedience. We would also continue to meet and pray each week and we would invite other community and religious groups to share in our activities. We would always proceed openly, notifying the corporations of our plans, hand-delivering our weekly leaflet to the front offices, and warning them when acts of civil disobedience were imminent.

Over the weeks, months, and years during which we've distributed nearly a hundred thousand leaflets, we have experienced a wide range of feelings. Sometimes our efforts have seemed futile. Apathy more than hostility can enrage anyone trying to make a dent in what seems a nearly impervious surface. Sometimes an insult has brought tears. Cold has numbed fingers and toes. We have often come to our weekly meetings feeling discouraged, but in the sharing of experiences we usually found ways to lighten up, to come up with a new idea, or to laugh together over our foibles.

On the other hand, once in a while we have received a "Thank you for doing this" or a friendly smile. And we've come to find out that corporations are not monoliths beyond human judgment and decision; they are made up of people and many are people we know: colleagues in the civil rights movement, former students, fellow students, neighbors, or members of churches supporting our vigils. We know a few executives' wives who are involved in peace work. And we've come to know the security people. We invited them to our nonviolent training sessions—and they came!

In the spring of 1985, we met with four Westinghouse officials. It was the second meeting of an "ongoing dialogue" agreed to by top management following nine days of civil disobedience in their lobby in March and April. During those nine days eighteen people were arrested as they carried messages in the form of homemade banners, sang songs, or gave speeches on the company's production of first-strike weapons parts. Eighty people later showed up in visible support of those arrested. The building manager then convinced the corporation, to which he is very loyal, that good security required discussion with us. His own views had undergone a real change in the preceding years.

In that meeting, River City member Liane Norman gave an impressive presentation outlining just what first-stike capability meant.

It was a careful, lucid picture, without rhetoric or moral posturing, of the direction weapons developments are taking. Norman pointed out that both the United States and the Soviet Union base their policies on capabilities, which they can see, rather than on intentions, which are invisible. "First strike" does not so much describe particular weapons as it does a system capable of destroying enemy weapons and communications command control centers with accuracy, coordination, simultaneity, and unanswerability. She pointed out that the Soviet response to a system perceived to give the United States a first-strike capability might well lead to their adoption of a launch-on-warning posture. The safety of the world would then be tied to the reliability of Soviet computers. Norman asked the Westinghouse officials to keep in mind the question, "Do you, as individuals and as members of a corporation, *consent* to the acquisition of a first-strike capability?"

In the discussion that followed, one official incredulously but courteously asked, "What do you expect us to do, stop making nuclear weapons?" Our answer was yes! But we pointed out that the arms race will end one step at a time, as it began. And Westinghouse can end its contribution one step at a time as well. If it's impossible to imagine a world without nuclear weapons all at once, perhaps one can imagine a gradual reduction. Westinghouse could refuse one new contract, which would be a public first step away from involvement with first-strike weapons.

We discussed the psychological impact such a decision might have. It might encourage others to take similar steps. Perhaps we and Westinghouse might lobby together for peaceful production alternatives in which their technical expertise might be used to solve pressing environmental problems. The question arose about stockholders. We imagined an educational program designed to create a base of support among employees and shareholders for new and safer policies. An educational precedent does exist: in 1960, after Westinghouse pleaded guilty to criminal price-fixing, Westinghouse devised a series of seminars on sound business ethics for its employees. This series continues to this day. Our discussions with corporate officials have forced River City Campaign members to come up with a concrete vision of steps leading toward a future without nuclear weapons.

While only two of the original members of River City Campaign remain, new people have joined us. Currently there are eight or ten regular participants. While our lives differ, we have come to care deeply for one another. One member is a young mother and artist, another a philosophy student, another a lawyer. We have one member who says she previously cared only about giving dinner parties and decorating her house; she considers her current work far more important. Another member is a teacher who drives an hour each way. Two members have changed careers from college professor and corporate worker to staff members of a peace institute. Other members are grandmothers. As we've shared hopes and fears, a bond has developed.

A similar bond has developed with the Westinghouse executives we've come to know. When I spoke to them of my experiences of psychic numbing, their eyes reflected a shared experience. They have eagerly agreed to talk about their own feelings at future meetings. Also on the agenda for the future is a discussion of options for action; we know that we're still very far apart on that one. Our blunt discussion of individual employees' criminal liability under international law raised hackles, as we knew it would. But the Westinghouse executives listen and they tell us reports on these meetings go to top management. Four years ago, our wildest dreams would not have included such a response from these corporate officials.

A few years ago a senior vice-president of Westinghouse looked on in red-faced horror as we trespassed in his lobby. It was Nagasaki Day, 1983. Several of us took turns naming—at the top of our lungs—the first-strike weapons components Westinghouse makes. After each piece we named, for example, "radar for bombers that will drop nuclear bombs," we chanted, "Hear the voice of conscience. Know what you do." As a result, two of us spent a week in jail. A few weeks ago I spoke in the backyard of the angry man's home as part of a neighborhood nuclear weapons study group! One Westinghouse employee contradicted me at a meeting with, "Do you *really* think our experiences are so different, Molly?" I do. In many ways. But we share a great deal too and that is the basis for my sense that change is possible.

Sometimes we are skeptical. The Campaign's checking account is down to a few dollars. Can we really persuade Westinghouse to give up lucrative contracts in today's business climate? Maybe we're being conned by a clever public relations department with these meetings, in hopes that we'll eventually go away. But we believe we have no grounds for hope unless we are able to make a leap, replacing our natural suspicion with trust—trust based not so much on present realities, or as a result of simple naiveté or gullibility, but on a vision we have to imagine, shape, and flesh out. Unless we act on the realistic expectation that Westinghouse employees can respond to the truth of what we say with their own version of the truth—which may include some things missing from our own vision—we can't really expect any kind of change. If we allow cynicism to prevail, then any hope we may have to end the arms race is a pipe dream or fantasy.

An early meeting with Westinghouse employees was largely a public realtions effort: one man claimed that they did not make nuclear weapons. This, we agreed, was true. No one makes nuclear weapons. Companies make components; these are shipped to Texas, where they are assembled at the Pantex plant in Amarillo. No one person *makes* a nuclear weapon and so no one person feels responsible. We tried to explain then that we had come to Westinghouse to take on the responsibility for these weapons and to invite Westinghouse employees to do the same.

Now this man recalls that statement. It made an impression. Another employee now admits our Campaign has changed his thinking. He is the one who got the corporation to commit to ongoing discussion.

We have no way of knowing, except for these glimpses, what is understood, what is remembered, what—if anything—works on the hearts, the minds, the consciences of the people we confront. We only know that our own lives have changed, that we have been brought to places we never thought we would be, and this has often happened because of another person who affected our thinking, helped us to understand.

In imagining how Westinghouse might change by taking steps that, linked to other steps around the world, could help back us out of the arms race, we've found that something unexpected has happened to *us*. The questions we are asking ourselves about our own nonviolence are deeper. We're recognizing more fully our own need for tougher spiritual roots. As militarism increases around us, we ask if we are ready to face consequences more serious than our previous brushes with lost jobs, despair, and jail.

We're beginning to see that the most important change is not up to others, but up to us as a community of individuals seeking to be peacemakers. Not only must we say no with our lives, but we must be willing to imagine possible alternatives to the evils that beset us, taking a leap of faith to do so. It is clear that the arms race does not exist apart from us; it will not magically end itself, nor can we end it by ourselves. We need the help of our adversaries. We also need to find practical, nonviolent ways to struggle for and defend freedom and justice.

There is little in our society that provides support and sustenance for what is essentially a spiritual task. Our understanding is based on the spiritual concept that we and all of creation are profoundly connected. We have no security in a system of deterrence that is based on a credible threat to destroy millions of our brothers and sisters, literally *all* of creation.

Neither can we reasonably expect to see immediate or effective results when the task is so great that it requires millions of people to respond. Yet our hope is based on the faith that the world can be changed and that it is God's will that we are being called to respond to in our resistance.

When this essay is published the talks with Westinghouse may have broken down, or we may be back in jail. We must develop that "revolutionary patience" (in Dorothee Sölle's words) that aims at the transformation of the world by remaining faithful, even when we see no results at all, knowing that it is in so doing that we will hold on to our humanity, living most fully that life which is gift, spirit, love.

Chapter 15

THE MORAL DILEMMA OF DEFENSE WORKERS

Robert Aldridge

When my daughter was going to the University of Santa Clara in the early 1970s she loaned me the book *The Respectable Murderers* by Monsignor Paul Hanly Furfuy. I would take this book with me to work at Lockheed, sit in the middle of a secret room where the reentry bodies of warheads for the Poseidon missile were being designed, prop my feet up on the desk, and read. In the book, Furfuy outlines how the church has been co-opted throughout American history by the pervading mores of the day—through the slave trade and the Civil War to World War II and the nuclear bombings. Furfuy gives what he calls the four mechanisms of moral deception: repression, rationalization, impossibility, and sublimation. These standards helped me to understand what I was doing and why. And once you become aware of how you're using these mechanisms, you can't fool yourself anymore. Then you've got to face the truth.

The first one, *repression,* is what psychologists call "denial," putting things out of your mind, not thinking unpleasant thoughts—"I don't want to think about that. Forget about it; it's negative. I want to think of something positive." I know that when I was working at Lockheed I was not interested at all in Hiroshima or Nagasaki. When we were building the MIRV warheads for the Poseidon missile, I put out of my mind the effect the Poseidon would have—the millions of fatalities that would result if that weapon were ever used. I didn't think about all the killing, maiming, mutilating, and orphaning that

Editors' Note: This article, which first appeared in slightly different form in the June 1984 issue of the *Catholic Agitator,* was taken from a talk given by Robert Aldridge at Loyola-Marymount University in Los Angeles on April 9, 1984.

the missile was made to do. This is repression, putting things out of mind.

But some things eventually become so persistent that it is hard to put them out of mind; they keep coming back. Here we arrive at the second mechanism—*rationalization,* which involves obviating uncomfortable facts with faulty logic. We do this all the time, telling ourselves, "I can't make a decision here; the experts know more about it than I do. I'm only following orders. I've got to do this to continue my job." A good example of rationalization was given to me by my boss when in 1973 I told him that I was going to resign. I told him all the reasons. He listened very sympathetically and said, "You know, you might be right. I think about these things all the time too. But I keep telling myself it's just a game we're playing; we're not really going to use them."

Eventually, we get to the point where we recognize our problem, and see that we should do something about it, at least theoretically, but then we often excuse ourselves by saying that it's impossible, that our contribution would be nothing. The third mechanism is *impossibility.* "If I quit, somebody else will do my job," I told myself many times. "I might as well be here and get the salary because it's going to go on. It's not going to stop just because I quit." After I left Lockheed, I wrote an article in a local journal outlining the reasons why I had left. One of my friends was still working there and he took it into the Engineering Department where I used to work and sent it around to my former colleagues. On the back of the article was a place to leave comments. When the article was returned to me with the comments, I saw that someone had written the following: "What I can do will have no effect at all, so I do nothing. Your ideology seems correct to me, but it must be accepted by the entire world before it would have any real meaning. The question is where to start." He felt that he wanted to do something, but that it would be impossible for him to accomplish anything.

The fourth mechanism is *sublimation*—lightening the guilt complex by some superficial activity. Before I left Lockheed, I was working in the peace movement against the Vietnam War. The war wasn't too threatening to nuclear weapons work at that time. But it came through to me that I was really just working for peace in my spare time and making bombs for a living. Understanding that mechanism helped me overcome it. These four mechanisms may help one to get through the fiction.

I want to mention just one more stumbling block, as I see it, and that is fear. Before I left Lockheed, I had a lot of fears about leaving. I've often analyzed these fears since then. I recognize now that the fear was mostly fear of the unknown, fear of something that is imagined to happen. When you start imagining all the negative possibilities, it gets very overwhelming. For example, I was in combat in World War II. When I was going through basic training I was scared stiff; but when I saw combat I was less afraid because I had actual, tangible things to deal with. Similarly, I found out after I left Lockheed that most of my fears about possible starvation, poverty, and so forth didn't materialize, and the few that did usually came one at a time and were relatively easy to deal with. The only good answer to fear is to realize that you are in a moral and spiritual battle. It is only the intangible faith within ourselves that can deal with the intangible fear.

The decision that reverses the arms race is not going to be based on politics or economics or technology. We've been arguing those things for decades and the arguments go on. What will change the arms race is going to be based on a moral, spiritual decision. It will end when a lot of people see that this is the worst situation that could possibly happen and choose to cooperate with it no more.

Chapter 16

WAR-TAX RESISTANCE: A CHRISTIAN RESPONSE TO THE DEMONS AROUND US

William Durland

Philip Berrigan sees Americans at a highpoint in demonism, possessed by the bomb and in slavish complicity with it in a lockstep toward our nuclear doom.[1] One effort to break out of this lockstep has been the refusal by thousands of Christians to pay for war by withholding that part of their tax money designated for military expenditures. (In 1986, 64 percent of every income tax dollar was so designated.) Following the example of the earliest Christians, these people of conscience have formed part of what is now referred to as "the Resistance Church."

The religious tax resistance movement is not restricted to the United States, however, but appears in other countries as well. To date there are over twenty-eight countries in which war-tax resistance is practiced. In Japan, for example, a movement is taking place, led by an organization called COMIT—Conscientious Objectors to Military Income Tax. Mennonites, Quakers, Catholics, and members of other denominations have banded together with Buddhists and people of no church affiliation to witness to the illegality of military preparedness. Article Nine of the Japanese constitution prohibits such preparations, but that nation violates its own laws nonetheless. Japan is not unlike the Soviet Union, the United States, and other superpowers, which have set the pace for violations of international agreements as well since 1945.

While the Nuremberg Principles call it a crime against peace to plan or prepare "a war of aggression, or a war in violation of international treaties, or [to participate] in a common plan for the accomplishment of any of the foregoing,"[2] the nations continue such plans. "First-strike" military preparations are part of U.S. foreign policy.[3]

Individuals are left to choose between violating national law requiring the payment of taxes for such purposes and complying with international law prohibiting such preparations. The Nuremberg Principles also state that individual responsibility attaches to such crimes.[4] It is not an excuse to say that one was following orders as long as a moral choice exists.[5] Further, the United Nations Charter recognizes the obligation to refrain from "the threat or use of force."[6] While the superpowers continue to play dangerously with their so-called deterrence policies, it is becoming more commonly recognized that deterrence is simply the nice political word for the threat to use force—a violation of the United Nations Charter. And for Christians the threat to kill is as evil as the killing itself, for sins are born in the heart. The early Christians knew too well that the only moral choice is to refuse Caesar what is God's.

In A.D. 70, Christians refused to pay the tax appropriated for Caesar's pagan temple in Rome and became the first Christian to resist paying tax for reasons of conscience.[7]

Christian disobedience under persecution was regularly defended on the broad ground of the supremacy of God's law to man's. . . . It is important to notice that this doctrine of disobedience is a principle perfectly general. The law of God, which the Christians put over against the law of the state, embraced a good deal more than the prohibition of idolatry and polytheism. It embraced a whole Christian ethic. . . . Numerous instances of this obstinate and avowed disobedience to government orders are mentioned in the literature of the period.[8]

The pardigm for Christian obedience and disobedience is found in the Gospels and the Old Testament. Matthew 12 is perhaps the best example of Jesus disobeying the religious (theocratic) authorities. In respect to the civil authorities, Richard Cassidy in his book *Jesus, Politics, and Society* writes: "If large numbers came to adopt his (Jesus') stance toward the ruling political authorities, the Roman Empire (or indeed, any other similarly-based social order) could not have continued."[9]

In his book *The Trial of Jesus,* Walter Chandler concludes that

Jesus was guilty of sedition under the Roman law of the time.[10] There is no doubt of the legitimacy of civil disobedience, including tax resistance or of the imperative for Christians to witness in this way.

The modern religious war-tax resistance movement began during World War II with the witness of people like Ammon Hennacy, a Catholic layperson, and Rev. Ernest Bromley, a Protestant minister. Bromley was prosecuted and imprisoned. A. J. Muste, Dorothy Day, and others paved the way for organizations like the War Resisters League, the Peacemakers, the Catholic Worker, and the Committee for Nonviolent Action. At one point during the Vietnam War there were estimated to be two hundred thousand telephone tax resisters and many thousands of income tax resisters. Only as an exception and not as a general rule were people criminally prosecuted and convicted. The exceptions during the 1960s and early 1970s included Juanita Nelson, Rev. Maurice McCracken, and Karl Meyer.

After the Vietnam War ended, the movement became dormant for nearly five years. In Philadelphia, lawyer John Egnal was a mainstay during those years in aiding Father David Gracie, an Episcopal priest, and Robin Harper, a Quaker, in their cases against the IRS, which sought to collect unpaid taxes with penalties and interest.

A new era began in 1978 with the birth of the National Center on Law and Pacifism (now called Center Peace). Their attorney and I presented four cases to the Supreme Court of the United States using various legal and theological arguments. The cases were designed to draw the highest court's attention to three things: the retained rights of citizens under the Ninth Amendment to the U.S. Constitution; international law violations by governments; and the free exercise and establishment of religion guaranteed by the First Amendment. Each case emphasized how the religious morals and conscience of the individual citizen are affected by violations of these amendments and the forced obligation to pay war taxes in complicity with them.

In *Anthony v. Commissioner of Internal Revenue,* 436 U.S. 904 (1978), Robert Anthony petitioned the Supreme Court to hear his argument in favor of his conscientious objection to the payment of military taxes under the free-exercise and establishment clauses of the First Amendment. Anthony, a Quaker, argued that forcing him to pay for war was the same as forcing him to shoot a gun and that interfered with his higher obligation to worship as a Quaker, such worship consisting of living pacifism as a way of life. To not live that pacifism would force him to accept a form of worship foreign to his conviction. Anthony was denied his rights before the U.S. Supreme Court.

Bruce and Ruth Graves followed Anthony in 1979 in *Graves v. Commissioner of Internal Revenue,* 1140 U.S. 946 (1979), and based their case on the free-exercise clause also, arguing that a constitutional right takes precedence over an IRS regulation and that "only the gravest abuses endangering paramount interests give occasion for permissible limitation" of the free exercise of religion. The Court denied the Graves case too, upholding an IRS regulation over the free-exercise clause.

The Rev. Howard Lull (an Episcopal priest), his wife, Barbara, and Peter Herby, a Roman Catholic peace activist, brought the Ninth Amendment argument to the U.S. Supreme Court in *Lull & Herby v. Commissioner of Internal Revenue,* 62 L.Ed. 643 (1980). They argued the retained rights under that amendment that prohibit government subversion of conscience. The early Christian church, they said, "forbade the receipt of money for magistrates polluted by war." The Supreme Court again denied the case.

Finally, Charles Purvis brought the fourth case in the series, *Purvis v. Commissioner of Internal Revenue,* 450 U.S. 997 (1981), arguing the violations of international law under many treaties to which the United States is signatory concerning wars of mass destruction. Purvis established that he was caught on the horns of a dilemma—either he would be in violation of international law by paying his war taxes or by not paying his war taxes he would be punishable under the domestic law of this country, the IRS Code. He chose not to pay, along with Anthony, the Graveses, the Lulls, and Peter Herby. And he suffered the same fate.

Although the Supreme Court would not listen to the arguments of Christian conscience firmly supported in constitutional principle, the movement grew. The Peace Church of the Brethren in Portland, Oregon, responded by letter to the IRS in this way:

Peace Church of the Brethren has been ordered to pay the Internal Revenue Service for income taxes owed by our pastor, Rick Ukena, and his wife, Twyla Wallace. Rick and Twyla have withheld the approximate portion of their tax liability devoted to military purposes as an act of moral and spiritual dissent to participation in and preparation for war. We, as a body of Christian believers, have thoroughly and prayerfully examined the levy issued against us, and have found no grounds consistent with our collective conscience and understanding of Christ's message, on which we can offer payment in their stead. . . . Our reasons for taking this stand are twofold. First, the church's intercession would negate Rick and Twyla's conscientious act of civil disobedience and would violate their right to personally bear the consequences of their decision, which they have accepted as their responsibility for choosing to affirm life. Second, as a body of believers, we are compelled by the same biblical teachings and example of Jesus Christ, to implement our faith and refuse to particpate in the making of war. We cannot perform corporately that which violates our Christian duty as individuals. . . . We have been placed in a position where a choice must be made between compliance with human laws aimed at destroying life and a higher order which commands us to love one another, even our enemies. We have no alternative but to obey God's law.

Perhaps the premier example of recent church cases is that of Tom Cordaro and St. Thomas Aquinas Church in Ames, Iowa. Cordaro is a lay campus minister and peace and justice coordinator who decided in 1979 that he could not in conscience pay federal income taxes that would be used to fund the nuclear arms race. Given his understanding of the gospel message of unconditional love, the statements of popes, Vatican II, and individual bishops denouncing the threat of nuclear war, Cordaro came to see his own participation, however unwilling, as greatly evil. He determined to resist paying war taxes, even if it would cost him time in prison.

In the fall of 1981, the IRS moved to collect Cordaro's back taxes. Since he had neither property nor bank account, they served a levy on the parish demanding that his salary be garnished to pay the debt. Rather than complying automatically, a pastoral team brought the matter to the December parish council meeting. After discussion the council unanimously resolved to refuse to pay the IRS levy and directed the administrator to write a letter to the IRS so stating, because they were not a tax collecting agency and because they saw underlying moral implications they had not had time to explore.

In early April, the Department of Justice wrote to Archbishop Byrne, urging him to secure the compliance of the parish within two weeks or a lawsuit would be filed against them. The council voted to engage counsel to contact the IRS, indicating the parish would go to court over the issue. But Archbishop Byrne decided otherwise. After the parish administrator protested the order to write a check for the tax debt, the archbishop asked to be sent a blank check so that he could write it. Archbishop Byrne issued a press release that contained no theological or pastoral comment upon the moral merits of the case, simply a statement of the legal situation, with the conclusion, "Accordingly, as president of St. Thomas Aquinas Church, I have instructed the officers to honor the levy to the extent authorized by law." While the parish administrator agonized over the final details of how to deal with the directorate and order in a way least destructive to his own conscience, he was informed that several parishioners had gathered the money to pay the tax debt anonymously.

Others are more hopeful about the stance the Catholic hierarchy will take. Arthur Jones in "An Alternative Pastoral Letter," which appeared in *The National Catholic Reporter* of April 14, 1983, envisions the National Conference of Catholic Bishops and the U.S. Catholic Conference developing "the groundwork and material for a regular and sustained campaign for nonviolent civil disobedience to continue on a regular basis until abolition [of nuclear weapons] is achieved. It is likely that such a campaign will include the refusal to pay taxes, with that money instead going directly to the poor."

In summer 1983, a "Resolution on Faithful Action Towards Tax Withholding" was brought for decision before the General Conference Mennonite Church in Bethlehem, Pennsylvania. The resolution was passed and the GCMC was the first denomination to take the step called for in the resolution. The resolution asked delegates to the conference to authorize the conference officers to test the constitutionality of the tax-withholding requirements of the United States and to assert the higher claim of Christ's law of love by refusing to serve as tax collectors in cases where individual employees have asked that their federal income taxes be withheld from their wages so that they may conscientiously refuse to pay for war preparations.

The witness of Charles Purvis on international law was taken a step further in 1983 when Catholics Eugene and Mary Doyle took their case to the Second Circuit Court of Appeals in New York on the grounds that Section 7852(d) of the IRS Code prohibits the assessment and collection of income taxes in violation of any treaty obligation of the United States in effect as of August 16, 1954. Such treaty obligations make it a violation of international law to plan or prepare for wars of mass destruction or threaten the use of such force. The Doyles' motivation was their loyalty to the gospel imperatives. The court stopped just short of declaring their arguments of conscience "frivolous."

"Frivolity" is the government's name for refusing to pay war taxes for reasons of conscience. In late 1982, the administration added new penalties to many existing ones. Bringing a case to the U.S. Tax Court that proves to be "frivolous" (i.e., the subject matter has been before the court at a previous time) will cost the plaintiff a $5000 penalty. To file an incorrect tax return (i.e., for war-tax resisters to claim a "war-tax deduction" that is not legal) constitutes a $500 fine. Hundreds of such fines have been levied since 1983 and several cases are still pending. So far no war-tax resisters have won their cases, but their efforts have not been deterred even though the government has resorted in recent years to seizures of cars and even homes.

In May of 1982, the National War Tax Resistance Coordinating Committee, a grass-roots organization, was formed, sponsored by the National Center on Law and Pacifism, the War Resisters League, the Peacemakers, and the Conscience and Military Tax Campaign. (The latter organization is dedicated to the passage of the Peace Tax Fund, which would legalize war-tax conscientious objection.) A clearinghouse was created for war-tax information and counseling and to coordinate local organizations. After three years of operation it is apparent that this organization is fulfilling its task of being just what its name describes.

Following the witness of Tom Cordaro and the St. Thomas Aquinas Church, a Roman Catholic church council in Indianapolis refused to comply with an IRS demand to pay federal taxes owed by its priest, the Rev. Cosmo Raimondi, based on "the sacredness of conscience."

In New Haven, Connecticut, the Summerfield United Methodist Church refused to hand over church records relating to its pastor, the Rev. Carl Lundborg, a war-tax resister. The IRS also ordered that church to withhold his salary, but the church did not comply.

In Cleveland, a presbyterian church sided with its minister, Charles Hurst, when the IRS ordered a levy of that pastor's salary. They wrote:

This levy is not an attempt to collect taxes. It is an attempt to collect a penalty or fine sought to be levied against Charles Hurst solely because of his expression of conscience with reference to payment of taxes for military purposes. We know our pastor. We know his deeply held conviction based upon his religious faith. It would border on blasphemy for us to cooperate in treating his action as frivolous.

By the mid 1980s the movement, originating through the witness of individual Christian resisters and thereafter moving to include church support for such resistance, began to express a corporate church position on war-tax resistance. Sojourners Community and its magazine, *Sojourners,* were leaders in this respect. Some of the examples of this transition are as follows: the Philadelphia Yearly Meeting of the Religious Society of Friends passed a statement saying that, "Friends are ready to give strong support to members led to refuse payment of taxes for military purposes."[11] In 1984 the Lutheran Peace Fellowship issued a call to Lutherans for war-tax resistance. They said: "We who abhor the devastation of modern warfare, pledge our resistance at the place where preparation for war must most directly intersect our lives, in our payment of taxes."[12] The statement entitled "Half Century After Barman," referring to the fiftieth anniversary of the Barman Declaration and the beginning of the Confessing Church movement in Nazi Germany in 1934, remembered the joining together of Lutherans, Reformed and United Churches at the town of Barman to issue a declaration that became one of the few public denunciations of Nazism at the time. The Lutheran Peace Fellowship call invited Lutherans to join "in some form of tax protest or tax resistance as a witness of faith against the false lordship of nuclear weapons and other instruments of mass destruction."[13]

In 1985 at a gathering of two-hundred top military leaders at the National War College a revealing statement was made by a high-ranking general. "The greatest challenge to all that we do now comes from within the churches," he said. "A whole new way of thinking is developing in the churches and we have to know what to do with it."[14]

The "battle lines" are drawn in these times, which may be the end times. Events such as cruise missiles deployed in Europe; the new U.S. Space Command bringing "Star Wars" to the heavens; the

United States, France, Italy, Great Britain, Syria, the Soviet Union, Israel, Lebanon, the PLO, Druse and Christian paramilitary, all facing each other at one time or another north of the Holy Land of God and only a few miles from the terrifying place of so many former wars and the predicted locale of the last battle—Armageddon!

"Around the world the Gospel of Jesus Christ is under attack," warns Rev. Frank Cordaro. "Not since the early centuries has being a Christian been a subversive act."[15] Dr. Paul Winter has been quoted as saying that in the final stages of history all of one's personal resources must be dedicated totally to the realization of the kingdom not to the security of the state.[16]

Perhaps in these times when the kingdom of God is said to be coming at any time, any hour, we must answer the question, "What belongs to Caesar?" with a resounding: "Nothing anymore! There is another who comes in the name of the Lord to establish a kingdom, a new heaven and a new earth. While we await his coming we will not join in your desecration and destruction. We will not wait as many of our Christian brothers and sisters did in Nazi Germany until it was too late. The Resistance Church refuses your blood taxes, refuses your oaths, refuses our bodies, refuses our spirits. What is left is yours!"[17]

NOTES

1. Philip Berrigan, "We Are One Family," *Catholic Agitator* (January 1982):2.
2. *The Charter of the International Military Tribunal* of August 8, 1945 (commonly called the Nuremberg Principles or Charter) Art. 6(c). See also William Durland, *The Illegality of War* (Colorado Springs: National Center on Law and Pacifism, 1983), 4.
3. See Robert Aldridge, *First Strike* (Boston: South End, 1983) and Durland, *The Illegality of War,* 11–12.
4. *The Charter of the International Military Tribunal,* Art. 6.
5. Ibid., Art. 7.
6. *United Nations Charter,* Art. 2, p. 1037.
7. Donald Kaufman, *What Belongs to Caesar?* (Scottsdale, PA: Herald, 1969), 21.
8. C. J. Cadoux, *The Early Church and the World* (Edinburgh: Clark, 1925), 251, 351, 354.
9. Richard Cassidy, *Jesus, Politics, and Society* (Maryknoll, NY: Orbis, 1980), 79. For examples in the Hebrew Scriptures see Exodus 1:15; 2:11–4:17, Jeremiah 27:5, Daniel 6, and Isaiah 40–55. See also Millard Lind, "Is There a Biblical Case for Civil Disobedience?" (William, Elkhart, IN: Associated Mennonite Biblical Seminaries, 1979).
10. Walter Chandler, *The Trial of Jesus* (Harrison: 1957), 71, 72, 79.

11. *Philadelphia Yearly Meeting News,* vol. 23, no. 4 (May 1984): 2.
12. Ibid., 1.
13. Ibid.
14. Jim Wallis, "The Rise of Christian Conscience," *Sojourners Magazine* 14, no. 1, January 1985, 12.
15. Rev. Frank Cordaro at the Faith and Resistance Retreat, Glenwood, Iowa, February 19, 1985.
16. Dianne Kennedy Pike and R. Scott Kennedy, *The Wilderness Revolt* (Garden City, NY: Doubleday, 1972), 151 quoting Dr. Paul Winter from his book *On the Trial of Jesus* (1961).
17. For a complete overview of war-tax resistance and religious conscience see William Durland, *People Pay for Peace: A Military Tax Refusal Guide,* (National Center on Law and Pacifism, 1984 with 1985 Supplement). On the subject of religious civil disobedience in general see William Durland, *Conscience and the Law* (Colorado Springs: National Center on Law and Pacifism, 1983).

Chapter 17

DECLARATION OF A DRAFT REGISTRATION RESISTER

Russell F. Ford

I, Russell F. Ford, state as follows:

1. I am now facing a possible maximum five years in prison for refusing to fill out and sign a 5-by-8-inch piece of cardboard (see attachment #1, Selective Service form 1).

2. I was born July 4, 1963.

3. I celebrated the American Revolution and my own eighteenth birthday on July 4, 1981. At that time I was aware of the personal implications of the Military Selective Service Act and knew that the prevailing view of the United States courts upheld the constitutionality of draft registration.

4. In refusing to register for the draft with Selective Service, I understood that this could be considered a crime under United States law.

5. In refusing to register, I was trying to prevent crimes that are actually at issue—the waging of interventionary wars and the use of nuclear weapons by the United States. I believe that my resistance to military preparations by the U.S. government is in accordance with the Fifth Commandment ("You Shall Not Kill"); the First Amendment (free exercise of religion, speech, and conscience or belief); and the Nuremberg Charter (the moral necessity not to participate in crimes against peace or humanity planned or perpetrated by one's own country). The defendant is not versed in legal matters and is uncertain

Editors' Note: This declaration was made by Russell Ford to Federal Judge M. Joseph Blumenfeld at the U.S. District Court in Hartford, Connecticut, on April 7, 1983, in support of a motion to dismiss charges that he had violated the Selective Service Act.

how the Fifth Commandment, Bill of Rights, and Nuremberg Charter relate to U.S. law.

6. I believe that war resisters are acting in the spirit of our history as Americans. If Harriet Tubman, a black abolitionist, could risk death guiding fellow humans through the Underground Railroad to freedom in the North and Canada, violating as she did the Fugitive Slaves Act, then certainly I can risk a few years imprisonment for violating another federal law. If enough of us act today, then perhaps our children will no longer see their children conscripted for war, as today we no longer sell children into slavery.

Samuel Adams, Harriet Tubman, Susan B. Anthony, and Rosa Parks did not think of themselves as saints or heroines. They were ordinary people who knew wrong and struggled against it. Yesterday they were criminals and traitors. Today we honor them and the hundreds who were with them. Yet today we jail disarmament activists for painting "U.S.S. Auschwitz: An Oven Without Walls" on a Trident missile submarine. We prosecute people for nonviolently sitting-in at the U.S. Capital Rotunda demanding that government and municipal buildings be used at night as emergency shelters for people with no homes.

7. For draft-age men to conform to Selective Service draft registration would be to demonstrate that we have not learned from the history of U.S. military involvement in Vietnam and the genocide carried out by this country against the people of Vietnam, Cambodia, and Laos. The draft is not practical without young men willing to submit to it. Conscription is necessary for the state to force men into the military for a war they would not choose to fight, as was the case in Vietnam. Opposition to the draft system is as important today in preventing a new war as it was to ending the war in Vietnam.

Registration is a step towards the draft—a testing of the political situation to gauge who is ready, who will object, how many will resist. According to the government's own figures, more than five hundred thousand men have not signed up though required to. Perhaps one million more did not give their social security numbers. Several million more have moved without telling Selective Service their new addresses.

As the government has been unable to convince the people that the law is in their best interest or in the interest of the country, the government has had to begin an enforcement program of doubtful legality (the defendant refers to decisions in the cases of David Wayte and Rusty Martin, putting in question the prosecution of selected vocal nonregistrants; and the recent injunction in Minneapolis federal court against enforcement of the "Solomon Amendment," a bill denying federal student aid to any person who does not prove compliance with the Selective Service).

8. An inspiration to my resistance has been my friendship with John Bach, housepainter, of Hartford. John was a student at Wesleyan University, as I have been, and in 1969 was convicted of refusing to cooperate with the Selective Service draft system. He was sentenced by the Honorable M. Joseph Blumenfeld, as result of which he was in prison for thirty-five months. Although that experience has certainly had a lasting influence on his life, it did not reform him, and neither has it deterred me from similar action.

9. I submit that to convict and jail me would be to repeat a mistake made fourteen years ago. Our consciences do not allow us to live our lives in any other way. We do not seek jail, but we cannot avoid it. It is your choice. We have not lied, we have not hidden our actions, we have not caused threat or harm to any living being. If it is illegal to refuse to fill out this Selective Service form, if it is illegal to make as clear as I know how that I will not kill, then it is the law that must change.

10. I submit that I have better ways to occupy the next thirty-five months of my life than continuing my witness in jail. The money spent to convict me and keep me in jail could be better spent for food, shelter, and education. I think that all of us— judge, jury, prosecutor, defendant, clerks, secretaries, guards, witnesses—would do better to involve ourselves working against real injustice, especially to search for ways to resolve conflicts without threat or violence. I ask you, a person of the law: how has history (and the law) judged the men who jailed

Rosa Parks for sitting in the front of a Montgomery, Alabama, bus? What purpose did you fulfill by keeping John Bach in jail for his refusal to participate in the Vietnam War?

11. I request that you dismiss charges, and join John Bach and me for lunch and conversation at a convenient time.

Respectfully submitted,
Russell F. Ford, pro se

Editors' Note: The U.S. Supreme Court ruled March 19, 1985, that the government acted lawfully when it selected only self-declared resisters for violation of the draft registration law. Written by Justice Lewis F. Powell, Jr., the seven-to-two decision held that the prosecution policy of "passive enforcement," which led to the indictment of eighteen nonregistrants, did not violate the draft resisters right of free speech under the First Amendment. The decision also upheld a ruling by the U.S. Court of Appeals for the Ninth Circuit in California. That court had reinstated the indictment of one of the eighteen, David Wayte, of Pasadena, California, after a federal district judge dismissed it on a finding of selective prosecution.

Between January 1980 and October 1986 twenty nonregistrants were indicted by the Justice Department. During this time, fourteen of these nonregistrants were tried and thirteen were convicted. Six of the indictments were eventually withdrawn by prosecutors.

Sentences for the convictions included lengthy periods of probation, fines, community serivce, and imprisonment. Seven people served prison terms ranging from one month to six months, and David Wayte was put under "house arrest" for six months. As of October 1986, two cases were still out on appeal.

For further information about draft registration resisters write to the Central Committee on Conscientious Objection (CCCO), 2208 South St. Philadelphia, Pennsylvania 19146.

Chapter 18

THE CONSPIRACY OF
SANCTUARY

Stacey Lynn Merkt

What speaks to us today as we live our lives in the face of hunger and plenty, the homeless and the mansions, the welcomed and the unwelcomed? Who or what do we listen to to make desisions about how to live responsibly? I cannot begin to list here the biblical passages that try to teach of the sanctity, the gift of life. I cannot begin to list the passages that exhort us to rout out injustice. It's our task to affirm life and in so doing denounce injustice.

Sanctuary offers protection to the refugee in our midst and publicly speaks out against our U.S. policies in El Salvador that have helped create a war there and thus refugees. More important, sanctuary is a faith response of God's people to injustice and those in need. Let's begin with a glimpse of why there is such a need for sanctuary.

El Salvador is a country the size of Massachusetts with a population of approximately five million. A small elite of fourteen families, along with the military, dominate land ownership, banking, commerce, and industry. That leaves 70 percent of the population living in poverty . . . with malnutrition, disease, illiteracy, early death, and no recourses. Throughout the last fifty years, numerous peoples' organizations have called for an end to these social injustices and the establishment of a true democracy. But these attempts to bring about change have been thwarted by the oligarchy and military. Seeing armed struggle as the last option available to bring about social reform, some of the major opposition groups banded together

---

Editors' Note: This article was written in early 1985 shortly before Stacey Lynn Merkt was sentenced for conspiring to transport undocumented Salvadoran refugees.

over the last eight years to form the Farabundi Marti Liberation Front/ Democratic Revolutionary Front (FMLN/FDR). The armed conflict between the Salvadoran government and the FMLN/FDR continues to intensify.

In an attempt to crush all domestic opposition, the Salvadoran government has recently escalated its war against the FMLN/FDR and has repressed all popular dissent. It has labeled as *subversives* not only those directly affiliated with the FMLN/FDR but also any group or individual advocating human rights and social change. This includes leaders and members of unions, teachers, students, doctors, nurses, clergy, religious, and those who help the poor. To be labeled subversive in El Salvador means to be labeled "communist," making you free game for the death squads. The death squads, known to be connected to the military, have carried out countless assassinations and are primarily responsible for the disappearances of thousands. Those who "disappear" later turn up dead, with obvious signs of torture.

The war against these "subversives" extends to the *campesinos,* the civilians. Women are seen as factories that produce guerrillas and therefore need to be eliminated. Children are seen as seeds of the guerrillas and therefore need to be eliminated. Currently, the increased bombings of the countryside are killing these civilians.

This is why people are fleeing El Salvador. Men, women, and children are risking the journey through Mexico every day. Already there are five hundred thousand refugees from El Salvador in the United States. What happens to the refugees once they are in the United States? If they are picked up by the border patrol (the police branch of the Immigration and Naturalization Service), their deportation process begins. The vast majority are indeed deported and face possible death. Why? One reason is that they no longer have their *cedula,* their I.D. The border patrol keeps it. Without a *cedula,* a person cannot prove that he or she is not a guerrilla and is thus killed by government forces.

Political asylum is supposed to be an option for the refugee who flees a country and is unable to return because of a well-founded fear of persecution for reasons of race, religion, nationality, or membership in a particular social or political group. Unfortunately, political asylum is not available for Salvadorans and Guatemalans. Less than 3 percent of the Salvadorans who apply for it are granted it. Extended voluntary departure (a stay on deportations while investigations in El Salvador would take place) has been pending in Congress for a year and a half. This status has been granted to nationals from eleven other countries in the past and is now in effect for nationals leaving Poland, Afghanistan, and Ethiopia. But it's not available to Salvadorans. That is because it does not coincide with our foreign policy. The United States has chosen to support the current, repressive government and thus does not support the thousands who flee that government.

I began working at Casa Romero, a hospitality house for Central American refugees, located in San Benito, Texas, in 1984. During the first twenty-seven months after the house opened, more than twenty-eight hundred refugees passed through. Comparatively speaking, this is a small number of refugees. But what this small number does for me is put names and faces on what we read as statistics. I have seen the hungry, the homeless, the stranger. And I have seen Christ. "Lord, when did we see you hungry and feed you; or thirsty and give you drink? When did we see you a stranger and make you welcome, naked and clothe you; sick or in prison and go to see you?" And the King will answer, "I tell you solemnly, in so far as you did this to one of the least of these brothers of mine, you did it to me" (Matt. 25:38–40, JB).

My response to the refugees comes out of a deep-down spot inside of me that sometimes seems pretty foolish and simplistic. I believe in a God of love, a God of justice. The Greatest Commandment tells me that I am to "love the Lord my God with all my heart, soul, and mind and to love my neighbor as myself." Love is an active choice, not some weak, pansy feeling. Love must be visible in my life. So when I see my sister or my brother in need, I cannot turn my face. My sister of El Salvador or of the Soviet Union. My brother who lives next door. We are one community.

Sanctuary is a faith response to these sisters and brothers in need. It has Old Testament roots. In Exodus, Moses was chosen by God to lead the Israelites out of slavery and exploitation into the promised land. This was no easy task! As they entered into Caanan, God, knowing his people, commanded them to set aside six cities of refuge (Num. 35). It was God's order to protect from further violence persons who accidently killed. It was a way of saying, "Stop! The violence stops here." The sanctuary is where the authority of God, the Giver of Life, is recognized as ultimate.

Today the need for sanctuary once again exists. Recognizing that the people fleeing El Salvador and Guatemala are fleeing for their lives, realizing that the U.S. policy of sending rifles, bombs, planes, advisers, and training creates the refugees, we, the church as a body without borders, must take a stand. Sanctuary's goals are twofold: to offer protection to the fleeing refugees and to offer a platform from which the voiceless can speak, so that the truth will be told and U.S. policy and involvement will be challenged. Currently over two hundred churches of various denominations have made public declarations of sanctuary, officially stating their intention to directly assist refugees and to public speak out against the causes of the war in El Salvador.

What is the administration's response to people trying to assist refugees? Indictments. I've come through two trials. In the first trial in March 1984 I was convicted of conspiracy to transport and of transporting Mauricio Valle and Brenda Sanchez Gallan. Their crime? Fleeing for their lives to seek refuge in the United States. In the second trial I was found innocent of transporting two refugees to the bus station but guilty of conspiring to commit that "crime." In this same trial Jack Elder, the director of Casa Romero, was convicted on six counts of charges ranging from conspiracy to bringing in, landing, and transporting refugees. In January 1985 he was acquitted by a Corpus Christi jury of transporting three refugees to a bus station.

What do we have in common? We are called "church workers." We are regular people who have heard of the atrocities in El Salvador. We have heard too much, seen too much. And we can't keep quiet when our God reminds us that "when an alien resides with you in your land, do not molest him. You shall treat the alien who resides with you no differently than the natives born among you; have the same love for them as for yourself; for you too were once aliens in the land of Egypt. I, the Lord, am your God" (Lev. 19:33–34, NAB).

Living faithfully is becoming subversive. I think people of faith in the United States have a unique opportunity. We are being asked to love by standing with the oppressed and confronting the oppressor, all the while realizing those fine lines within ourselves. The violence of war, the violence of the underlying causes of war, the injustices of hunger, disease, the few having all while the majority have none—we of the United States have the luxury of addressing these violences without dying. The costs for us are courtrooms (and their injustices) and prison time. I do not take either of those things lightly. The cost of doing nothing, sitting idly by is too high. If I examined Scripture in light of today's realities in Central America and the United States and do not act in some small way, I would not sleep at night. My hope lies in the ripples that come from one small insignificant person seeing her task and doing it. The hope has already been born, killed, resurrected. We are witness to that.

The following was my reflection as I awaited my probation hearing on March 26, 1985, and my sentencing on March 27, 1985:

"He has nothing on!" cries the little boy as the Emperor swaggers down the road in the parade. It's a children's story (an adult's parable) by Hans Christian Andersen, "The Emperor's New Clothes." It's the story of two weavers (liars) who come to the Emperor offering to weave the finest cloth ever seen, so fine that the only ones who couldn't see it were either stupid or didn't know their job. The rules are set. It is mandatory for everyone to see these nonexistent clothes. And so though no one sees the clothes, everyone lives within the set rules, too afraid to question or speak out. Everyone sees the clothes. Till the boy's cry. The cry turns into a murmur. The crowd turns it into a shout.

So many parallels to today jump out of this story for me. The people held on to their lies. They were afraid. The rules were set. Their decision to see clothes when there were none was based on the fear of not conforming, of not being able to speak out for the truth.

What does this have to do with refugees? The fine cloth we are given by this administration is nonexistent. We are told that the Salvadoran government does not make war on its people; it only quells a few Communists. Our role in this war is minimal; we send economic rather than military aid. And the refugees that continue keeping Casa Romero overflowing are economic refugees, not people fleeing war. Political asylum continues to be a fruitless recourse, but the only one offered.

The days between conviction and sentencing have been full ones for me. Full ones inside me. I think I have felt every feeling known to exist, but anger, fear, hurt, and depression are my top four. In a nutshell, anger comes from the lies and injustices; fear factors down to being afraid of the unknown; hurt stems from being continually attacked by the U.S. government; and depression occurs because of the sameness of the situation. When will it change?

For me it has become a time of letting go, of relaxing and accepting. It is a time for loosening my grip on what we've called our security. In letting go, I return. What I seek to return to is the faithful loving God that I have known for years, the God of Hosea who woos his straying people time and time again to say: "I will break bow, sword and battle in the country and make her sleep secure. I will betroth you to myself forever, betroth you with integrity and justice, with tenderness and love; I will betroth you to myself with faithfulness and you will come to know Yahweh. . . . I will love the Unloved. I will say to No-People-of-Mine, 'You are my people,' and they will answer, 'You are my God' " (Hos. 2:18–23, JB).

We take a stand, risk, and face consequences not so that our commitment or faithfulness to God can be seen, but so his faithfulness and commitment to us can be seen. I've come full circle. We love because he first loved us. There is hope . . . the hope that sustains me. I remember the God who is faithful to his people. I act in community with the thousands of people who, propelled by faith, give assistance to the refugees. I and all of us here do not act alone. Our community begins with our brothers and sisters of El Salvador and Guatemala. If I go to prison, I do not go alone.

The truth is spreading. Just before the trial in Houston a bipartisan Congressional committee accused the government of misinformation about our involvement in El Salvador. We have more "advisers" in that country than the limit of fifty-five we have admitted to. And sometimes they do more than advise. Much of the supposed economic aid we send is really military aid, which means we feed the war, not the people.

The fabric is ripping. There are rips that we can see and tiny tears not yet visible. The seeds that have been sown with blood in El Salvador spring up here as we stand up for justice, love, people. My choice is to persevere. Let's remember the words of Archbishop Oscar Romero: "To each one of us Christ is saying: if you want your life and mission to be fruitful like mine, do like me. Be converted into a seed that lets itself be buried. Let yourself be killed. Do not be afraid. Those who shun suffering will remain alone. No one is more alone than the selfish. . . . Do not fear death or threats. The Lord goes with you."

Editors' Note: In June 1985, The Fifth Circuit Court of Appeals overturned Stacey's first trial conviction and remanded that case for a retrial. On June 2, 1986, U.S. Judge Ricardo Hinojosa dismissed Stacey's indictment after the U.S. prosecutor motioned to dismiss the case claiming that there was difficulty in obtaining witnesses.

Stacy's second trial, with Jack Elder, resulted in her conviction on a single count of conspiracy. On March 27, 1985, U.S. Judge Silemon Vela sentenced her to 179 days in jail and three years on probation. A condition of her probation is that she not live at Casa Romero. Her conviction was affirmed on her initial appeal. She was reappealing the conviction as of August 1986, and her legal status was uncertain pending the outcome of that appeal.

In the same case, Jack Elder was convicted on six counts of conspiracy, and was sentenced to one year in prison for each conviction and three years on probation with the same condition that he not live at Casa Romero. After telling the judge that he would not abide by that probation condition, he was re-sentenced to five-and-a-half months in a halfway house instead of three years on probation.

Meanwhile, in a separate case, Lornita R. Thomas, who replaced Jack Elder as director of Casa Romero, was sentenced to two years in prison after being convicted of transporting illegal Central American refugees. She was scheduled to be released from prison in December 1986.

In another landmark case, eleven people were federally indicted on various charges relating to Sanctuary work. On May 1, 1986, after a six-month jury trial in Federal Court in Tucson, Arizona, eight of the eleven people were convicted of conspiracy and smuggling undocumented Central American refugees. Six of these people were sentenced to five years probation, and two were sentenced to three years probation. The other three people were acquitted.

In July 1986 there were estimated to be about 300 sanctuary churches and synagogues in the United States, nineteen sanctuary cities, twenty sanctuary universities, and one sanctuary state—New Mexico.

Chapter 19

JOURNEY TO FORT BENNING

Larry Rosebaugh

The people of Brazil sing a song entitled *"Hoje e Domingo o dia de Senor"* —"Today is Sunday, the day of the Lord." it is a joyful, spirited song that depicts the true meaning of Sunday. It is the one day of the week in Latin America that is waited for, anticipated, and planned for by all.

Even when torn by war and hunger and broken spirits, they do not forget *"Domingo,"* the Lord's day. To the people of Guatemala, El Salvador, Nicaragua, Peru, Bolivia, Brazil, and all the countries of Central and South America, a sense of family, community, faith, and hope persists that cannot be destroyed. And in the heart, if not in the village church, *"Domingo"* remains the day set apart to give thanks and praise to God.

It is no coincidence, then, that such thoughts come to me today on a bright sunny Sunday morning. The setting in which I write, however, is a federal prison located on a tract of desert land thirty miles outside the city limits of El Paso, Texas. But Sunday does not

Editors' Note: On July 30 and 31, 1983, Roy Bourgeois, Linda Ventimiglia, and Larry Rosebaugh were apprehended and given "bar and ban" letters at Fort Benning for leafletting Salvadoran soldiers. On August 9, 1983, the three ignored this order and entered a wooded area at Fort Benning, across from the restricted barracks area where 530 Salvadoran soldiers lived. They scaled a tall pine tree and broadcast a message taped by the martyred Salvadoran archbishop Oscar Romero via a large portable tape recorder. After half an hour, they were apprehended by military police and were charged with criminal trespass, impersonating officers, and, in addition, Roy was charged with simple assault. They were expelled from the base at 2 A.M.

Two days later, they were taken into custody by the FBI and imprisoned. During this time they began a forty-day liquid fast to appeal for an end to the training of Salvadoran soldiers at Fort Benning. They were subsequently tried and convicted in federal court and received eighteen- and fifteen-month prison sentences.

This article was written at La Tuna Federal prison in Texas in October 1983 while Larry Rosebaugh was serving a fifteen-month sentence.

lose its meaning within these walls, for giving thanks cannot be limited by concrete walls and barbed wire fencing.

Two and a half months ago, Fr. Roy Bourgeois, Linda Ventimiglia, and I were arrested by FBI agents and charged with criminal trespass for entering the Fort Benning military base in Columbus, Georgia. Our concern was the 530 Salvadoran officers being trained at Fort Benning. Once trained, they would return to their country to continue the massacre that has already claimed the lives of over forty-five thousand civilians in less than four years.

No one craves taking up residence as a guest of the federal government. However, I am thankful for the opportunity to have been "called" to Fort Benning, thankful for the opportunity, along with many others locally and across the country, to march, to vigil, to fast, and to proclaim our no to U.S. military intervention in El Salvador. And finally I am thankful for the chance to plead in the words of the martyred Archbishop Romero to the Salvadorans in training at Fort Benning: "I beg you, I beseech you, I order you in the name of God, stop the killing. Lay down your arms now. Stop the killing of your sisters and brothers and accept the asylum we offer you!"

Roy, Linda, and I sit in three different federal prisons presently. We are thankful for the chance to join sisters and brothers everywhere in a conscious effort to end the insanity our government wages in our name. The following is some personal background that may help shed light on why I, in this case, am now where I am.

In 1974, I found myself setting out from my parents' home in St. Louis, Missouri. Destination: Recife, Brazil. I was ordained a Catholic priest in 1963 after five years of study in Pass Christian, Mississippi, with the Oblates of Mary Immaculate, a missionary order founded to work and live among those abandoned the world over.

Active in civil rights work, the peace movement of the 1960s, and various forms of service in the inner cities of Chicago and Milwaukee, I felt it time to follow my Order's call to serve the poor in Recife. It followed, too, to hitchhike across Mexico, Central, and South America. To hop a plane and arrive in Brazil in fourteen hours seemed to go against the notion of identification with the poor to whom, by vow, I had committed my life. I was accustomed to hitchhiking, and it would give me a chance to acquaint myself with the conditions and culture of the people.

Needless to say, the two-month trip to Rio de Janeiro has left lasting impressions on me. After settling in Brazil, it was possible to understand even better the suffering and misery I observed on my trip across Latin America.

I spent the first several months in Recife walking the railroad tracks or, more properly, the government property that extends fifteen yards on either side of the tracks. By law it was not permissible to buy or sell this land. Despite the hazardous living conditions for children and adults alike, the poor had no other choice but to settle here. Their shacks were lined up for miles, just feet apart from each other. Even though they lived with open sewers, faulty electricity, and of-tentimes bad water, my newly acquired friends welcomed me warmly.

The kids helped me a lot with my Portuguese and introduced me to the rest of their families. The adults loved to talk for hours over a cup of coffee and would share whatever little they had to eat. "How many children do you have?" I would ask. The reply was always, "four, five, six, here"—meaning still alive—and "at least that many more who had died before the age of five," they would add.

One day I was paying a visit to Jose and Maria and their ten children. They lived in one room with only two beds. As I ap-proached, I noticed a group of men, women, and children coming up the embankment in front of their house. Leading the group were three or four persons carrying a wooden casket that measured about four and a half feet long. The night before, Maria and Jose's nine-year-old boy was rushed to the hospital with stomach cramps. He died that same night. Diagnosis: death from malnutrition. When I entered the house, Maria was sitting cuddling her six-week-old daughter, Fatima. Smiling, she looked up and greeted me.

Early in the 1960s, Archbishop Dom Helder Camara, of Recife, Brazil, renowned spokesperson for the rights of the poor, and others introduced the notion of the small Christian "base community" among the poor in Brazil. For centuries, religion had taught the poor that poverty was something to be endured as God's will and for the salvation of one's soul. But now this notion would change. Meeting with their neighbors, people would come together to reflect on the Scriptures in light of the reality around them. They would soon realize the root causes of their oppression and how to liberate themselves from its bind.

These base communities were not a concept that could be put into practice easily. Lay leaders, men and women, young and old were chosen, trained, and sent back to their communities. The communities began to take shape. People were taught to see their struggle as one between the "haves" and "have-nots," between themselves and those 2 percent who own 70 percent of the land, between themselves and the owners of the giant corporations, foreign and home-based, who drive them off their land forcing them into the large cities where jobs are nonexistent and their human misery is only intensified.

In their newly formed communities, people also learned that the Sunday Eucharist was a place to celebrate their common struggle and future hopes. Their music spoke of the long hot hours in the fields, of young children cutting sugar cane along with their parents, of their pitiful wages at the expense of the rich land owners.

Before the "base communities" existed, few men attended church services in Latin America. However, when religion came to be seen as an integral part of daily life and gave hope to a more humane and decent future, men began to surface in the churches. Prayer and action based on faith in Jesus Christ was seen as worth living and dying for.

At the heart of the "base community" is the notion of nonviolence. In the countryside of northeastern Brazil, whole villages of *campesinos* schooled in nonviolence and the concept of the "base community" gather to voice their absolute no when government officials arrive to claim the land for cattle grazing. Accompanying the poor on horseback are often the local priest, nuns, lay leaders, and the bishop, who comes as an added strength during these confrontations.

Over the years members of these "base communities," sisters, and priests, have disappeared and been tortured and killed. Yet the people recognize this as the price to be paid for their eventual liberation.

Today in Brazil, there are as many as eighty thousand Christian "base communities" and five hundred thousand are estimated to exist across Central and South America. In 1968 the Catholic Conference of Bishops of Latin America met in Medellin, Columbia, and chose to make a "preferential option for the poor" the primary objective of the church in Latin America. Ten years later in Pueblo, Mexico, this option for the poor was reinforced with more vision and clarity.

In the 1960s, Dom Helder Camara stood as the main figure in the struggle for justice in Brazil. His voice, which continued to cry out in defense of the poor, was soon silenced. Between 1968 and 1978 he could not be heard on radio or seen on television. His name could not be mentioned in the Brazilian press, so much was he feared by the powerful. However, this personal persecution only fostered the rise of other church leaders, Protestant and Catholic.

Today, it is the united voices of the bishops and church leaders in Brazil who are first to be heard when injustice is incurred. It is the church in Brazil, Catholic and Protestant, and its commitment to the poor that threatens the government the most. Bishops, clergy, religious, and lay members of the Christian community are called "Communists" and "subversives" and accused of homosexual activities on the front page of the newspapers. In other countries of Latin America, the story runs much the same.

In Nicaragua, it was the men and women of the "base communities" who rose up to lead the struggle against the tyrannical regime of Somoza. In El Salvador, Archbishop Oscar Romero was assassinated three weeks after writing President Carter demanding that all U.S. military aid be prohibited from entering El Salvador. He believed in the people's right to determine their own destiny and that outside military intervention only prolongs the oppression of the people.

Fr. Miguel d'Escoto, Maryknoll priest and the present Minister of Foreign Affairs in Nicaragua, says that the armed revolution that occurred in Nicaragua could have been prevented had the bishops been united in their condemnation of the Somoza dynasty. However, in Latin America, bishops are often chosen from the ruling class, who for centuries have determined the direction of the church. With the bishop's conferences of Medellin and Pueblo things are changing, but slowly.

Despite the disappearance, torture, and death within the "base communities," the people continue meeting to pray and reflect on the gospel. The Acts of the Apostles, with the accounts of imprisonment and persecution, reads as an existing reality to the people of Latin America. Big corporations, foreign and native, are being condemned by the church for their exploitive and deplorable practices.

Coca-Cola in Guatemala was condemned for its hazardous working conditions and unjust wages. The people have come to see the exportation of coffee, cattle, and sugar cane to North America and Europe as a grave and fatal social sin that must be resisted.

We went to Fort Benning to be a voice for the poor and voiceless of Central America. We went to plea on behalf of the Salvadoran people in the words of their own Archbishop Romero: "Lay down your arms, stop the killing, and cease the oppression once and for all."

The cry of Communism is once again heralded by the U.S. government as an excuse to protect the interests of the rich at the expense of the poor in Central America. The cry of Communism legitimizes the killing of an innocent people.

Let us listen to our own people returning from Latin America after years of service and identification with the poor. Let us discover the truth of what is really happening from those who have shared the true spirit of Christianity with members of the "base communities," who strive to make the gospel a reality in their lives today.

Confinement now for the three of us is a time when we sit longer and chew the words of world realities more thoroughly. We begin to feel the conditions we hear of in the Philippines, Grenada, Lebanon, Honduras, and all of Central America. And we ask why even more intensely!

We see our brothers and sisters confined to meaningless existences and our blood begins to stir. Each news item of torture or disappearance deeply touches our nervous system. We know an identification not before sensed, between the imprisoned here and with sisters and brothers everywhere. The Third World is obviously not confined to existence outside our own borders.

Sometimes the most important thing we can do is merely to share the experience of being imprisoned. It is not so much in doing, meeting, and solving problems, but in being with, and being without, and, most significant, in just *being*.

The poor and oppressed of our own cities, of the rural areas of

Appalachia, of Native American reservations across the United States have much to teach us. We must listen and share in their oppression. By doing this, we join hands with sisters and brothers the world over.

Chapter 20

JOURNEY TO MISSOURI

Martin Holladay

This is the tale of a journey, symbolic and actual. It is a journey from Lebanon to Vermont to Missouri, where I now find myself in jail awaiting trial for hammering on the concrete lid of a nuclear missile silo.

The poets of the Old Testament referred to Lebanon as a land particularly blessed with beauty and fruitfulness: the land as an ideal, a flower of creation.

> Let grain abound throughout the land;
> on the tops of the hills may it sway.
> Let its fruit flourish like Lebanon;
> let it thrive like the grass of the field.
>
> Psalm 72:16

> Your plants are an orchard of pomegranates
> with choice of fruits, . . .
> with every kind of incense tree,
> with myrrh and aloes
> and all the finest spices.
> You are a garden fountain,
> a well of flowing water
> streaming down from Lebanon.
>
> Song of Songs 4:13–15

I grew up in Lebanon before the civil war. My actual memories of the country's crystalline natural beauty mingle with nostalgia to form an ache for Eden that parallels that of the poets' hymns. Anyone who traveled much in Lebanon before 1975 should be able to identify with this feeling. The orchards of Lebanon bear a cornucopia of fruit, mythic in variety and perfection of flavor; and in spring the melting snow brings forth wildflowers that carpet the hills.

The land of Lebanon is to me a land of unfailing abundance, like the waters of Afqa, which cascade as a full-formed river from the mouth of a mountain cave. The beauty and miraculous fertility of Lebanon are real manifestations of the limitless love of God.

This Lebanon belongs to my youth. Because it is now many years and thousands of miles distant, and because its hills have been transformed by war, this Lebanon of memory has become symbolic and irretrievable. From Lebanon I am banished as from the original garden.

For the last ten years, I have lived in the woods of northeast Vermont. There I am sometimes a carpenter, but chiefly a gardener. In Vermont I built my house and raise what food I can: eggs, potatoes and other vegetables, apples and berries. This is my post-Eden existence:

> By the sweat of your brow
> you will eat your food
> until you return to the ground.
> Genesis 3:19

This verse makes clear the human identification with the soil. But what are the ramifications of our sweaty bond to the land?

The ideal of the relationship between farmer and land is that of the relationship between lovers. As the farmer becomes intimate with and nourishes the land, to that degree the land responds and brings forth abundantly. The fulfilled relationship between farmer and land must nourish both. The manual labor necessary for cultivation strengthens the bond of intimacy felt by the farmer. Tenderly the farmer props up and terraces the land where it sags from the rain, makes it rich with compost where carelessness has impoverished it, restores plants to plots made barren.

As God is our lover—"even the very hairs of your head are all numbered" (Matt. 10:30)—so the farmer becomes lover to the land, until every wrinkle and fold is known. The farmer then is grieved to see the beloved degraded, grieved to be parted from the beloved.

Everyone who has left houses or brothers or sisters or father or mother or children or fields for my sake will receive a hundred times as much and will inherit eternal life (Matt. 19:29).

This list of beloved ones—those from whom we are grieved to be parted—culminates in "fields."

As the fulfillment of the relationship between lovers is sexual, so too is that of the farmer and the land. The essential agricultural act is the planting of seed, the land swells with germination. We see why in all cultures the earth has been considered female.

As my relationship with the land in Vermont was deepening, I became aware that the government of this country is moving in a different direction. The accelerating nuclear arms race is based on a much different relationship to the land than that of the farmer.

The first requirement for the nuclear arms race is a belief in the legitimacy of violence. All violence is a revolt against God, for the murderer assumes the role of judge and kills one who was created in God's image. Our nuclear program is blasphemous, for it reflects our willingness to destroy creation. We stand ready to destroy not only our sisters and brothers who are Christ with us, but the very fertility of the soil: to destroy the mountains of Lebanon. Our sin has evolved from the tasting of fruit to setting fire to the garden.

My increasing awareness that the nuclear threat reaches everywhere, even to the backwoods of Vermont, brought me to a most difficult fork in the road. Eventually—not without heartache—I gave away my chickens and took leave of the land. I traveled to Missouri, to the missile fields.

In Missouri the soil is deep and black, richer and easier to farm than the thinner, stonier, steeper soil of Vermont. Here I saw farms— homes and barns, cattle and hogs, and fields stubbly with last year's corn.

In the farmers' very fields are missile silos. Until one knows what they are, they are inconspicuous. One sees a level area about a hundred yards square surrounded by a chain-link fence. Inside a circular slab of concrete and a few steel poles. The surrounding farmland is plowed right up to the fence. The missile is invisible, underground.

If one drives the back roads of Missouri, the first silo one sees is followed a few miles down the road by another, and then another. There are over a thousand Minuteman missile silos in the Midwest, and a hundred and fifty in Missouri alone. They are scattered through the countryside like razor blades in a loaf of bread.

Part of the reason for our profound failure to deal with these nuclear weapons on a moral level is that it takes an act of the imagination to understand the reality of our huge arsenal. The traveler sees only a fenced, level area marked with a "No trespassing" sign. But the reality of that site is a Minuteman II missile with a range of eight thousand miles, armed with a 1.2 megaton nuclear warhead, one hundred times more powerful than the Hiroshima bomb. The missile site represents an explosion beyond imagining, a rain of fire and poison such as the world has never known, a nightmare of melting cities and burning flesh.

It is my awareness of a rising tide of violence that brought me here: the violence that has now covered Lebanon; the violence of nuclearism, which now indicts all Americans, even rural Vermonters; and the violence here in the farmland of Missouri, where it is as stark as a launching site for a Minuteman missile. For each silo the earth has been excavated and replaced with concrete, steel, and plutonium. The missile is in the cornfield; our separation from the fields is now triumphant.

That our culture is moving away from an intimate relationship with the land has become a cliché. Yet the movement from making love to rape is fundamental and bespeaks a wrenching moral degradation and turning away from God. The phallic nature of our missiles is inescapable, and their deadly intent certifies that there is no beloved, only victims. The insertion of a sixty-foot nuclear missile into a buried silo is a graphic image of rape. We are sowing a different crop now, and none can imagine the harvest. "They sow the wind, and reap the whirlwind" (Hos. 8:7).

On February 19, 1985, the trial of the Silo Pruning Hooks began in Kansas City. Helen Woodson, Larry Cloud Morgan, Rev. Carl Kabat, and Rev. Paul Kabat were on trial for hammering and praying on the concrete lid of a missile silo in response to the words of Isaiah 2:4, "They shall beat their swords into plowshares." That morning I expressed my support for their action by entering a different silo, beating it with a hammer and chisel, and pouring blood. "The earth will disclose the blood shed upon her; she will conceal her slain no longer" (Isa. 26:21). The small sound of my hammer was a farmer's anguished "No."

Where do we find our hope, and how does the healing begin? Jesus gave us two great commandments. The first is: "Love the Lord your God with all your heart and with all your soul and with all your mind" (Matt. 22:37). We are grounded in this commandment by the fact that we must eat and are therefore indissolubly linked to the soil that feeds us—to the earth, God's creation. This commandment does not call us merely to make a statement of preference for God, a declaration devoid of responsibility. Our love for God requires us to love justice and therefore to implement it, to love all creation and therefore to defend it.

The second of the two great commandments is to "Love your neighbor as yourself" (Matt. 22:39). We are grounded in this commandment by the fact that we are each of woman born and therefore indissolubly linked to the human family. In our love for our neighbors, violence has no place. We are called to disarmament, a disarmament of the heart. But our love for our neighbors also calls us to protect them, to prevent harm, to intervene to save them.

Do what is just and right. Rescue from the hand of the oppressor the one who has been robbed. Do no wrong or violence to the alien, the fatherless or the widow, and do not shed innocent blood in this place.

Jeremiah 22:3

Editors' Note: Martin Holladay was tried in U.S. District Court in Kansas City, Missouri, April 22–25, 1985. He was convicted of destruction of government property and sentenced to eight years imprisonment. In September 1986, his sentence was reduced to the time he had already served—nineteen months—and he was released.

Chapter 21

FROM AMBLER TO AVCO: A REFLECTION ON THE AVCO PLOWSHARES WITNESS

Agnes Bauerlein

The blessings of a large family were never more clear to me than on the afternoon of July 4, 1982, when we gathered for a family picnic at our home in Ambler, Pennsylvania. My grandchildren splashed playfully in the backyard swimming pool, surrounded by doting aunts and uncles. Their mothers chattered nearby under the shade of an oak tree. A volleyball game raged in the background while my husband snoozed in oblivion, the newspaper covering his face.

On that holiday I was perhaps more acutely aware of my blessings because I knew that I probably would not be part of that tranquil domestic scene for some time to come. Later on, as we gathered around the table, my heart skipped a beat at the thought of being involved in an act of civil disobedience/divine obedience that might possibly mean a long separation from my loved ones.

Slowly, over many previous months of serious thoughts and prayers, I had decided to protest the proliferation and continuation of the nuclear arms buildup in a stronger way than I had previously done. I had decided that civil disobedience would be my way of saying no to an insane arms race that threatens all life on our planet.

I left home on a July morning of 1983 to join my six compatriots in preparation for our symbolic disarmament action. Our time was spent in sharing, prayer, and solitude. Under the theme "faith in the face of fear," we celebrated the Eucharist. We all had our own fears and anxieties, which we openly expressed with each other. We broke the bread and shared the wine in remembrance of Christ. And in faith we accepted what would come the next day.

Sleep did not come easy that night and, at 5:30 that following morning, July 14, I watched a magnificent sun rise over the ocean and saw it as a good omen. For the last time we met in a circle, prayed for guidance and, after some hurried hugs, left for our destination.

Walking into AVCO, a plant in Wilmington, Massachusetts, that manufactures components for the MX and Pershing II missiles, we carried our household hammers, our blood, photos of our families, various prayers, and statements of peace and justice. On behalf of our thirty-seven children, twenty-four grandchildren, and all future generations, we also issued an indictment against AVCO and its co-conspirators, including the "national security state" and the armed forces, for committing crimes against God and humanity by manufacturing for profit weapons of mass destruction. Our intent in issuing this indictment was to show that our acts were justified under divine and international laws—laws that call upon all people to prevent crimes against humanity from occurring.

Entering the building went smoothly, contrary to our expectations. Doors were literally opened for us and we were met by greetings of "Good Morning." Once inside the building, I was overwhelmed with a feeling of oppression. This factory of mass destruction brought images of violence, death, and hell to my mind as we wandered through the vast open area, looking for a suitable place to commit our action. Fear took hold of me. It was not a fear of being caught, but a fear of not being able to express my sense of despair through this action. Still, I knew the truth *must* be told. Faith led us through an unfamiliar building into an assembly room filled with large crates where we found parts to the MX. We poured our blood over these and symbolically hammered this particular nuclear "sword" into a "plowshare," praying that our action would bear fruit. Strangely enough, we were in there for quite a while. Even our singing and hammering, sounding like a bell of justice, drew no one's attention. Eventually, though, we were discovered and apprehended by AVCO's security and local police—but not before we were able to carry out a direct act of disarmament and expose the nature of AVCO's work.

Later that day, after we were arrested and processed, we were all jailed. The men were taken to Billerica jail in Massachusetts. The four of us women spent the next ten days at the Framingham jail before being released on our own recognizance at the pretrial hearing. Certainly feelings of oppression and powerlessness are very clearly dominant ones for prisoners. But had I not sensed that same oppressive factor at AVCO where workers were "free"? Had I not sensed the very subtle oppression of the kind of work being done there? Had I not sensed the powerlessness of the workers who "must work to support their families"? The atmosphere of prison kept calling me into prayer, for there the stark realities of life are strong and brokenness is a continual reminder of our need to be in touch with the Spirit of God.

Questioning injustice has always been second nature to me. As a child living in Nazi-occupied Holland during World War II, I remember asking my father why the police didn't do something to protect the Jews who were so blatantly subject to persecution. Reading Dorothy Day in the *Catholic Worker* in the 1950s and 1960s, I wondered why the Roman Catholic hierarchy was not listening to her convictions of pacifism and nonviolence.

My personal acquiescent acceptance of the events that led to a war in Southeast Asia will forever remind me that commitment to family does not preclude commitment to the rest of humanity or the call of conscience. So many years of bottled-up, unanswered questions finally erupted in February 1981 when I became closely involved with supporting the Plowshares Eight during their trial. Their example showed me that I must take responsibility for the world I live in and act on my faith, regardless of the consequences. They filled me with hope for the future. To realize that I had the freedom to act on my convictions was very liberating. I now can foresee a world for my children and grandchildren. I realize that the earth doesn't have to be governed by fear and violence. I simply decided that raising and nurturing eleven children was too much of an investment to leave unguarded. In opting for a life without nuclear weapons, I decided to take action myself and not let the future of my family be decided by someone else. I also wanted my children to know that questioning authority is right and that acts of conscience should be the norm.

During our mid-December jury trial in 1983, I tried to speak about my conscience convictions. The expert testimony offered in our defense also served to communicate my belief that our actions were morally and legally right. Having myself experienced the horrifying effects of Nazism, it was deeply moving to hear the testimony of Dr. Richard Falk, who told the jury that, under the Nuremberg Accords and international law, actions like ours are required not only to prevent future crimes such as those perpetrated by the Nazis, but also to prevent the use of weapons of indiscriminate mass destruction from ever occurring. Also in light of the imminent danger posed by nuclear weapons, Daniel Ellsberg testified that our actions were reasonable and necessary to help lessen the risk of nuclear war and initiate the process of disarmament. These witnesses and others who testified all reconfirmed for me that I have a moral and human duty to act to prevent nuclear war.

Despite hearing testimony on the justification of our acts, the judge declared that all of the expert witnesses' testimony was irrelevant to the case. He also ruled that issues of conscience and moral and international law could not be considered by the jury in rendering a verdict.

The jury found the AVCO Plowshares members guilty of trespassing and "wanton" damage to property. The seven of us were immediately taken to jail and shortly thereafter released on our own recognizance, pending an appeal for another trial.

Perhaps my youngest son Matthew, then aged ten, summed it up best of all when I questioned him on his feelings of my possible prolonged absence. His answer was thoughtful and simple. "I don't like it when you are away and I will miss you, but I know why you are doing it and the more of you that are doing it, the better it will be for us kids."

Chapter 22

THE SILO PRUNING HOOKS

Silo Pruning Hooks Action Statement

War is one of the oldest facts of history. Since the beginning of time, human beings have slaughtered each other in a mindless orgy of greed, power, and national pride. Today however, as never before in history, our vast arsenal of nuclear weapons threatens all life on earth, the very existence of God's creation. Surely today, the words of the Lord in Genesis (4:10) echo in our ears: "Why have you done this terrible thing? The blood of your brother [and sister] cries out to me from the earth!"

In the fertile earth of Missouri, graphically depicted in the movie *The Day After,* lies a demonic force of death. Each missile silo conceals the power to destroy millions of lives, and thus our rich fields have become the final, bloody burial ground for all humanity.

Our Christian faith calls us to accept personal responsibility for ending the cycle of violence that threatens us all. In their "Pastoral Letter on War and Peace," the bishops remind us: "Peacemaking is not an optional commitment. It is a requirement of our faith. We are called to be peacemakers . . . by our Lord Jesus. We are called to move from discussion to witness and action." We can no longer bury weapons of mass destruction in God's earth and, with them, bury our conscience and our faith in the nonviolent Christ who proclaimed love of enemy and God's kingdom of justice and peace. Today, Christians must act as peacemakers, "beating swords into plowshares and spears into pruning hooks" (Isa. 2:4 NAB), disarming our hearts, our lives, and our nation.

Editors' Note: This statement was issued by the Silo Pruning Hooks at the time of their disarmament action, November 12, 1984. The four members of this plowshares group include Fr. Paul Kabat, O.M.I., Fr. Carl Kabat, O.M.I., Larry Cloud Morgan, and Helen Dery Woodson. They used a jackhammer and air compressor to damage the silo cover lid of a Minuteman II missile silo in Knob Noster, Missouri.

Faithful to that mandate, we have come today to begin the disarmament of one missile silo. In cutting the fence, we remove the barriers to peace symbolized there. In pouring our blood, we expose the murderous intent inherent in the weapon and in our government's war policies. In hammering the silo cover and instruments, we render temporarily useless a weapon of mass murder, and in damaging the warning system, we express our intent to place our trust in the Lord of Life rather than in "gods of metal" (Lev. 19:4, TEV).

In so doing, we express our love for our brothers and sisters throughout the world and call upon them to act in conscience to achieve disarmament. We affirm the responsibility of each person to stand firmly in the way of the forces of death with life-giving witness and action. And we pray that, through the grace of God, our act may enflesh the total disarmament of body, mind, and spirit to which we are called.

> Sow for yourselves justice and reap the blessing
> Plant new ground in peace
> For it is time to seek the Lord.

Personal Statements of the Silo Pruning Hooks

In this journey called time, the Native people have learned many things, followed many paths, and our vision has been dimmed. We know of Nazi, Hitler, and Jew; we have heard the cries at Dachau and Auschwitz. We know of Korea and death—Hiroshima and Nagasaki. We hear the cries of the Japanese people and wonder why.

We suffered on our own land with indignity, forced from the earth we love and respect, taught to march and kill with no respect for creation and the creatures that are also our relatives.

Today we are at the Portage of Peace. Our journey must turn away from wrong and killing. We must look to the Grandfathers for guidance and stop at all costs these Mountains of death that will end all life as we have known.

We must walk instead the path of good and sharing with all our relatives. All creatures, all hills, and the warmth of the desert must once again be made pure.

—Larry Cloud Morgan

After more than twenty-five years in the priesthood and over fifteen years of justice and peace ministry centered in the state of Minnesota trying to express connections between the various concerns and issues of oppression, I have decided it is time for me to make an obvious confrontation with crisis.

The global corporate state with its militarism, its oppression, and its basic injustice has to be confronted by more and more people. I have confronted it with my words. Now it is time to confront ultimate evil with my body. So it goes.

—Fr. Paul Kabat, O.M.I.

Over fifty years of age, twenty-five years of priesthood, missionary work in the Philippines and South America, and the Gospels have taught me that personal responsibility for everything done in our name is a requirement for anyone attempting to be a Christian.

As citizens of God's kingdom on earth, we are called to stand against, with our bodies and souls, the usurpation of God's prerogatives on earth. At one time only God could destroy the earth, but now we creatures can destroy it and all life many times over. We offer our pinch of incense to Caesar by our taxes, by our refusal to do clear public actions against idolatry of nuclear annihilation and the starving of our brothers and sisters.

Our country's carpet-bombing of Dresden and the nuclear destruction of Hiroshima and Nagasaki have prepared us to accept the preparation for mass murder done in our name. Like the German people who accepted the legality of the Holocaust, we, by our lack of clear public actions, accept the possibility of the final idolatry.

I am celebrating my silver anniversary of the priesthood by beginning the disarmament of one missile silo; I invite you to do the same with the other 1048. "Choose life that you and your children may live" by breaking the laws that protect the nuclear idols of our time.

—Fr. Carl Kabat, O.M.I.

In any act of civil disobedience/divine obedience, there is a connectedness, a sense in which the witness flows from the very heart of life, from the sources of grace within one's experience. For me, this has been my children and the church.

"Much will be expected from one to whom much has been given," and it is in gratitude for the gifts of my large family and my faith that I act today. Yet, this is not an easy step for any parent of young children. The risks—lengthy separation from my family, physical danger, misunderstanding—fill me with fear. I can only speak the truth with my life, that above all else, we owe our children a safe and peaceful world in which to grow up.

In faith, the call to divine obedience transcends personal pain or fear. It speaks of great hope, hope that we as brothers and sisters in the beloved community can become peacemakers no matter what the sacrifice. It is in this hope that I act here today, because ultimately, I can do no less.

—Helen Dery Woodson

A Special Plea for Life

Larry Cloud Morgan, Whitefeather of the Ojibway, Grandson of Loonsfoot and Red Bird Woman
With the Silo Pruning Hooks

In the Name of the Native American People I ask the government of the United States of America, so called by the great-great-grandchildren and grandchildren of immigrants who came to my land 492 winters past, to take from our Mother the Earth these machines of fire that destroy earth and human life throughout the lands of all people.

I act today, as the Old Ones have said I must, to take our stand, to make our land calm once again.

The trees must remain green, the waters must be crystal, the sands are to be pure and warm once again.

The sage and sweet grass, where the deer and elk lay their heads, must once more be safe and soft for them. Where the children shall walk and grow must be peaceful and warm; no bad shall they hear, and only good things their eyes shall see.

The circle we form, which knows no color and knows no end as our feet touch our Mother the Earth, shall not feel the hurt and destruction of fire.

The winds are pure, and the Grandfathers have told us the time is now when peace must come from the North Wind, where the Old Ones have gone and only they, with the Great Spirit, know what is tomorrow.

What Did You Accomplish?

Paul Kabat

Perhaps one of the most demoralizing questions to be asked of an activist like me is, "What did you accomplish?" It's like asking a young couple shortly after the birth of their first baby, "What did you accomplish?"

The simplest answer to that question put to me is that I hope the Silo Pruning Hooks have made a significant contribution to the future of humanity. Obviously any accomplishment is still very much in the future, is still to happen, is still *in via,* on the way.

In spite of my fantasies I do not expect my act or my resulting years in prison to have any cosmic effect on history, just as I am aware that the quiet deaths of many children in Fourth World situations around the world do not make any real difference to us Americans or to the political and economic leaders of our nation. Millions of children phase out silently and are buried in obscurity. So also, the Silo Pruning Hooks will not be much noted as time and events go by.

Being realistic, I know that 99.9 percent of all Americans are not aware of our action and do not even want to know about it. If I were to run for a national office, I would have no name recognition at all. Certainly I am no Ted Kennedy or Gary Hart, no Jesse Jackson or Geraldine Ferraro. Nor am I a Pete Rose, or a Joe Montana, or a Chris Evert Lloyd, or a Madonna, or whoever is being featured on the cover of *People* magazine this week, this month, or this year. Does that mean that unknown people like you and me should sit back and let the world go by without us as we eat, drink, and survive from day to day until some form of death brings us to our internment?

Success is not measured by passing notoriety or some kind of public acceptance. My success is to live an authentic and humane life to the best of my ability. For me it was humane and authentic to try to disarm a nuclear missile at N-5 near Kansas City, Missouri, before it was discharged toward some distant target to kill millions of fellow human beings.

I wish thousands of other Americans would join me in similar acts of disarmament to put a stop to the arms race and to discourage our political and economic leaders from destroying other human beings. There seems to be no other way to bring the insane nuclear arms race to a halt, to turn the process of omnicide around.

In spite of some six thousand disarmament meetings of world officials since August 6, 1945, not one weapon has been disarmed through negotiation. On the contrary, every day our stockpile of nuclear arms grows by three or more weapons in this country. Every day we travel deeper and deeper into the state of insanity.

As far as I know the four of us Silo Pruning Hooks are the first people ever to try to disarm a loaded nuclear facility directly. Even though we knew there were six feet of concrete between us and the missile and that our efforts would be more symbolic than effective, we felt that somebody had to make a first move to productive disarmament. We knew we would never get near the warhead even if we could be on the site for a week, much less the few minutes we were actually there. We still had to make some kind of effort to disarm that nuclear bomb.

So what did we accomplish and what will we be accomplishing by our life in prison? Who knows?

At least we are a continuing testimony of our concern for humanity and for real disarmament. Because we are religious people we hope we have had some redemptive and salvific value for eternal life as well as intercessory power before the throne of God. Because we are a thinking and acting people we hope we are having a thoughtful and productive effect on other thinking and active people. Because we are human beings we hope we are bringing more humanity into a world going mad with many forms of violence and oppression.

Maybe we will not accomplish anything of cosmic worth by our efforts and our ongoing imprisonment. Maybe little will be changed and little remembered of what we tried to do. However, I know what I did and why I did it. I feel more human and more authentic and

even more productive than I ever did before in life. I hope I can be
satisfied with those results. Whatever else may be produced is *extra
wurst* ("extra sausage"), as Father Chester Kozal, O.M.I., used to
say. That good man and teacher of mine survived some years in the
Dachau concentration camp. I hope I can survive ten years in an
American prison system and can do whatever God is calling me to
do and be.

With that I will leave the final accomplishment to God. "Not my
will but yours be done."

For the Silo Pruning Hooks
Helen Dery Woodson

Forgetful earth
by human treachery now damned
her creatures' modest need neglect
gives but a grudging portion for her children's fill
and in unfruitful labor thus
anticipates the sterile scape of death.
Her victims
sprung like rotting teeth from dragon's horny jaw
their eyes scratched senseless in the stony waste
seek answer from her barren breast.
And will you give a million tons of fire
instead of bread? How long
O Lord?
How long?
Where still unshattered sacred voices fly
where martyr's copious blood yet feeds
the fragrant soil
our hammers rang with urgent song
may hardened steel be bent
in mercy's grasp
and concrete split beneath perduring truth.
May earth again redolent
pungent, sweet
revoke her mindless curse
and yielding to her Lord's unceasing love
let peace and justice sear her bleeding heart.

*(Written in the Jackson County Jail, Kansas City, Missouri, November,
1984).*

Chapter 23

FOR LOVE OF THE CHILDREN

Elizabeth McAlister

As I was sitting in the Syracuse Public Safety Building (a euphemism for jail in these quarters), some of the reality of what I and my friends had done began to well up in me. It was accompanied, as reality usually is, by terror. Probably one of the hardest things for us human creatures is facing reality. Like so many others, I don't like to think about things like death—my own death or the death of people close to me. I certainly don't like to think about war and that kind of death and, above all, I don't like to think about nuclear war and the death of all we have known.

But I found myself thinking about all of these things while in jail. Once in jail, life becomes radically stripped down; so many of the distractions are gone. It becomes a little bit harder to run away from oneself and from reality and terror. Parenthetically, this is one of the reasons I think jail is an important experience for me—and probably would also be for a lot of people who have never thought about jail in relation to themselves.

I thought about jail in relation to myself only once while growing up. While I was a postulant in a religious community in 1959, I read of the life of St. Bernard of Clairvaux. I read of Bernard as a warrior who experienced his conversion to Christ through a long period in jail, and I thought then that I would need such a jail experience for me to become "holy." But it seemed utter fantasy that such would be my lot. Reality being stranger than fantasy, I have seen the insides of a goodly number of jails, but without the experience of becoming holy.

I was in the Public Safety Building this time because I and six friends had entered Griffiss Air Force Base in Rome, New York, on Thanksgiving 1983. We went inside the building that housed, among other things, a B-52 bomber that was being outfitted to carry a full complement of cruise missiles. Some of us hammered on the bomb bay doors of that B-52, poured our own blood on the fuselage, spray-painted the phrases "320 Hiroshimas" and "Thou Shalt Not Kill" and "If I Had a Hammer" on it, and taped to it photos of our children, and a "people's indictment" of Griffiss Air Force Base that we had drawn up. The other half of the group did similar work in a nearby storage area for B-52 engines. They painted "Omnicide" and "Stop Cruise" in strategic locations.

The government responded to our acts by indicting us for sabotage, for destruction of government property, and for conspiracy. And so I was sitting in jail looking at the possibility of spending twenty-five years there. That much reality can be frightening, especially when the one facing it has three young chidren aged nine, eight, and two whom she loves deeply.

Into this atmosphere and these ruminations, a friend sent a cartoon. It depicted two children talking. The first asked if the second had seen *The Day After* on TV. The second child responded, "No! My parents wouldn't let me. They thought it would be too scary! Did you see it?"

"Yes," responded the first.

"Did you find it scary?"

"Not as scary as my parents did," said the first.

"Oh!" said the second. "What did they find the scariest part?"

"The very end," said the first, "when I asked them what they were going to do to stop it."

I sent the cartoon to my older children, Frida and Jerome, along with the letter I was writing them that day. *The Day After* was tele-vised on November 20; our action was on November 24. Their Dad and I had watched the film with them (as well as with other members of the Jonah House community) and we had talked with them af-terward about the meaning of the film. We talked too about the action I was about to undertake (though not the specifics because children don't need that kind of information; they don't need to be responsible for it). We told them that I had been preparing with several others to engage in a disarmament or "Plowshares" action in the coming week. It would mean that I would probably be in jail for some time and be apart from them. Our children have grown up with these realities as part of the air they breathe; they have seen many people in the community in which we live, including their mom and dad, imprisoned for resistance to nuclear annihilation. But to have mom do something like this and to face her possible absence from their day-to-day lives for an indefinite amount of time—this was a large step.

Both of the older children said that they understood, in a new way, why this resistance was so necessary. They were willing to accept the personal sacrifice of my absence as their part in trying to stop a nuclear war from happening, as their part in trying to avoid the suffering that the movie displayed in an understated but none-theless very clear way. They committed themselves to assume more responsibility around the house and especially to be helpful in dealing with the questions and fears of their little sister who was not able to understand as they were. It was a moment of extreme closeness for the four of us, a moment of accepting together whatever might come, and we concluded our conversation with prayer and big, big hugs.

We all back down from moments like that. The children re-main(ed) querulous, somewhat selfish, lazy; they remain(ed), in short, young children. But we don't back down completely. Some-thing of the clarity of a moment like that stays with us, enlightening a dark time. While the children fear prolonged separation, they are proud of their mom and of themselves for offering something, for sharing something of the suffering of children in less privileged en-vironments. They are, as we are wont to tell them, First World chil-dren but they have some consciousness of Third World children, which, we hope, will affect their lives and the choices they make in them.

Little Katie is another story. Not because she's our child do I say it; she's a beautiful little person. She is as full of life and joy and love and curiosity as any two-year-old (maybe a little more than many—but that gets too subjective). And watching her grow is watching a miracle unfold. It is hard to think about missing all that. And, for her part, I have to agonize over the potential damage to her spirit. At the same time as she is a deterrent to this kind of risk, she is a spur to it. Nursing her as I did for almost two years—she showed no inclination to be weaned—I heard the persistent question welling up within me: "Will this child be able to grow up?"

To nurture such innocent life and know, as I do, the threat to her life, to know, as many have sought to tell us, the threat to all life on this planet means to make some choices. The options are few and clear: first, I could choose to hide somewhere, anywhere, with my children, to remain protective of them, isolated. But I know there is nowhere we can go. I guess I also know that it would not be possible for me for very long to choose a "security" for my children that cannot be an option for other or for all parents.

Second, I could pretend that the threat is not there at all; I could live without seeing or hearing or thinking about it. That is all too possible to do. But that would mean making my own body and soul and those of our children part of the problem—part of the numbness, indifference, and resultant selfishness that enables the machinery of war to mushroom out of all control. It would also mean surrendering the few clues I have arrived at throughout my life about what it means to be a decent, responsible, caring human being.

Or third, I can ask how I can best love my children and I can answer by working to provide for them and the millions like them a hope for the future. I cannot say that I hope for a future for them without, at the same time, being willing to do something to make that hope become a reality.

The action we took at Griffiss Air Force Base was the sixth such Plowshares action. These actions sprang from our prayerful reflection on the biblical mandate out of Isaiah and Micah to "beat swords into plowshares, and spears into pruning hooks." They sprang from our shared realization that even as the arms race has been built weapon by weapon, decision by decision, disarmament needs to occur weapon by weapon, decision by decision, or as one person expressed it, "dent by dent." Our hope in doing these Plowshares actions is not so much that we will successfully destroy a particular weapon. Our hope is that in our effort to be obedient to the Spirit, to life, the Spirit might become more present in our world, empowering more and more people to act in whatever ways they can to say a clear no to such destructive weaponry, to say a clear no to policies that call for the use of such weaponry.

The first Plowshares action took place at the GE facility in King of Prussia, Pennsylvania, in September, 1980. The group of eight participants included my husband, Phil Berrigan, his brother Daniel, two other members of the Jonah House community, and four friends. One of the women who acted at King of Prussia is the mother of six children. The AVCO Plowshares included four grandmothers; they had collectively thirty-seven children and twenty-four grand-children. Many of the men and women who have participated in these actions have done so as parents. Each would articulate it differently, but all acted so that the children might have some hope of a future. It would be a great service if these parents' voices could be heard more in our days.

It is so clear how torn up people are today. If we try to look squarely at what is happening in our world, we become so full of despair, of hopelessness, that we cannot live. And so we withdraw into numbness. I read a lot of Robert Lifton in the Public Safety Building and could identify with so much of what he writes. Then Dan Berrigan sent me a book called *Bringing Forth in Hope* by Denise Priestley (New York: Paulist, 1983). I devoured the book, feeling that it said things for me that I had not been able to say for myself. She writes at one point:

It is very difficult for me and for others to get a handle on how to stop this evil, and that is part of its destructiveness. Everything is presented as so interdependent that there are no longer any limits or boundaries, and the whole system becomes overwhelming. . . . There is no more powerful or destructive weapon than the creation of this kind of confusion in and among people. . . . We begin to believe that this is the only reality that exists, and the possibility and hope for a new way of being is pushed further and further out of our consciousness.

Against this ennui, the seven of us at Griffiss (as well as others who have acted for justice and peace before and since our action) felt hope as an urgent imperative calling us to enunciate (albeit in fear and in trembling) a testimony to life. We sought above all, to enunciate hope, to announce that while this is a time when death appears to reign supreme, it is also a time of hope. The promise of new life is at hand for our world if people reach out and grasp for it, if people in solidarity with one another reach out and dismantle the weapons that block our access to life.

Editors' Note: This article is adapted from one that appeared in Daniel Berrigan, ed., *For Swords into Plowshares, The Hammer Has to Fall*. (Highland Park, NJ: Plowshares Press, 1984).

PART FOUR

Appendices

The personnel access hatch of a Minuteman missile silo damaged by Martin Holladay in the Plowshares Number Twelve disarmament action on February 19, 1985, near Odessa, Missouri. Holladay broke off the hatch's handle with a hammer, spray painted the word "NO!" on the concrete hatch lid, and poured blood around it. He was sentenced to eight years in prison for this action. *Photo from the Office of Special Investigation, Whiteman Air Force Base, Knob Noster, Missouri.*

Appendix 1

FIRST-STRIKE WEAPONS
Robert Aldridge

"First strike," as used in this book, means a massive, disarming attack with little or no retaliation. "First-strike capability" means possessing the weapons and technology to inflict such an attack. The five following elements can be broadly defined as a first-strike capability against an opposing superpower. Contributing U.S. technologies are given in parentheses.

1. Anti-satellite (ASAT) weapons to destroy critical early warning, communications, navigation, and reconnaissance satellites. (The current ASAT program and planned improvements.)
2. Missiles capable of decapitating enemy command posts and destroying land targets such as missile silos, submarine pens, bomber fields, communications centers, and storage depots. (MX, Trident II, Midgetman, Pershing II, cruise missiles, and accuracy improvements to Trident I and Minuteman III).
3. Anti–submarine warfare forces capable of quickly sinking the 15 percent of Soviet missile-launching submarines at sea. (The Arctic Surveillance Program and other ongoing projects.)
4. A defense against ballistic missiles, cruise missiles, and bombers to intercept any surviving enemy weapons that are launched in retaliation. (The Strategic Defense Initiative or "Star Wars" program.[1] Also the Strategic Air and Cruise Missile Defense Program.)
5. A command, control, communications and intelligence network to integrate and coordinate the four above elements. (The Strategic Computing Program and many other projects.)

A "perceived" first-strike capability might arise from a mature second element—missiles to destroy land targets. For instance, Moscow might perceive that the United States could destroy Soviet land-based missiles and still have sufficient weapons in reserve to threaten devastation of Soviet cities if the Soviet Union retaliates. This is the so-called window of vulnerability that the Reagan administration used to justify U.S. strategic force "modernization." This window of vulnerability is much more credible, however, when applied against the Soviets, who have about 80 percent of their strategic nuclear warheads in missile silos as opposed to roughly 20 percent for the United States. Therefore, only missiles capable of first strike will be discussed in this appendix.

Missile-X (MX) is a land-based intercontinental ballistic missile (ICBM) that carries ten 330-kiloton warheads over 7000 nautical miles, to land within 400 feet of as many targets. Initial operation was scheduled for December 1986 with 100 deployed by 1989. The first 50 are going into existing Minuteman silos, but Congress has halted production beyond that until a less vulnerable basing scheme is approved. Putting MXs into silos indicates a lack of concern about their vulnerability, probably because they are planned for striking first. The main contractors are Morton Thiokol, Aerojet, Hercules, Rockwell International, Northrop, Honeywell, Lockheed, AVCO, General Electric, Westinghouse, GTE, Martin Marietta, Logicon, Autenics, Rocketdyne, TRW, and Boeing. A December 1984 Air Force estimate of $21.6 billion for 100 missiles is expected to increase.

Trident II (also called D-5) is the next generation of submarine-launched ballistic missile (SLBM) and is in full-scale development. It will only fit into the new Trident submarines, of which at least 20 are planned—each holding 24 missiles. The missile will fly over 4,000 nautical miles to deliver eight 475-kiloton warheads within 400 feet of as many targets. By getting closer to Soviet shores, however, these missiles could reach their destination in 10 to 15 minutes. Initial operation is planned for December 1989 in the ninth Trident submarine, which will be based at Kings Bay, Georgia. Initial operation at the Bangor, Washington, base is scheduled for August 1994. All twenty subs should be operational by the end of this century, at a cost of at least $85.3 billion (May 1984 General Accounting Office estimate for 20 submarines with missiles and support facilities plus backfit of Trident II missiles into the first eight submarines). Lockheed is a major contractor for the missiles, General Dynamics for the submarines, and Westinghouse for the launch tubes.

Midgetman is planned as a small, single-warhead ICBM. It is scheduled to begin full-scale development in 1987, with initial operation in the early 1990s. The prime basing concept is a hard mobile launcher vehicle on which two industry teams are competing— Boeing/Goodyear and Martin Marietta/Caterpillar. Morton Thiokol, Aerojet, Hercules, Rockwell International, Northrop, Honeywell, AVCO, Litton, Ford, GTE, General Dynamics, United Technologies, and General Electric also have been involved in the Midgetman program. A rough General Accounting Office estimate for 500 missiles deployed in hard mobile launchers is $44 billion (1982 dollars), but so much of the program is still undefined that those figures are very preliminary.

One hundred and eight Pershing II launchers have been deployed in West Germany. No further deployment has been publicly announced. The Pershing II is an intermediate-range ballistic missile (IRBM) which, from present bases, can reach first-echelon command and control centers around Moscow in 12 to 14 minutes. The contractor for this Army weapon is Martin Marietta. Its single, selectable-yield, maneuvering warhead places a 10-to-50-kiloton blast within 150 feet of an underground command center. This is the first operational missile with a target-homing, maneuvering warhead. (Similar warheads are being developed for Trident, MX, and Midgetman, which, if used, will further increase accuracy.)

Cruise missiles comprise a large family and are potentially the most accurate of all weapons. Although they are slower than ballistic missiles, taking several hours to reach their targets, they seem to have better capability of penetrating a fratricide environment caused by nuclear explosions. Should ballistic missiles flying high and fast be unable to complete a first strike, cruise missiles coming in low and slow may be able to finish the attack.

Air-launched cruise missiles (ALCMs), built by Boeing, became operational on B-52 bombers in December 1982 and are also scheduled for the B-1 bomber. Each of these jet-powered missiles carries a 200-kiloton warhead. By October 1986 1,763 are to be deployed, to be later supplemented by some 2,537 advanced (stealth) cruise missiles (ACMs) built by General Dynamics. Ground-launched cruise missiles (GLCM), also built by General Dynamics, became operational in Europe in December 1983. Four hundred and sixty-four GLCM launch tubes are planned for NATO countries. They carry a selectable-yield, 10-to-50-kiloton warhead, and can reach any part of the Soviet Union west of the Ural Mountains.

Three types of sea-launched cruise missiles (SLCMs) are being deployed. One is a short-range antiship model with a conventional warhead. Another is a long-range land-attack model with a 200-kiloton nuclear warhead. The third is also a long-range land-attack model but with either a single conventional warhead or conventional submunitions. General Dynamics is the contractor; McDonnell Douglass is a second source. Of the 3,994 SLCMs planned, 758 will be the nuclear version and, although reports differ, they will be distributed on something like 82 surface ships and 101 submarines.

Accuracy improvement programs to existing Trident I and Minuteman III missiles could also add to a perceived U.S. first-strike capability by about 1990. Evidence indicates that these missiles have been or could be equipped to receive in-flight navigation corrections from the Navstar satellite global positioning system. This would give a target accuracy of about 300 feet. (Trident II, MX, and Midgetman would also have this accuracy if they used Navstar fixes.) There are currently 550 Minuteman III missiles carrying three 70– to 335-kiloton warheads each and by 1990, when the full compliment of 18 Navstar satellites are in orbit, there will be 384 Trident I missiles capable of attacking eight targets, each with 100-kiloton bombs.

These weapons, combined, will provide sufficient numbers to constitute a first-strike capable force, which will be destablizing in two ways. First, they will destablize treaty negotiations by demonstrating a lack in sincerity toward arms reduction. Second and most dangerous, they will make the nuclear standoff in times of international crises so unstable that Soviet leaders may decide to use their weapons in a preemptive attack before they are destroyed by the United States. First-strike weapons are more likely to start a nuclear war than deter one.

Soviet silo-based missiles do pose a threat to U.S. silos. Although not as accurate as U.S. weapons, they partially compensate by having bigger bombs. On the other hand, their SLBMs seem too inaccurate for first strike, but the Kremlin is reportedly developing a family of cruise missiles comparable to ours. However, the Soviet Union is far from attaining the other first-strike elements and, as discussed above, the difference in strategic warhead distribution makes the United States less able to perceive a "window of vulnerability" to its forces. Therefore, although the Soviets are striving desperately to emulate U.S. gains, they are nowhere near a credible first-strike threat.[2]

NOTES

1. The Strategic Defense Initiative (SDI or "Star Wars") details a layered defense against Soviet ballistic missiles that spans the time from two to three minutes after their launch to within a few seconds of impact. The defensive weapons range from killer lasers, subatomic particle beams, and electromagnetic rail guns to nonnuclear kill interceptors and nuclear warheads. Optical detectors, radar, and laser-radar sensors are being investigated. SDI is currently a five year research program just to see if the concept is feasible estimated to cost twenty-six billion dollars. Some estimates have placed an operational system in the neighborhood of a trillion dollars.

    Investigation by critics shows that "Star Wars" would not effectively shield the United States from a wholesale Soviet assault. It would be more reliable for intercepting a small portion of the Soviet nuclear arsenal that escaped destruction during a U.S. first strike.
2. For further information about Soviet and American nuclear weapons, contact the Center for Defense Information, 1500 Massachusetts Avenue NW, Washington, DC 20005.

Two Views of
United States Federal Spending
Fiscal Year 1986

29%
National Defense

41%
Direct Benefit Payments
for Individuals

10%
Grants to States and Localities

15%
Net Interest

5%
Other Federal Operations

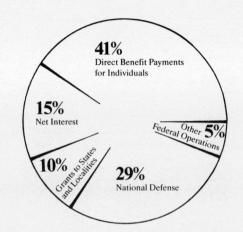

One: The Administration's View of Spending

The above pie chart is the Reagan Administration's view of the budget. Some would say this is a distortion of how our income tax dollars are spent because it includes Trust Funds (e.g. Social Security) and buries the expenses of past military spending in non-military parts of the pie.

The practice of combining "Trust Funds" and "Federal Funds," which began in the 1960s during the Vietnam War, makes the human needs part of the budget seem larger and the military portion smaller. Trust Funds are raised separately and spent separately. What you pay on April 15 goes only to the Federal Funds part of the budget unless you are self-employed.

These figures were taken from the Budget of the United States Government—FY 1986 (released by President Reagan on February 4, 1985).

We have used "Outlays," rather than "Budget Authority," figures because we wanted to reflect what was to be spent for FY 1986 alone.

Source: War Resisters League, 339 Lafayette Street, New York, N.Y. 10012

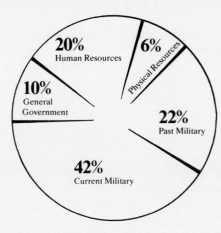

42%
Current Military: $310 Billion

Military pay $73
Retired pay $10
Operation and Maintenance $80
Procurement $83
Research & Development $34
Nuclear Weapons (DoE) $8
International military assistance $9
Coast Guard $3
NASA (military portion of 50%) $3
Other $7

22%
Past Military: $163 Billion

Veterans benefits $26
Interest on national debt (80% due
to military spending) $137

6%
Physical Resources: $40 Billion

Energy, natural resources and
environment, agriculture,
commerce and housing credit,
transportation, community and
regional development

20%
Human Resources: $146 Billion

Education, training , employment,
social services, health, income
security, general fiscal assistance

10%
General Government: $76 Billion

International, science. NASA
(civilian), justice, government,
interest on the national debt (20%)

100%
Total Federal Funds: $735 Billion

Two: A Closer View of How Income Tax Money is Spent

The percentages on this pie chart are Federal Funds, calculated after removing Trust Funds (such as Social Security).

"Current military" spending adds together money allocated for the Department of Defense plus the "defense" portion from other parts of the budget. Spending on nuclear weapons (without their delivery systems) amounts to about 1 percent of the budget. Including delivery systems, the "nuclear" portion increases to about 10 percent of the budget.

"Past military" is represented by veterans' benefits plus 80 percent of the interest on the national debt. Analysts differ on how much of the debt is military—created. Estimates range from 50 percent to 100 percent. We feel that 80 percent may even be conservative.

THE NUCLEAR CLUB

Countries that have built and tested nuclear devices	Those believed capable of building a nuclear bomb	Potential developers of a nuclear bomb in five years or less
United States	Brazil	Pakistan
Soviet Union	Argentina	Iraq
Britain	Israel	Libya
France	Canada	Egypt
China	South Africa	Japan
India	West Germany	Taiwan
	Sweden	South Korea

Source: Arms Control Association, Washington, D.C. For a more comprehensive examination on worldwide nuclear proliferation see Leonard S. Spector, *The New Nuclear Nation* [New York: Vintage Books, 1985].

WHY DO WE HAVE AN ARMS RACE?

Sidney Lens

Most of the antiwar movement has emphasized the armament aspect of the arms race—urging the American government to rid itself, either through negotiations with the Russians or unilaterally, of such horrifying weapons as the MIRV, Pershing II, Trident, MX, and so on. But weapons are not the cause of the dispute between the superpowers; they are the *result* of that dispute. We must come to grips with this fact if we are to be effective.

The conflict between the two great powers centers on how the postwar world should be organized. Contrary to conventional wisdom, the Cold War is not the result of "Communism" or "totalitarianism." We get along quite well with some Communist countries—Yugoslavia, Hungary, China, Romania. And we can hardly make an issue of "Soviet totalitarianism" since many of America's non-European allies are totalitarian—South Africa, Chile, Pakistan, Indonesia, Paraguay, and others. Nor can the arms race be attributed to Soviet "expansionism." All nations want to expand their influence. It is inherent in the nation-state. Indeed, no nation in history has expanded its power more than the United States since 1945. There is something more fundamental behind the Cold War and arms race—something that goes back to World War II.

The American gross national product and capital goods industry almost doubled during that war. The nation then had the capacity to produce enough capital goods to satisfy the needs of virtually the whole world economy, but both the victors and the vanquished in World War II lacked the resources to buy our wares. Unless we could revive the world economy, American leaders said, we would face a depression at home on the order of the one in 1929, with unemployment at 15 to 20 percent. To avoid this outcome the United States sought to organize the world around the principle of "free trade." An American industry, far more efficient than its competitors at the time, could easily undersell all other nations if tariffs were low and if there were no quotas or other barriers on trade. Washington also insisted that the world accept the dollar as the international medium of exchange. The United States doled out many billions in loans and grants to allies willing to accept this worldwide economic pattern. It worked fairly well for the corporate classes in the United States, Western Europe, and Japan for more than a quarter of a century. American exports grew from $3 billion before the war to $43 billion in 1970 (and $220 billion by 1983), and its foreign investments reached similar peaks.

To organize the world according to its own interests the United States has practiced a form of global imperialism. Franklin Roosevelt expressed the hope that as America took the place of Britain, France, and other imperial powers, it would practice a "benign" imperialism. For many reasons, it hasn't worked that way. The United States has dominated world affairs since 1945 by an *interventionist policy* that has been both subtle and cruel. Interventionism has taken five forms:

1. *Economic aid* to those nations, developed and underdeveloped, who were willing to accept the principles of "free trade" and adopt the U.S. dollar as the international medium of exchange. Even the Soviet Union was invited to join the system and offered billions in recovery loans if it would give up its monopoly of foreign trade. For Moscow, however, that would mean catastrophe: American industry, much more efficient, would enter Soviet markets freely, undersell Soviet enterprises, and put them out of business. The Soviet Union (and its Central European allies) would be reduced to raw material–producing countries. Moscow rejected the U.S. offer, and thus began the Cold War.

2. *Military aid and training* to nations willing to accept the American system. With that military aid conservative and rightist foreign allies of Washington were able to fend off revolutionary threats from their people. At one time the United States was supplying arms and training military forces in sixty-nine countries.

3. The *use of the Central Intelligence Agency* on a day-to-day basis to shape foreign governments the way Washington wanted them

shaped. The CIA in effect has been an instrument of war. It not only has overthrown governments that our government did not like (in Iran, Guatemala, the Dominican Republic, Brazil, Chile, Indonesia, and other places) but has also helped conservatives remove liberals and radicals from their union posts, broken strikes (in Marseilles, for instance), and forced governments out of power by buying off some of their leaders (in Ecuador for instance). CIA intervention has included attempts to assassinate leaders such as Fidel Castro and Patrice Lumumba, the financing and organization of invasions by exiles (in Cuba, Nigaragua), and support for reactionary governments in Iran, El Salvador, and elsewhere to prevent their overthrow.

4. *Direct action.* Where CIA and paramilitary intervention has been unavailing, the American government has moved in directly—overtly—with its own troops, as in Korea and Vietnam.

5. Finally, *the policy of "containment"* elaborated in 1947 by Harry Truman and George Kennan. The Soviets, it is said, must be "contained" to prevent them from helping revolutionary forces in the process of breaking away from the American empire. The Soviet Union, though no longer a revolutionary state itself, helps revolutionary movements and nations on the theory that "the enemy of my enemy is my friend." Since the United States has been trying to weaken Soviet influence and—as Kennan stated in his 1947 article—to force it to change its form of government, the Soviets have retaliated by giving aid to movements and governments that are in the process of seceding from the American empire. To "contain" the Soviet Union, Washington has spent $3 trillion on its military forces and built a stockpile of nuclear weapons capable of destroying the whole world.

The five forms of American interventionism are a coherent package, having the single purpose of fashioning the world economy and political system in such a way that helps American corporate interests enrich themselves. Communism per se has nothing to do with it. It is not the "evil empire" that Washington objects to, but a country that has been giving aid and comfort to other countries who refuse to be part of the American world system.

From this greatly abbreviated analysis it is clear that we cannot end the threat of war merely by working for a freeze or for cutting off funds for the MX—both worthy objectives in themselves. What we must do is challenge the underlying cause of the arms race—imperial domination of the world by the United States and its allies—and the strategy of interventionism that flows from it. To put it another way, we must support nationalists and radicals who are trying to free themselves from foreign domination as an integral part of the struggle against nuclear war. The two goals are integrally related, and what we do to help the people of Indonesia, Thailand, South Africa, Chile, El Salvador, and other places free themselves from the yoke of internal dictators and foreign domination is just as important as our campaign to slash the military budget.

The arms race is not caused because "we can't trust the Russians" (we can't trust *any* government, including our own, nor should we). Nor is the arms race the result of the atom bomb per se.

It is a complex of five techniques of intervention aimed at building an American empire, on the one hand, and the Soviet resistance to that policy, on the other. If we focus on the problem in this way, we get a clearer idea of how the campaign against the war in Vietnam or against the American-supported Pinochet dictatorship in Chile relate to the ultimate task of assuring world peace.

Appendix 2

ON OBEDIENCE TO GOD AND GOD'S LAW: AN EXCERPT FROM THE GRIFFISS PLOWSHARES TRIAL BRIEF

W̄e state with clear conscience that our action at Griffiss Air Force Base was an act of obedience to the law of God, indeed an act of religion and worship of God.

It is our conviction, which we will seek to prove, that such action is protected by the First Amendment to the U.S. Constitution, which states the "Congress shall make no law respecting an establishment of religion, or prohibiting the free exercise thereof . . ."

We went to Griffiss Air Force Base and we come into this court because we are Judeo-Christians (biblical people) seeking in our lives to be faithful to God's law. Our responsibilities/duties as biblical people have been the subject of careful study and reflection among us. In the course of this study and reflection, we find our religious faith and practice (which should be protected by the Constitution) in conflict with the conduct of our government, especially as regards its sanctions of nuclear war preparations, and the monies, the re-sources, *the trust* it puts in them. In short, we are compelled by this government into a stance of false worship of its weapons unless we act against them as we have sought to do.

Editors' Note: This brief was proffered at the trial of the Griffiss Plowshares, seven men and women who, on Thanksgiving Day, 1983, entered Griffiss Air Force Base in Rome, New York, and hammered and poured blood on a B-52 bomber converted to carry cruise missiles.

Three articles from the Decalogue, the Law of God, are especially germane in this regard, as is the mandate from Micah. We wish to cite them and demonstrate how our lives in nuclear America are twisted into disregard of these laws and of the God of the Bible.

A.

"I am the Lord your God who brought you out of the land of Egypt, out of the land of slavery. You shall have no other gods to set against me" (Deut. 5:6–7, NEB).

"You shall demolish their [reference to 'pagan peoples' inhabiting the lands of Canaan] alters, smash their sacred pillars and cut down their sacred poles. You shall not prostrate yourselves to any other god . . ." (Exod. 34:13–14, NEB).

B.

"You shall not make carved image[s] for yourself . . . you shall not bow down to worship them" (Deut. 5:8–9, NEB).

"You shall not make yourself gods of cast metal" (Exod. 34:17, NEB).

C.

"You shall not commit murder" (Deut 5:17, NEB).

D.

"They shall beat their swords into plowshares and their spears into pruning hooks; nation shall not lift sword against nation nor ever again be trained for war" (Mic. 4:3, NEB).

A. "You Shall Have No Other Gods to Set Against Me"

While the Constitution claims that "Congress shall make no law respecting an establishment of religion, or prohibiting the free exercise thereof . . ." (Amendment 1), a religion has been established in and by this country that violates the conscience of its citizens. *The cult of national sovereignty is the major religion.* This cult, as we will show, has all the dimensions of a religion, and worship of the *imperial god* is required of all. The nation-state/empire has become our god. For when one analyzes the implications of sovereignty (as in national sovereignty), it means divinity and nothing less.

We do not quarrel with patriotism, with love for one's own country. We do not quarrel with the need to respect—and require respect for—one's real needs as a country. Our difficulties are rooted in the reality that, in these days, we are citizens of a country with imperial claims, policies, and weapons. And the more imperial a nation seeks to become, the more it threatens religious freedom, because in its lust to be number one, it does not stop at usurping the authority even of God.

It may be truthfully argued that the United States does not make overt claims that our nation or its leaders are gods. (Such would be too unsophisticated.) Still, our country and its leadership (as well as other "imperialist" countries and their leaderships—the Soviet Union, China, etc.) sees itself as the "engine of history." McGeorge Bundy called the United States "the locomotive at the head of mankind [sic] pulling the caboose of humanity along behind." Any engine-of-history outlook requires the displacement of the *one* who is the *Lord of History*.

People are lured into this absolutizing of the state. We live in a situation analogous to the ancient attempt to have God and "other gods." And the people today seek to give God and the nation-state each its just due. But the "just due" required by the nation-state is *full allegiance* and support of its military purpose. Such is not possible. The God of the Bible describes himself as a jealous God. He will not take his place alongside family, country, occupation. Nor is the nation-state content to exist alongside God or "other gods." It demands preeminence and so propels us into conflict. We live in a situation where we must exercise our consciences and choose the sovereignty of God OR the sovereignty of nation.

B. "You Shall Not Make Carved Images for Yourself or Worship Gods of Metal"

> The gods of the nations are idols of silver and gold
> made by the hands of men.
> They have mouths that cannot speak
> and eyes that cannot see.
> They have ears that do not hear
> and there is no breath in their nostrils.

> Their makers grow like them
> and so do all that trust in them.
>
> Psalm 135:15–17, NEB

We assert that the nation-state as "god" has created idols that all its citizens, in the name of loyalty and patriotism, are required to *worship* and to *trust in*. This is a violation of our freedom of religion and *worship*.

In July 1945 at the "Trinity" (so-called) test at Alamogordo, J. Robert Oppenheimer was amazed and confounded by the bomb's demonstration of "godlike" power. At the dawn of the atomic age physicists assumed a mythic (religious) standing in the public imagination. It was thought that they had achieved the godlike knowledge of the primal serpent's promise. In turn, the weapons were named for gods: Poseidon, Titan, Trident—"Devil Gods!"

That these weapons are the object of worship is demonstrated by the awe with which they are regarded. Enter the Air and Space Museum in Washington, D.C., to see this enfleshed, or attend one of the many air shows or arms bazaars at military installations and hotels across the country and experience the "worship" offered this technology.

Then, we are required to trust in the security these weapons offer us and our way of life—not to trust in God as the Bible requires. (This is verified in the daily pronouncements of our president, our military, arms manufacturers, and media people). And they demand more and more of the resources of our country and its people at the expense of the real needs—the needs of justice, of men and women and children at home and abroad. (Forty-two thousand children die daily from hunger-related causes while we spend billions yearly on arms.)

The Psalm quoted above warns: "Their makers shall grow like them and so do all who trust in them." We assert that these weapons were created out of a spirit of insensitivity to the humanity of their victims. The weapons themselves—the bombs, missiles, and their carriers—have no feeling, no conscience, no imaginative sensitivity toward those against whom they are targeted. So, in imitation of our "gods," the nation (and other nuclear powers as well) has given way under an enveloping insensitivity, hardness, emptiness. There is in the nation and its weapons a gravitational field that draws people to itself and absorbs them into that senselessness whose ultimate fulfillment would be nuclear obliteration.

Part of the meaning of war, we are convinced, lies in its being the chief ritual of our national religion. In war, we find all the elements common to religious worship:

—The scene of war is the altar. Radio and TV (modern technology in general) enable millions to worship at the altar. Technology enables the state to become totalitarian, to absorb completely the lives of citizens. (Note the attention the news media gives to any so-called national emergency: the Korean jetliner, the invasion of Grenada, etc.

—The original meaning of "victim" was one sacrificed to a deity. Victims still fall within that little remembered etymological meaning. Even, in this regard, with the term "holocaust" or "whole burnt offering," we look eye to eye at human sacrifice on a scale one cannot begin to imagine.

—And war has its priests and high priests, its fire, smoke, ash, its blood, and song.

When we think of it, nuclear holocaust becomes a terrible parody of Pentecost with its mighty wind, its tongues of fire, although in the instance of war, they reach from earth to heaven rather than heaven to earth.

Then, we reflect, a liturgy of worship is often envisioned and enacted in order to help heal the wounds of division within a community of worship. Again we see the parody repeated in this country (and, we must assume, in other countries) where wars have been used to conceal, evade, and cover up the wounds, divisions, injustices within the nation—to create a false unity. Wars have more often than not been used to rescue presidents from declining domestic support.

The worship required by the God of the Bible who compels our lives is not only different but opposed to the worship the nation-state requires of its citizens. For example, hear these words of our God about the offering he requires (Isa. 58:7–11, NEB):

> Is it not sharing your food with the hungry,
> taking the homeless poor into your house,
> clothing the naked when you meet them
> and never evading a duty to your kinsfolk?

> Then shall your light break forth like the dawn
> and soon you will grow healthy like a wound newly healed;
> your own righteousness shall be your vanguard
> and the glory of the Lord your rearguard.
> Then, if you call, the Lord will answer;
> If you cry to him, he will say, "Here I am."
> If you cease to pervert justice
> to point the accusing finger and lay false charges,
> if you feed the hungry from your own plenty
> and satisfy the needs of the wretched
> then your light will rise like dawn out of darkness
> and your dusk will be like noonday;
> the Lord will be your guide continually
> and will satisfy your needs in the shimmering heat . . ."

Clearly, we are told, to know God, to worship God requires that we practice justice to one another and especially to those most needy. Clearly, we are told, while there is injustice among people, their worship and prayer cannot have God as their object. So Jesus says in Matthew 5:23–24, NEB: "If, when you are bringing your gift to the altar, you remember that your brother has a grievance against you, leave your gift where it is and first go and make peace with your brother. Only then come back and offer your gift."

The injustice upon which nuclear weapons are based, the weapons we are asked by our nation-state to worship, are suggested by former president Dwight David Eisenhower: "Every weapon that is made, every warship that is launched is a theft from those who hunger."

C. "Thou Shalt Not Kill"

God enjoins us against killing other human beings. Genesis 9:5–6 established this even before the covenant was made with Moses: "I will require satisfaction for the death of a fellow-man . . . for in the image of God has God made man." Human beings are the one image of God the Bible allows. Human beings, all created in the image of God, must not destroy the image of God incarnate in another. Nor does God allow us (i.e., human beings) to avenge murder; it is God who requires satisfaction for murder. "Your brother's blood . . . is crying out to me from the ground" (Gen. 4:10, NEB).

"So the Lord put a mark on Cain in order that anyone meeting him *should not kill him*" (Gen. 4:15, NEB).

The command against killing includes the preparation for killing. Even the law makes the intent to commit a crime equivalent to the crime itself. We find the killing of human beings in war and preparations for war to be against God's command, and so we are commanded to resist war preparations to be obedient to God. We believe that war is the key issue for coming to grips with who we are before God.

Why the killing, why the mass disregard of the sacredness of human life created in the image of God? To the degree that each of us tends to proceed as if we were the center of the universe (individually or collectively, i.e., as a nation-state), we find that whatever is not in our immediate experience (the dimensions of the suffering of other human beings, for example) remains abstract or remote. A biblical word for this absorption in self is *blindness,* which is closely related to murder and which brings on the furies of war.

With the cruise missile and other weapons of our first-strike arsenal, we face megakill—a ghastliness of intent for murder hundreds of million fold. An intimation of hell is found in the lack of feeling, the petrification with which this murder is viewed by our leadership, the military, and the general public. In truth, in the nuclear arms buildup, what has happened is that the general public has granted to our government the authority to enter into immense sacrificial destruction of our right to life, liberty, and the pursuit of happiness.

We believe that this idolatry of patriotism must be unveiled not when it leads to open warfare, but when that possibility has been accepted by the government itself (that is, now, when first-strike capability is lauded, planned for, when the policies to justify it are promulgated; when we develop and deploy first-strike weapons in Europe as well as here at home), because it is not so much the killing that is the deepest sin of militarism.

In all of this, we have, as Paul warns in Romans 1:25, "given up the truth of God for a lie."

D. "Beat Swords into Plowshares"

The context in Micah in which this command is addressed to us is the context of a courtroom in which God stands as a witness

against us: "Listen you peoples . . . That the Lord your God . . .
May bear witness against you . . ." (Mic. 1:2, NEB). Above all, this
is the court and judgment that we fear.

The crimes for which God testifies against us are as follows:

— "They covet land and take it by force; if they want a house,
they seize it; they rob a man of his home and steal every man's
inheritance" (Mic. 2:2, NEB).

— "But you are no people for me, rising up as my enemy to my
face, to strip the cloak from one that was safe and take away
the confidence of returning warriors, to drive the women of my
people from their pleasant homes and rob the children of my
glory forever . . . you that . . . would commit any mischief,
mischief however cruel" (Mic. 2:8–10, NEB).

— "Listen you leaders of Jacob, rulers of Israel, should you not
know what is right? You hate good and love evil, you flay men
alive . . . you devour the flesh of my people" (Mic. 32:1–2,
NEB).

— "Listen to this, leaders of Jacob . . . you who make justice
hateful and wrest it from its straight course, building Zion in
bloodshed and Jerusalem in iniquity. Her rulers sell justice, her
priests give direction in return for a bribe, her prophets take
money for their divination" (Mic. 3:9–11, NEB).

The words "Listen" and "Hear" are addressed to us. A deeper
listening is incumbent upon us; we are compelled to listen, and this
listening has its roots in obedience. We cannot listen and conclude
that these crimes were the crimes of Israel, crimes in which we have
no part. We, in this nation and culture, must recognize that our
megatons are in existence because we "covet land," "rise up as enemy of God . . . and drive women from their homes—rob children
of God's glory," and "make justice hateful, . . . build our cities in
bloodshed and iniquity."

God calls us out of this infidelity and back into obedience. His
judgment has as its aim not punishment but redemption. The injunction follows—it is the path to restoration: "They shall beat
swords into plowshares and their spears into pruning hooks; nation
shall not lift sword against nation nor ever again be trained for war."
It is clear. Justice and peace will be available, but not until there is

disarmament. "On that day, says the Lord, I will gather all who are lost . . ." (Mic. 4:6, NEB). In short, then will come the restoration, the passover into a new sense of justice.

In our act at Griffiss, we were seeking to listen to and receive God's judgment, to act in obedience to God's will and (we believe) the deep longing in the human heart for justice. We know that that is impossible as long as these weapons exist—between us peoples as well as over the heads/lives of all people.

Our action at Griffiss Air Force Base was a simple act of obedience, of religion, and of worship.

NOT GUILTY

Shelley Douglass

On June 21, 1985, we listened to the court clerk say "not guilty" nineteen times. Something special had happened in Kitsap County, Washington—for the first time in a jury trial related to the Trident submarine base at Bangor, a jury had brought back a "not guilty" verdict.

The verdict represented years of waiting and communicating, years of involvement in the Trident campaign. People had resisted the building of the Trident base, the arrival of the first Trident submarine, the transportation of missile motors for the Trident missiles. Since 1983 there had been many people on the tracks in front of the White (Nuclear) Train as it carried hydrogen bombs into the base to be loaded onto Trident submarines.

There had been other trials before this one, trials that prepared the way for this verdict of "not guilty." Ted Dzielak, Lynn Greiner, and John Midgley, members of the National Lawyers Guild, had for several years worked faithfully with Ground Zero, and later with the Agape Community, trying to bring the truth about the arms race into the courtroom. They had tried to create an opening for international law to gain a hearing and for the jury to render a verdict based on the fullness of the law.

Seeds grow unnoticed, silently. The seeds planted through the years since the Trident campaign first began and the faith of the people who planted them bore fruit on June 21, 1985, when a jury in Kitsap County found nineteen people who had sat or knelt in front of a train carrying hydrogen bombs to the Trident submarine base at Bangor on February 22, 1985, not guilty of a crime.

The defendants had been charged not only with trespass but with conspiracy to commit trespass. Four other people who were not on the tracks in front of the train were charged with conspiracy to commit trespass for the part they played in preparations for meeting the train. These people had represented the Puget Sound Agape Community in meetings with Pat Jones and Chuck Wheeler from the Kitsap County Sheriff's Department and Tom Lawson and Don Roetering from Burlington Northern Railroad.

The defendants believed the conspiracy charge was an infringement of their First Amendment rights and an attempt at intimidation. In a pretrial hearing Judge W. Daniel Phillips ruled that the conspiracy charges should be dismissed since the meetings held with the authorities were not conspiratorial but for peaceful purposes and since the state's case had no substantial grounds for conspiracy.

When the trial began on June 18, Judge Phillips ruled that a defense based on necessity and international law would not be permitted. However, since the charge of criminal trespass contains within the statute the words "knowingly enters or remains unlawfully," the defendants were able to testify as to what they knew, what they did knowingly. In other words, they testified as to their state of mind.

Because many of the defendants were knowledgable about the Trident submarine and weapons system, the U.S. policy regarding nuclear weapons, the route of the train, the function of the Pantex plant in relation to nuclear weapons in this country, and many other facts, they were able to communicate a great deal of information to the jury. They were also able to convince the jury that they were not guilty of any crime. They sat or knelt on the tracks because they could not do otherwise; they were there to uphold moral and international law.

Some expert witnesses were able to testify to corroborate a particular defendant's state of mind: Mary Fujita, who is a victim of the atomic bombing at Hiroshima; Daniel Ellsberg, who spent years planning American strategies for nuclear war; Sam Keen, who has studied the psychology of enemy making and seen its effects on our spirits; and Mona Seehale, who left her job at the Strategic Weapons Facility Pacific at Bangor and testified that she did so because of the witness of people like the defendants, people who acted on their consciences and challenged her to do the same. Robert McAfee Brown, a theologian who would have addressed moral law, and Richard Falk, Professor of International Law at Princeton University, were not permitted to testify.

During the months of preparation for trial, the nineteen defendants and the lawyers who worked with them became a community. The trial lawyers, Kate Pflaumer, Bill Bender, Mike Fox, and Russ Hauge, exhibited a flexibility, creativity, and expertise that was reflective of the larger "behind the scenes" legal team as well. During the trial it was clear that defendants and lawyers were speaking as one and that they deeply shared two things in common: a love and reverence for life and a profound need to defend it by nonviolent means.

After all the testimony was heard, the jury deliberated for two and a half hours, returning a verdict of "not guilty" for each of the nineteen defendants. Sallie Shawl, one of those acquitted, wrote later, "In February the train was stopped by love manifested in the relationship between the Puget Sound Agape Community, Burlington Northern security personnel, and the Kitsap County Sheriff's Department; in June the train was stopped by the truth as heard and then spoken by a jury in Kitsap County."

THE NECESSITY DEFENSE:
A REPORT

Thomas Lumpkin

Civil disobedience acts of conscience have, in the measure of thier truthfulness, an inherent power that in no way depends upon the various judgments made by judges and juries. Nevertheless, on a number of occasions in recent years nuclear resisters and protesters of U.S. Central American policy have claimed a legal justification for their acts. Most often they have presented their cases as clear and obvious applications of what is known in U.S. civil law as the defense of necessity or duress. In response, some judges have simply refused the claim. In several instances, however, a defense of necessity was allowed in theory, but in fact a judge or jury imposed so narrow an interpretation on its meaning that it was inapplicable to the acts of resistance. In a very few cases the necessity defense has been the basis for sane and heartening judicial statements and decisions of acquittal. It is my pleasure to report one such instance of my own experience.

On December 28, 1984, a commemoration of the Holy Innocents feast was held at the headquarters of the Williams International Corporation in Walled Lake, Michigan. Williams International is responsible for the small fanjet engines that are an essential component of modern U.S. cruise missiles. During the service Dan Lagrou was arrested for pouring his blood upon the company's fence and charged with malicious destruction. Marietta Jaeger and I were among four arrested and charged with trespassing. Upon our arraignment at the 52nd District Court in Walled Lake, the three of us chose to have "not guilty" pleas entered. We were set for trial on March 22, 1985, before Judge Martin Boyle, one of the court's three judges. None of us requested lawyers, preferring to make our own defense.

Initially we had asked for a jury trial. By having a jury Dan and Marietta hoped their testimonies would educate and convert (in the best sense of both words) seven more people to the realities of the cruise missile and their local corporation's involvement with it. I was inclined to make a legal case for our innocence using the necessity defense.

In the weeks preceding our trial, I realized that only one of the half dozen previous Williams International civil disobedience cases had come before Judge Boyle, and it had been a jury trial. Judge Boyle remained the only one of the three district court judges who had not yet ruled himself on the actions at Williams on the basis of the necessity defense. I thought we should give him the opportunity. Dan and Marietta agreed and we collectively changed our request for a jury trial to a bench trial about a week before our scheduled court date.

My understanding of the necessity defense is that the defendants must show, first, there is a situation posing a serious and imminent danger to life and limb; second, they believe their act of breaking civil law is a necessary and effective remedy to that situation; and third, they were compelled, or under duress, to so act.

To substantiate the first requirement, we called upon two expert witnesses, a physicist at the University of Michigan and a political scientist at Wayne State University. Professor Daniel Axelrod from the University of Michigan testified on the nature of modern-day cruise missiles, the critical role of Williams International in their development, and the role of the cruise missile in U.S. nuclear strategy. Professor Maurice Waters from Wayne State testified on the particularly destabilizing impact of the cruise on arms control.

Our argument for the second requirement was a historical and sociological one, and we made it ourselves. (We had sought expert witnesses in these areas but none were available on our short notice.) We claimed no reasonable and effective remedy exists to the present and imminent danger posed by the cruise missile that does not *include* acts of civil disobedience. We argued that, historically, no significant social change in our nation's past had occurred without elements of civil disobedience (e.g., the right of workers to organize, of women and blacks to vote, the curtailment of the Vietnam draft). Sociologically, we argued that public opinion has an impact on U.S. public policy, and civil disobedience has been a sociologically significant component in determining public opinion.

To substantiate compulsion, each of us simply explained the motives that led us to civil disobedience. We spoke of *moral* rather than *physical* compulsion. We were not physically compelled to go to Williams (i.e., we acted in full and free command of our faculties) but, because of who we were and what we knew, we (to use Daniel Berrigan's phrase) could not *not* do what we did.

At the trial's conclusion, Judge Boyle began by taking up Dan's charge of malicious destruction. He focused on the "malicious" requirement of the law and found himself convinced that no malicious intent existed.

His testimony is clear and convincing that he did not act out of malice. He may have acted wrongfully. He certainly acted willfully but in the eyes of the law he did not act maliciously. . . . We can't go beyond the language of the statute, and the court would have to find Mr. Lagrou not guilty for that reason.

Turning to the trespass charges against Marietta and myself, he said:

Now with respect to the other two, answers are not so easy. Again, there's no question they trespassed. . . . The prosecutor suggests that there's some inconsistency in their conduct as to suggest they did not act under duress and that their . . . testimony from the witness stand [does] not support that conclusion either. Well, of course, the defense of duress is not often used in this context. . . . But in the commentary of the standard jury instructions it's stated that there's a meagerness of case law on this subject . . . so just because it's never been applied to a circumstance such as this doesn't mean that it can't be.

Judge Boyle went on to respond to our arguments:

Now the defenses listed in the jury instructions provide first that the threatening conduct must have been sufficient to create in the mind of a responsible person the fear of death or serious bodily harm. . . . I don't think anybody would deny the risk of nuclear annihilation exists. It's been expressed by the President of the United States, and politicians talk about it more than they act upon it, and one has to be almost totally ignorant not to be aware of it. . . . It's not unreasonable to believe that Ms. Jaeger and Mr. Lumpkin have a reasonable fear of death. Now they didn't express that so much for themselves. They expressed it for the children . . . for society, but . . . the fear of death for society, it seems to me, would justify a defense of duress a whole lot quicker than the fear of death for an individual.

And they must have committed the act to avoid the threatened harm. Perhaps that's the most difficult standard to establish in this circumstance because, as the prosecutor's questions suggest, how futile must their action be when one or two persons stand against the kind of power we're talking about. . . . But these defendants are of a mind that political persuasion, while it may be helpful, is not going to be effective. They cite experiences in the history of this country, and we're all familiar with them, and they're not only of recent history. They run through the course of our history, and sometimes the defendants of yesterday are the heroes of today. . . . Can two people stop the nuclear arms race? Probably not, but they suggest that they do this in the hope that others will join them. There can't be any question that if enough people take their side, the nuclear arms race is going to end. . . . There are some who say that there is absolutely no prospect of the administration or the Congress to bring this matter to a successful conclusion and that the track record proves it and that the only possibility, however remote, the only possibility of survival lies in protest. If people believe that, who can say they are wrong? These people in my opinion believe that, and I don't judge anyone else who goes out there and enters upon the property until I've heard them explain themselves.

By now it was clear Marietta and I were also going to be acquitted. Judge Boyle made a few more observations before concluding with his verdict:

And I don't propose to respond to the suggestion that such a defense cannot be accepted if we are to have any control in society. Do we have any control in society now when we have fifty thousand nuclear arms?

How is Williams to operate if their property is not protected? Well . . . if we have to surround our nuclear weapons plants with military personnel, that's the price we'll have to pay for nuclear arms. If we have to turn the military against the people, that's the price we'll have to pay . . . if enough people feel like Ms. Jaeger and Mr. Lumpkin.

These people have acted in good faith. They've acted out of compulsion. . . . While what they do presents a problem for the order of society, it does not constitute a criminal offense. I accept their defense and find each of them not guilty.

Needless to say, it was a great feeling to be acquitted (for once!). Yet it must be obvious that the necessity defense (and certainly "not guilty" verdicts) is incidental rather than essential to the work of civil resistance. Our trial appearances are just one part of a witness that begins with the act of civil disobedience itself and often extends into jail and/or prison time, with various kinds of support work carried on throughout. The necessity defense is simply one way to be considered within the entire spectrum of ways to witness in court.

THE NECESSITY DEFENSE
ALLOWED: DEFENDANTS FOUND
NOT GUILTY BY JURY

On November 13, 1984, twenty-two people were arrested for blocking the entrance to the Great Lakes Naval Training Center in Wake Forest, Illinois. The purpose for the demonstration was two-fold: to protest U.S. naval activities in Central America and to protest the Navy's part in nuclear weapons proliferation, such as stationing nuclear submarines in the Carribean and supplying artillery with nuclear capability to the Central American region.

All of the twenty-two were charged with mob action—a sort of misdemeanor conspiracy charge that involves knowingly assembling with one or more people to break the law. About half were charged with resisting arrest because they did not get up and walk when arrested. Sixteen of those arrested went to trial but charges against eight were subsequently dropped and a ninth was dismissed. The seven remaining were allowed to present a defense based on the principle of necessity.

After a one-week trial defendants were found "not guilty" by the jury. In his charge to the jury, the judge instructed them to find the defendants guilty of either mob action or resisting arrest if the prosecution proved that they did not act out of necessity.

In addition, the judge gave the following instruction to the jury regarding international law:

—International law is binding on the United States and on the State of Illinois.

—The use or threat of use of nuclear weapons is a war crime or an attempted war crime because such use would violate international law by causing unnecessary suffering, failure to distinguish between combatants and noncombatants, and poisoning targets by radiation.

NOTE

1. People v. Ann Jarka. Nos. 002196–2212, 002214, 002236–2238, Circuit Court of Lake City, Illinois, April 1985.

(*Source:* Robert Aldridge and Virginia Stark, "Nuclear War, Citizen Intervention, and the Necessity Defense," *Santa Clara Law Review* 26, no. 2 [Spring 1986]: 324–325.)

UNITED STATES V. LAFORGE AND KATT

Excerpts from Jury Instructions and Sentencing Statement of U.S. Judge Miles Lord

At trial defendants were allowed a necessity defense and the court instructed the jury as follows:

During their case in chief, the defendants have been allowed to attempt to assert a defense in this case which has been variously referred to as the defense of necessity or justification.

The defense of necessity or justification requires evidence of each and every one of the following essential elements:

1. That the criminal conduct of which the defendants stand accused was taken to prevent a greater harm to themselves or others, which was imminent to occur;

2. That there was no effective legal alternative method or course of action available to them that could be taken to avert this so-called harm, and;

3. That there was a direct causal relationship between the criminal conduct taken and the avoidance of the alleged harm. It is not necessary that the steps be completely effective in order to use this defense; in other words, it wouldn't be necessary that they destroyed all nuclear weapons, but that they had an effect upon them.[1]

Editors' Note: On August 10, 1984, John LaForge and Barbara Katt grained entry to the Sperry Defense Systems Division plant near St. Paul, Minnesota and, with hammers, damaged a Trident submarine guidance system. They were arrested and ultimately convicted of destroying government property. Maximum sentence for the $36,000 damage was ten years and a five-thousand dollar fine. The judge sentenced each defendant to six months in jail and then suspended that sentence on condition of six months probation.

Defendants were found guilty by the jury. At sentencing Judge Miles Lord made a lengthy statement, excerpts from which follow:

It is the allegation of these young people that they committed the acts here complained of as a desperate plea to the American people and its government to stop the military madness which they sincerely believe will destroy us all, friend and enemy alike . . . Can it be that those of us who build weapons to kill are engaged in a more sanctified endeavor than those who would counsel moderation and mediation as an alternative method of settling disputes?

Why are we so fascinated by a power so great that we cannot comprehend its magnitude? What is so sacred about a bomb, so romantic about a missile? Why do we condemn and hang individual killers, while extolling the virtues of warmongers? What is the fatal fascination which attracts us to the thought of mass destruction of our brethren in another country? . . . Have we given thought that, in executing that decree, we will also die? . . . [H]ave we so little faith in our system of free enterprise, our capitalism, and the fundamental concepts that are taught us in our constitutions and in our several bibles that we must, in order to protect ourselves from the spread of foreign ideologies, be prepared to die at our own hands? . . . I would here in this instance, attempt in some way to force the government . . . to remove the halo—which it seems to hold over any device which can kill—and, instead, to place thereon a shroud, the shroud of death, destruction, mutilation, disease, and debilitation.[2]

NOTES

1. No CR 4-84-66, U.S. District Court, Minnesota, partial Transcript of Proceedings, Portion of the Court's Final Jury Instructions, November 8, 1984.
2. Id. Transcript of Sentencing, November 8, 1984.
(*Source:* Robert Aldridge and Virginia Stark, "Nuclear War, Citizen Intervention and the Necessity Defense," *Santa Clara Law Review* 26, no. 2 [Spring 1986]: 322–323.)

JUDGES MUST SPEAK OUT FOR PEACE: AN INTERVIEW WITH WEST GERMAN JUDGE ULF PANZER

Ground Zero: What responsibility do yo think judges have in regard to nuclear weapons policies?

Ulf Panzer: In a democratic state, law, justice, and peace are different terms with the same meaning. In enforcing the law we work for justice, and justice and peace go together. There is no justice without peace, and no peace without justice. So judges in a democratic state must speak out if they see peace in danger, even if it's their own government that endangers the peace. That doesn't make any difference. We have to speak out.

Ground Zero: How did "Judges and Prosecutors for Peace" begin?

Panzer: It all started in Berlin in the fall of 1981 when 140 judges and prosecutors from West Berlin put an advertisement in a local

---

Editors' Note: Ulf Panzer is a judge of criminal law in a district court in Hamburg, West Germany. He is also a moving force in a group of eight-hundred judges and prosecutors from all over West Germany who strongly oppose nuclear arms.

Members of "Judges and Prosecutors for Peace" have marched together through Bonn to protest Pershing II and cruise missiles as a violation of Germany's constitution. Many of them participated in the blockade of a U.S. Air Force base at Mutlangen.

This interview was conducted in July 1985 by James Douglass of the Ground Zero Center for Nonviolent Action.

newspaper declaring the Pershing II and cruise missiles—and nuclear armament in general—to be not only immoral but also illegal, unconstitutional, and not in accordance with binding rules of international law. This led to similar advertisements all over West Germany, which were signed by about 500 judges and prosecutors.

One of my fellow judges in Munich got the idea that we should unite. So he wrote to all the judges and prosecutors who had signed the advertisements, and our movement developed. We now meet twice a year from all over Germany. There have been three common actions: two nationwide advertisements and a peace forum of 500 judges and prosecutors in our capital, Bonn.

We invited leading law professors in the fields of international law and constitutional law to our forum. We discussed the legal aspects of nuclear armament. Then we formulated a resolution we submitted to all members of our Parliament. We asked them to protest the deployment of Pershing II and cruise missiles and to use all their influence to get the two superpowers back to the negotiating table in Geneva.

Ground Zero: I understand that you also marched through Bonn.

Panzer: Yes, we held a march right through the downtown area of our capital—an old-fashioned demonstration with bands, banners, scrolls, chanting peace slogans, singing peace songs. And we read our declaration to the openmouthed citizens of Bonn who couldn't really believe that we were genuine judges and prosecutors daring to hold a demonstration.

What we judges and prosecutors are saying is that we refuse to participate in militarizing our society. There's a silent, aggressive militarization happening. We just refuse to cooperate with that.

Ground Zero: How do you reply to the criticism that as a judge demonstrating for peace you have compromised your office by becoming political?

Panzer: The office of judge is a political office, and law is applied politics. Every case we decide is a reflection of our politics. Take the case of a shoplifter. In that case we apply politics. We protect other people's property. It's our policy to do that.

There is no such thing as an apolitical judge. Every judge reads the paper and forms a certain political opinion on many issues. And to be silent on the question of nuclear war is just as much a political statement as to oppose it, to speak up against it.

I am convinced that if the judges in your country and our country would unite and say we are so glad to have nuclear arms, no government official would say a word because it would reflect official opinion, maybe also the opinion of the majority of the country. But as soon as you oppose certain things, then they come and say you have violated a judge's neutrality. There is no such thing as a neutral judge.

Ground Zero: If a peace group of judges and prosecutors were to develop in the United States, I'm sure there would be pressure put on them to cease their activities. Has that been your experience?

Panzer: Some of my colleagues—forty judges in Lubeck and two leading judges in Berlin—were reprimanded by their courts' presidents and by the Secretary of Justice. But we filed a lawsuit against these reprimands, and there was a very good decision by an administration court in Kiel. The ruling was that the reprimands had to be withdrawn.

The court said that the Secretary of Justice had to take into consideration that the status and image of a judge had changed considerably in recent years. We don't live under the Kaiser any more. We live in a democracy, and in a democracy judges are independent from the government.

The court said judges have freedom of speech, freedom of expression. We owed our democracy in Germany partly to judges who spoke out against the aristocratic government in 1848, when the first democratic state was formed on our territory and Germany became a republic.

So that was a victory for us. Ever since then, the government continues to frown at our public engagement but it can't do anything about it.

Ground Zero: How has the history of the Third Reich influenced your stand against nuclear weapons?

Panzer: Judges were an instrument of the leaders of the Third Reich, a very docile instrument. Many judges in Germany—almost all of them—committed immense crimes during the Nazi regime. We feel that by being silent today we judges would be guilty again.

In the Third Reich, we allowed ourselves to be used to legitimate the most cruel crimes. We feel that we are right at the point of being used again to legitimate instruments of mass murder, of omnideath really. We do that in our courts by declaring them to be legitimate property, which they are not. Or we do it by jailing or at least in Germany by fining people who try to stop those weapons from destroying us. We don't want to be part of that legitimating process any more.

But I have to add, of course, that we are a minority among West German judges. We are about 10 percent. Ninety percent have a different opinion.

Ground Zero: I wish 10 percent of the judges in this country would take such a stand.

Panzar: It has had quite an impact, especially on the "ordinary people." In Germany the peace movement is characterized as criminal by government officials and the conservative press. They claim we are criminals, that we are antidemocratic, even that we are paid by Mr. Gorbachev.

That was a little more difficult to maintain when we judges came into the peace movement. You can't really say that we get our paychecks from the Kremlin, or that we are antidemocratic when we are enforcing democratic laws.

It also helped to encourage other people when they saw on TV that judges and prosecutors were holding a demonstration. They obviously thought it can't be so criminal, after all, to protest nuclear armament. So they went into the streets too.

Ground Zero: Have their been acts of nonviolent resistance to nuclear weapons in Germany that judges have upheld in court?

Panzar: There have been some. But they are all being appealed by the state. So there are no final decisions yet.

I have to explain that a little. As a judge you can follow your conscience in such a case and declare a defendant not guilty, being certain, however, that the prosecutor will appeal that decision, which is possible in Germany. And the second court will overturn your decision. That means the defendant has to pay the court fees and defense attorney fees twice. And the second court will also punish the defendant.

So some of my colleagues—I haven't been given a civil obedience case yet—have declared the defendants guilty but have only admonished them, without giving them any punishment. So we walk a tightrope. If we make a really outstanding decision, it will probably be overturned, and we give stones instead of bread to the defendants.

Ground Zero: You just used the term "civil obedience." Can you explain why you used that term rather than "civil disobedience"?

Panzer: We are convinced that the true crimials are those who produce and possess nuclear arms and who may some day use them. If you protest or resist nuclear arms, you are on the right side of the law. So the term "civil disobedience" just isn't appropriate. You are obeying the law by resisting nuclear arms.

Ground Zero: In describing an act of nonviolent resistance as "civil obedience," are you referring to obedience to the constitution of the Federal Republic of Germany or obedience to international law or both?

Panzer: I'm referring to both. But as far as our constitution is concerned, our federal constitutional court didn't accept a complaint saying that nuclear arms were not constitutional. Apart from that there is, of course, the question of international law.

The United Nations Charter clearly says that not only is war prohibited but that violence is prohibited, and even the threat of violence. The strategy of nuclear deterrence is nothing but the threat of massive violence: "If you push your button, then I'll push mine." Bearing in mind that nuclear war means a kind of "peace"—the eternal peace of all of us because there won't be any human beings left on this planet—such war truly is a crime against the law of humanity.

So international law says nuclear arms are prohibited. There are many declarations and protocols violated by nuclear arms: Geneva, The Hague, the Kellogg-Briand Pact . . . The United States has signed all those treaties.

Of course, international law can't be enforced because there is no institution that can enforce it. International law is based on respect and acceptance. I'm sorry to say that the United States government accepts some World Court decisions in The Hague—those that are in its favor. Those decisions that are not in the alleged interests of the United States it just won't accept.

Ground Zero: In the absence of an authority to enforce international law, do you see acts of civil obedience beginning to take on a power of enforcement?

Panzer: I always compare the question of nuclear arms with the question of slavery. When you had slavery in the United States, it was within the bounds of national law to buy and sell a human being. That was unquestioned for quite a while. But then the opinion in society changed. People started to resist slavery. People went to jail for resisting slavery. A war was fought partly over the issue of slavery.

Today we know that slavery is a crime against humanity. It is abolished by all civilized countries. I think the same must happen with nuclear arms.

Law in its operation is a conservative thing. It functions to keep the status quo. It is an instrument of power really. It's very rarely that law changes the opinion of a society. It's almost always the other way round, that society changes and the law follows. That is our only hope: that the protest of nuclear arms will grow and grow, and the law will follow, and we will abolish nuclear arms—and eventually, all armament.

Ground Zero: In the United States it is a common experience for people who engage in acts of civil obedience to go to jail, and for increasing lengths of time if they repeat such acts.

I know you are familiar with the Silo Pruning Hooks action at a Minuteman II missile silo in Missouri, for which Helen Woodson and Carl Kabat received eighteen-year prison sentences, Paul Kabat ten-years, and Larry Cloud Morgan eight-years. How do these kinds of sentences compare to the sentences of people in West Germany who are engaged on acts of civil obedience?

Panzer: By German standards such sentences are unbelievable. We made a resolution protesting those sentences, signed by 130 of my fellow judges in Germany—only 130 because I couldn't reach any more at the time. What is astonishing about those sentences is that the legal structures in Germany and the United States are pretty much the same. Yet we have this tremendous difference in sentences.

I can compare one Plowshares case in Germany, in Mutlangen, where Pershing II missiles are deployed. Ironically, one of the defendants there was also Father Carl Kabat.

The Silo Pruning Hooks received sentences ranging up to eighteen years for destroying the concrete lid of a silo and hammering on a missile. The damage that was done there amounted to about $12,000. A year ago in Germany, Father Carl Kabat and three German peace activists invaded the Mutlangen Pershing II missile site and destroyed a Pershing II missile launcher. The damage that was done there amounted to about $11,000.

In Mutlangen, they were convicted on charges of trespass, attempted sabotage, and destruction of property. The judges in their sentencing statements said they had to pay high respect to the honest and credible motives of the defendants and to their religious beliefs. They said it was a crime, nevertheless, because our laws don't allow such forms of resistance. But they said it was a minor crime and that the court itself saw the danger of the deployment of Pershing II and cruise missiles in our territory. So the defendants were only fined, with the fines ranging from $70 to $600 with respect to the different incomes of the defendants.

Usually in Germany you get fined for civil obedience. We don't have any imprisonment for that yet. In your country many people go to jail for civil obedience. On this trip I've been to Minneapolis, Denver, and Spokane, and most of the people I've met have served minor prison sentences for civil obedience. It's quite unbelievable for a German.

Ground Zero: Do you see any parallels between U.S. attitudes toward nuclear arms and attitudes that led to the Third Reich?

Panzer: I am a German, so I am very reluctant to compare U.S. nuclear arms with the crimes of the Third Reich. There may be a similarity, but I think I am in no position to say that. I do think that both of our countries today have a kind of velvet or silent fascism. And I'm not so sure that in Germany it couldn't all happen again. I'm really not. In West Germany we have neo-Nazis. Thank God, they are really a minority. I'm not afraid of them too much. But I am afraid of conservative right-wingers.

That's why the visit of your president to Bitburg was so dangerous. It did a lot of harm. He encouraged the wrong kind of people— those who say, "Let's forget about our past and concentrate on the future. Let the past be buried. That was forty or fifty years ago."

But you get a blurred vision of the future if you forget about your past. I think you create the first foundation for those things happening again.

The president of the United States also has a distorted view of our recent German history. That history wasn't just the action of one man, Adolf Hitler. Almost all of our fellow citizens participated. By saying that only Adolf Hitler and his party were responsible, the president encouraged and strengthened the conservative or maybe even fascist powers in our country.

Ground Zero: You have said how much the complicity of judges with the Nazis has influenced your decision to resist nuclear weapons and break your complicity with the nuclear state. What happened to those judges after World War II?

Panzer: No judge from the Third Reich has ever been convicted of a crime for imposing sentences of death because the defendant made a joke about the Führer. Not one judge. And there were thousands of such cases. It was all legal.

The British forces that occupied Hamburg tried to install a new administration and court after the war. But they couldn't find any members of the legal profession who hadn't taken part in the crimes of the Third Reich. So they tried to appoint at least as many new judges who hadn't taken part in the crimes. It didn't work out because they didn't have as many.

So it was two judges to one: two judges who had committed crimes of different severity, who had acted as judges in the Third Reich, and only one judge who had a clear conscience. And that continued for years and years. They applied credit laws the same way they had applied cruel and criminal laws in the Third Reich five or six years before. They moved up, of course, into higher positions.

Today most of them are retired or dead. And it is unknown. Nobody talks about it.

THE NUREMBERG PRINCIPLES

Principles of International Law Recognized in the Charter of the Nuremberg Tribunal and in the Judgment of the Tribunal

As formulated by the International Law Commission, June–July 1950.

Principle I
Any person who commits an act which constitutes a crime under international law is responsible therefor and liable to punishment.

Principle II
The fact that internal law does not impose a penalty for an act which constitutes a crime under international law does not relieve the person who committed the act from responsibility under international law.

Principle III
The fact that a person who committed an act which constitutes a crime under international law acted as Head of State or responsible government official does not relieve him from responsibility under international law.

Principle IV
The fact that a person acted pursuant to order of his Government or of a superior does not relieve him from responsibility under international law, provided a moral choice was in fact possible to him.

(*Source:* United Nations General Assembly Resolution 95 (1). The Principles were formulated by the International Law Commission at the request of the General Assembly.)

Principle V

Any person charged with a crime under international law has the right to a fair trial on the facts and law.

Principle VI

The crimes hereinafter set out are punishable as crimes under international law:

a. Crimes against peace:

(i) Planning, preparation, initiation, or waging of a war of aggression or a war in violation of international treaties, agreements, or assurances;

(ii) Participation in a common plan or conspiracy for the accomplishment of any of the acts mentioned under (i).

b. War crimes:

Violations of the laws or customs of war which include, but are not limited to, murder, ill-treatment or deportation to slave-labor or for any other purpose of civilian population of or in occupied territory, murder or ill-treatment of prisoners of war or persons on the seas, killing of hostages, plunder of public or private property, wanton destruction of cities, towns, or villages, or devastation not justified by military necessity.

c. Crimes against humanity:

Murder, extermination, enslavement, deportation, and other inhuman acts done against any civilian population, or persecutions on political, racial, or religious grounds, when such acts are done or such persecutions are carried on in execution of or in connection with any crime against peace or any war crime.

Principle VII

Complicity in the commission of a crime against peace, a war crime, or a crime against humanity as set forth in Principle VI is a crime under international law.

THE NUREMBERG PLEDGE OF LAWYERS AND JURISTS

Deeply concerned by the commission of many crimes of state and by the terrible danger of an annihilating nuclear war:

We, the undersigned, pledge to work in our professional roles and as citizens for the effective application of the Nuremberg Principles, that acts in violation of these principles are punishable as crimes whether committed by a head of state or by an ordinary soldier or civilian, whether done under governmental order or not, and that crimes against peace, war crimes, and crimes against humanity are to be condemned, prevented, and prosecuted by the enforcement of international law.

More concretely, we pledge to resist the commission of crimes of state, including especially preparations for war waged with nuclear weapons and seek the establishment of a legal framework in international society to assure the impartial and rigorous application of the Nuremberg Principles.

On this fortieth anniversary of the Nuremberg Judgment we call on lawyers and jurists throughout the world to join us by signing this pledge and we invite members of political, military, scientific, religious, business, and all other professional associations to join us in this struggle on behalf of law and peace by drafting and circulating similar pledges to their colleagues and by playing active roles on behalf of the Nuremberg Principles in the constitutional order of international political life.

The Nuremberg Pledge of Lawyers and Jurists was adopted at Nuremberg on November 24, 1985, by vote of the two thousand participants at the International Association of Democratic Lawyers Conference.
(*Source: Ground Zero,* Spring 1986, p. 3)

UNITED NATIONS RESOLUTION ON THE PROHIBITION OF NUCLEAR WEAPONS

The General Assembly,

Mindful of its responsibility under the Charter of the United Nations in the maintenance of international peace and security, as well as in the consideration of principles governing disarmament,

Gravely concerned that, while negotiations on disarmament have not so far achieved satisfactory results, the armaments race, particularly in the nuclear and thermonuclear fields, has reached a dangerous state requiring all possible precautionary measures to protect humanity and civilization from the hazard of nuclear and thermonuclear catastrophe,

Recalling that the use of weapons of mass destruction, causing unnecessary human suffering, was in the past prohibited, as being contrary to the laws of humanity and to the principles of international law, by international declarations and binding agreements, such as the Declaration of St. Petersburg of 1868, the Declaration of the Brussels Conference of 1874, the Conventions of The Hague Peace Conferences of 1899 and 1907, and the Geneva Protocol of 1925, to which the majority of nations are still parties,

Considering that the use of nuclear and thermonuclear weapons would bring about indiscriminate suffering and destruction to humankind and civilization to an even greater extent than the use of those weapons delcared by the aforementioned international declarations and agreements to be contrary to the laws of humanity and a crime under international law,

Believing that the use of weapons of mass destruction, such as nuclear and thermonuclear weapons, is a direct negation of the high ideals and objectives which the United Nations has been established to achieve through the protection of succeeding generations from the scourge of war and through the preservation and promotion of their cultures,

1. *Declares that:*

(*a*) The use of nuclear and thermonuclear weapons is contrary to the spirit, letter, and aims of the United Nations and, as such, a direct violation of the Charter of the United Nations;

(*b*) The use of nuclear and thermonuclear weapons would exceed even the scope of war and cause indiscriminate suffering and destruction to humankind and civilization and, as such, is contrary to the rules of international law and to the laws of humanity;

(*c*) The use of nuclear and thermonuclear weapons is a war directed not against an enemy or enemies alone but also against humankind in general, since the peoples of the world not involved in such a war will be subjected to all the evils generated by the use of such weapons;

(*d*) Any State using nuclear and thermonuclear weapons is to be considered as violating the Charter of the United Nations, as acting contrary to the laws of humanity and as committing a crime against mankind and civilization;

2 *Requests* the Secretary-General to consult the Governments of Member States to ascertain their views on the possibility of convening a special conference for signing a convention on the prohibition of the use of nuclear and thermonuclear weapons for war purposes and to report on the results of such consultation to the General Assembly at its seventeenth session.

(*Source:* United Nations General Assembly Resolution 1653 (XVI) on the Prohibition of Nuclear Warfare, 1961. Note: The United States voted against this resolution.)

INTERNATIONAL AGGRESSION AND NONMILITARY DEFENSE

Ronald J. Sider and Richard K. Taylor

In the war crimes trials at the end of World War II, SS Colonel Rudolf Hess, commandment of Auschwitz, testified that the Nazis had killed three million persons in his concentration camp alone. The crematoria of Auschwitz were able to reduce to ashes more than five thousand bodies in less than a day. In six years, Hitler's followers exterminated six million Jews and innumerable others.

Yet today we place in the hands of world leaders the power to exterminate hundreds of millions of people in the course of a few hours of "nuclear exchange." Unleashed, the superpowers' bombs and rockets would create thousands of crematoria—not packed furnaces, but crowded cities.

Christians and reflective people everywhere are realizing more and more that nations rely on the potential use of Hitler's means—terror and mass extermination—to accomplish their ends. People are turning against nuclear weapons not only out of fear of terrible destruction. They are also unwilling to support military strategies that would make them complicit in killing and maiming on a scale far beyond the carnage wrought by Hitler. People fear being targeted, having to live in the bull's eye of another nation's nuclear weapons. But for the person of moral sensitivity, it is perhaps even more appalling to be a nuclear targeter—one who must sanction the possibility of burning to ashes millions of God's children in keeping with the nuclear policy of one's own nation.

Peace-minded Christians from both the "just war" and pacifist traditions are responding to this situation by supporting pragmatic proposals for mutual, verfiable disarmament. But they realize that a freeze of strategic weapons would still leave the superpowers with enough nuclear warheads to create more than fifteen thousand city-crematoria. Major postfreeze nuclear disarmament, achieved through superpower negotiations, would take years; meanwhile, each side would retain the power to destroy human life far more quickly and massively than did Hitler's death camps.

Not surprisingly, Christian pacifists respond to this moral horror with total rejection of war. Obedient faith in Jesus Christ, they say, means to heal rather than wound, to love enemies rather than destroy them, to pray for persecutors rather than make them suffer. This commitment rules out war and preparations for war.

But the moral enormity of modern war is having an impact far beyond pacifist circles. A notable case in point is the recent pastoral letter of the U.S. Catholic bishops, which condemns nuclear war as immoral. Other Christians go even further, concluding that nuclear war constitutes "murder" according to the "just war" theory. And since preparation for murder is also murderous, it is wrong even to possess nuclear weapons. Numerous Catholic and Protestant non-pacifists joined with pacifists in signing the declaration "A Call to Faithfulness," which committed them to the "total abolition of nu-clear weapons" and "noncooperation with our country's preparation for nuclear war." From April 20 to 24, 1983, about one hundred fifty church leaders representative of the Christian church worldwide met in Sweden to discuss the nuclear arms race. In their final dec-laration, the vast majority condemned the very possession of nuclear weapons. Clearly, "nuclear pacifism" has growing numbers of ad-herents among Christians in the "just war" tradition.

The nuclear freeze can be seen as an important first step toward the abolition of nuclear weapons, but it is not enough. If Christian values compel us to conclude that possession of nuclear weapons is immoral, it would seem imperative to call for a complete, unilateral, and immediate renunciation of such weapons.

Predictably, those who disagree with this position are appalled. "Don't you realize that nuclear deterrence is the cornerstone of our defense policy?" they ask. "Would you have the United States do nothing to counter aggression? Would you let nuclear-armed totali-tarian dictatorships have their way?" To these critics, unilateral re-nunciation would open the way for the Soviets greatly to expand their influence and to impose tyranny on weaker states. They find support for their views in the long history of Christian thought that teaches "the right of legitimate self-defense."

We agree that nations have a right to defend their independence and cherished values against outside threats. The extent of the "Soviet threat" can be debated, but it is incontestable that powerful nations regularly try to impose their will through military means. Biblically rooted Christians believe that "wars and rumors of wars" will persist and that "nation will rise up against nation" until Christ returns (Matt. 24:6–7). Political science joins this biblical view in a realistic analysis of the world's power struggles. History gives countless examples of one state's attempting to extend its influence by threatening another. Tyranny is far from dead. Some means of response has been and will be necessary.

Christians are not exempt from the call to resist the spread of oppressive governments. Biblical faith calls us to "seek justice, correct oppression, defend the fatherless, plead for the widow" (Isa. 1:17). The "oppression" we are called to "correct" presumably includes that which an invading totalitarian country might try to impose. Among the "fatherless" we are called to "defend" are surely those vulnerable people whom an expanding despotism might seek to crush.

Few would argue that Christians should have stood by and done nothing while Hitler's Nazism was spreading. Few would dispute the fact that Communist leaders such as Stalin have exterminated millions. Realism suggests that immense threats to cherished values and institutions will continue to arise, whether in a Soviet guise or some other.

The fact that American values and institutions are deeply flawed and that the United States sometimes acts oppressively in international affairs does not alter the fact that the current American system is preferable to any that an outside despot might try to enforce. "Government of the people, by the people, and for the people," though inadequately realized in the United States, is preferable to government by a hostile foreign power.

Christians, then, are under a dual mandate: to be peacemakers, but also to resist evil, injustice, and oppression. We are to "hold fast to love and justice," as the prophet Hosea reminds us (Hos. 12:6).

This text suggests that, however strongly we may critique the imperfections of our nation, we should also defend its positive values and institutions against the intervention of a hostile foreign power.

Does this bring us back to "square one," the need to support military defense, even when "defense" with modern weapons involves us potentially in mass murder and the capacity to extinguish the human race? What if a means of defense could be found that does *not* rely upon military weapons, nuclear or conventional, and yet gives hope of protecting a nation's cherished liberties in the face of outside aggression? Such a means could serve as an alternative to military defense and war. Christians advocating defense of this kind would call not for disarmament but for *transarmament—transforming* the nation's defense system to one relying on nonmilitary means.

Even to pose the question sounds startling. A nonmilitary defense system sounds like a contradition in terms. But there are scholars, military experts, theologians, and peace advocates who believe nonmilitary defense to be a viable option. Its proponents include General André de Bollardiere, one of France's most highly decorated generals, and Captain Sir Basil Liddell Hart, military editor of the *Encyclopaedia Britannica,* widely acknowledged as one of the foremost military writers of our time. Even the governments of several European countries (Sweden, Norway, Denmark, the Netherlands) have taken an interest in these ideas, studied them and, in at least one case, run army exercises based on nonmilitary defense. Gene Sharp, an American proponent of such defense, has lectured at the U.S. Army War College. His writings on nonviolent response to aggression have received favorable reviews in several American military periodicals.

Proponents of nonmilitary defense point out that the current arms race is based on a "symmetric"strategy adopted by each of the superpowers. Each tries to match or surpass its opponent with weapons of the same kind—warhead against warhead, rocket against rocket, tank against tank. But successful resistance to outside tyranny has occasionally been mounted through an "asymmetric" strategy—pitting *non*military means against the opponent's military forces.

Such an asymmetric strategy was employed in Hungary's battle against Austrian Rule in the mid-1800s. After crushing a Hungarian military uprising in 1849, Austria put Hungary under martial law, divided it into military districts, suppressed its parliament, and repealed its constitution. Militarily defeated, Hungary seemed to have no alternative but to submit to foreign rule.

Political and religious leaders, however, united in a strategy of absolute resistance without violence. They advised Hungarian citizens not to recognize Austrian rule and to treat Austrian officials as "illegal persons." Austrian decrees would not be obeyed. Hungarians would follow their own constitution and laws. Church services and government meetings would be held even when Austrian officials forbade them. Ferencz Deak, a Hungarian jurist and leader of the resistance, said, "We can hold our own against armed force. If suffering be necessary, suffer with dignity."

The variety of tactics used in the Hungarian resistance cannot be detailed here. Suffice it to say that Austria finally was forced to reopen the Hungarian parliament and to restore the constitution. Hungary won complete internal independence. It resisted all Austria's attempts to destroy its churches' autonomy.

Advocates of nonmilitary defense are often asked if such tactics could succeed under a more brutal oppression. They reply by pointing to little-known instances of successful nonmilitary resistance to Hitler's demonic schemes. In Bulgaria, for instance, Bishop Kiril told authorities that if they attempted to deport Bulgarian Jews to concentration camps, he himself would lead a campaign of civil disobedience, lying down on the railroad tracks in front of the deportation trains. Thousands of Jews and non-Jews resisted all collaboration with Nazi decrees. They marched in mass street demonstrations and sent a flood of letters and telegrams to authorities protesting all anti-Jewish measures. Bulgarian clergy and laity hid Jews. Christian ministers accepted large numbers of Jewish "converts," making it clear that this was a trick to escape the Nazis and that they would not consider the "vows" binding. Because of these and other nonmilitary measures, all of Bulgaria's Jewish citizens were saved from the Nazi death camps.

Similar nonmilitary resistance in Norway prevented Vidkun Quisling, Hitler's representative, from imposing a fascist "corporative state" on the country. Finland saved all but four of its Jewish citizens from the death camps through nonmilitary means. Denmark's asymmetrical resistance was so effective that Adolf Eichmann had to admit that "the action against the Jews of Denmark has been a failure."

The authors of a growing literature on nonmilitary resistance to tyranny are cataloguing and analyzing asymmetrical campaigns in many parts of the world and in various periods of history. These include the Indian independence movement led by Mohandas Gandhi, Germany's nonmilitary resistance to invasion by France and Belgium in 1923, successful Latin American campaigns to overthrow dictatorships by nonviolent means, and the recent Iranian revolution, in which massive street demonstrations overthrew the militarily powerful shah. A new organization, the Association for Transarmament Studies, has been established to further these studies and to explore their relevance to the nonmilitary defense of the United States.

None of these historical examples, of course, proves that nonmilitary means can be substituted for military ones in the defense of a nation. But they do show that people have thwarted tyranny and defended their most precious values without violence or military weaponry. They point to a power to resist oppression that does not rely on the ability to kill and injure.

The success of nonmilitary movements cited is all the more remarkable when we consider their primitive and unrefined nature as compared with military defense. Most nonmilitary movements have not had the advantage of advance planning or preparation. A more carefully thought-out nonmilitary defense could perhaps produce even more powerful results, just as training and strategizing help the military to be more effective.

It is also instructive to look at the part that Christians have played in nonmilitary defense. The Norwegian Evangelical Lutheran Church played a key role in the resistance to Quisling's fascism. Protestant leaders in Hungary spearheaded the resistance to Austrian occupation. Examples abound of church people who have taken leadership in the nonviolent defense in their country's way of life.

Perhaps this is not so surprising when we consider the Christian tradition. Christianity grew up in a region occupied by foreign invaders who used fierce military power to enforce their rule. In territory under the brutal heel of imperial Rome, Jesus instructed his disciples to love their enemies and to turn the other cheek. The Christian reponse to Roman tyranny was not to "roll over and play dead." Early church members responded to unjust Roman decrees with protest and noncooperation. Cecil John Cadoux writes:

One Christian tore down the first edict of persecution posted up by Diocletianus; another fearlessly seized the governor's hand as he was in the act of sacrificing and exhorted him to abandon his error; another strode forward in open court and rebuked the judge for his ruthless sentences. A Christian woman, dragged to the altar and commanded to sacrifice upon it, kicked it over.[1]

Though generally pacifists, Christian leaders were far from passive in their response to persecution. They poured forth a torrent of protest, defiance and censure against the persecutors and their decrees. But unlike those who chose a military path of resistance, they acted without violence and with a willingness to endure suffering. St. Chrysostom, a church leader of the fourth century, summarized the balance between resistance and nonviolent suffering:

What then, ought we not to resist an evil? Indeed we ought; but not by retaliation. Christ hath commanded us to give up ourselves to suffering wrongfully, for thus shall we prevail over evil. For one fire is not quenched by another fire, but fire by water.[2]

However, the early Christians did more than simply refuse to kill their enemies; they sought to love them. As Justinius said, "We pray for our enemies and try to persuade those who hate us unjustly." And as St. Cyprian said to his persecutors, "It is not lawful for us to hate, and so we please God more when we render no requital for injury. . . . We repay your hatred with kindness."

It seems that the early Christians had found Hosea's secret of how to "hold fast to love and justice" (Hos. 12:6). Their commitment to justice made them speak and act against Roman oppression. Their immersion in the love of Christ led them to love their enemies and to suffer rather than kill. Their powerful example of nonmilitary resistance finds echoes at many points in the life of the church through history.

What do these historical examples say to us today, confronted as we are with the need to defend important values against totalitarianism and the moral and practical impossibility of defense with nuclear weapons? Perhaps they say that we should be working not only for disarmament but also for transarmament. Perhaps we should be seeking a method of defending freedom and democracy that draws directly upon the nonviolence exemplified by Jesus.

How could transarmament come about? Public and congressional debate would first have to take place. Private and governmental agencies to carry out nonmilitary defense would have to be created, along with a plan for the economic readjustment that would come with conversion from military to nonmilitary defense. Military personnel and weapons industry workers would have to be retrained for civilian work. Large sectors of the U.S. population would need to be trained in the philosophy, strategy, and tactics of nonviolent resistance to aggression. Since American military weapons would no longer be available to protect vulernable allies, they would need help in adopting their own nonmilitary defense systems.

How can those of us who reject a reliance on nuclear weapons for defense begin to work for an alternative defense system? First, we can educate ourselves about nonmilitary defense.[3] Then we can talk to people about nonviolent resistance as a moral means of national defense that has at least as much "practicality" as nuclear deterrence. We can persuade colleges and universities to do research on the topic. We can encourage public debate. We can urge nonmilitary defense upon political candidates and our representatives in Congress. We can form groups that use nonviolent means to attack existing social injustices. We can use nonviolent demonstrations to oppose specific nuclear programs while educating the public about an alternative means of defending precious values.

Would such an alternative defense system "work"? Can nonmilitary defense be justified on purely pragmatic grounds? Although it *has* worked in the past, there is certainly no guarantee that it will work in all circumstances. But then, the same can be said for military means of defense, which have their own mixed record of success and failure.

Would nonmilitary defense be risk-free? Certainly not. It would require a willingness to suffer and sacrifice. A population using it could well face imprisonment, torture, mass executions. But military defense also requires suffering and sacrifice, as the fifty million deaths of World War II so vividly illustrate. What if even five million people had been willing to die in a nonviolent struggle against Hitler?

Having nuclear weapons or not having them—both postures involve awesome risk. We face a chasm of uncertainty and risk never known before. For the Christian, obedient faith in Jesus Christ is the only bridge over the chasm. Does Jesus want us now to prepare ourselves massively to kill or massively to love our enemies?

NOTES

1. Cecil John Cadoux, *The Early Church and the World* (Edinburgh: Clark, 1925), 531.
2. C. G. H. MacGregor, *The New Testament Basis of Pacifism* (Nyack, NY: Fellowship Publications, 1954), 154.
3. For an excellent resource for study see *U.S. Defense Policy: Mainstream Views and Nonviolent Alternatives* (available from International Seminars on Training for Nonviolent Action, Box 515, Waltham, MA 02254).

PART FIVE

Resources

To culminate a year of resistance at the Pentagon organized by the Atlantic
Life Community, these children led about 1,000 people in a vigil encircling
the Pentagon building on New Year's Eve in 1980. Their presence signalled
hope for future change in U.S. military policy, hope for future peace. *Photo
by Tom Lewis.*

PEACE AND DISARMAMENT GROUPS

Groups Working on an International, National, and Regional Level for Disarmament and Social Justice

T he following is a list of groups that might be helpful in assisting new and established groups in their work for peace and justice. This is not a comprehensive list; it would be extremely difficult to list all the numerous antinuclear groups, which vary greatly in emphasis and action. Many of the groups below have information concerning regional groups with which they are affiliated.

Agape Communities. A network of spiritually based communities in the Northwest, West, Southwest, and South who are involved in a nonviolent campaign to stop the transport of nuclear weapons by the "nuclear train." Contact Ground Zero Center for Nonviolent Action, 16159 Cleer Creek Rd. NW, Poulsbo, WA 98370.

American Friends Service Committee (AFSC). An organization with regional offices around the United States involved in education and nonviolent action for nuclear disarmament and social justice. It publishes a wide variety of resources on peace and disarmament. 1501 Cherry St., Philadelphia, PA 19102.

Association for Transarmament Studies (ATS). A worldwide organization providing resources for the study and discussion of civilian–based defense. it sees "transarmament" as a desirable future possibility for nations if and when they are able to rely on prepared nonviolent action to deter and resist aggression. 3636 Lafayette, Omaha, NE 68131.

Atlantic Life Community (ALC). A network of individuals and spiritually based resistance communities throughout the eastern United States involved in nonviolent direct action for disarmament at the Pentagon, the White House, and nuclear weapons facilities. Contact Jonah House, 1933 Park Ave., Baltimore, MD 21217.

Catholic Worker. A Catholic network of over fifty communities in the United

States committed to the "works of mercy and peace" from a gospel-pacifist perspective. It publishes a monthly newspaper. For Catholic Worker houses in your area contact 3 Catholic Worker, 36 E. First St., New York, NY 10012.

Center Peace (formerly known as the National Center on Law and Pacifism). An ecumenical pacifist group focusing on theological and legal counseling for war-tax resistance and providing books and other resources on conscientious objection to war. It published *People Pay for Peace,* an excellent guide on war-tax resistance, by William Durland and it publishes a newsletter. c/o "Pendle Hill", Wallingford, PA 19086.

Clergy and Laity Concerned (CALC). An interfaith organization with local chapters throughout the United States dedicated to religious political action for peace and justice. It distributes a wide range of disarmament and justice resources. 198 Broadway, New York, NY 10038.

Coalition for a New Foreign and Military Policy. A coalition of social action, religious, labor, and peace groups working for a peaceful, demilitarized U.S. foreign policy. It distributes a variety of resources. 712 G St. SE, Washington, DC 20003.

Disarmament Campaigns. A Dutch group that distributes information about disarmament campaigns occurring worldwide. Anna Paulownaplein 3, PB 18747, 2502 ES The Hague, Netherlands.

Educators for Social Responsibility. An organization with local chapters working with educators, parents, and students to introduce a war and peace curriculum into the school systems. 23 Garden St., Cambridge, MA 02138.

Fellowship of Reconciliation (FOR). A religious pacifist organization working for disarmament and social justice. It has numerous local and denominational fellowships, a "U.S.-U.S.S.R. Reconciliation Program," and a "Children's Conflict" program. It publishes *Fellowship,* a monthly magazine. Box 271, Nyack, NY 10960.

Infact. This national grassroots organization, which led the successful seven-year Nestlé boycott, is now coordinating a nationwide boycott against General Electric for its role in producing nuclear weapons. 186 Lincoln Street, Room 203, Boston, MA 02111.

International Physicians for the Prevention of Nuclear War. An international organizations of doctors from the United States, the Soviet Union, and other countries working to reverse the arms race. It provides audiovisual and other educational resources on the medical aspects of nuclear war. It won the Nobel Peace Prize in 1985. 225 Longwood Ave., Boston, MA 02115.

International Fellowship of Reconciliation (IFOR). A transnational religious community of different faiths committed to nonviolence as a principle of life for a world community of peace and justice. It has affiliates in over thirty countries and publishes a magazine five times a year with a strong focus on human rights and disarmament. It disseminates information about nonviolent movements worldwide. Hof Van Sonoy 15-17, 1811 LD, Alkmaar, The Netherlands.

Lawyers' Committee on Nuclear Policy. A nonpartisan organization involved in educating the legal community and the public about the illegality of nuclear weapons under international law. It acts as legal council to Nuclear Free Zone campaigns and efforts to oppose naval homeporting. 225 Lafayette St., Suite 513, New York, NY 10012.

Mobilization for Survival (MFS). A coalition of groups emphasizing grassroots action toward reversing the arms race and meeting human needs. It provides information and resources on disarmament and groups working around the country to resist U.S. nuclear military policy. It is the contact for the National Weapons Facility Network 853 Broadway, Room 418, New York, NY 10003.

New Call to Peacemaking. A coalition of the historic peace churches— Quaker, Mennonite, and Brethren—involved in work for peace and disarmament. Box 1245, Elkhart, IN 46515.

National Inter-Religious Service Board for Conscientious Objectors (NISBCO). A coalition of religious groups who oppose all forms of compulsory national military service. It provides resources on countering military recruiting and on draft counseling, including a booklet, *Words of Conscience: Religious Statements on Conscientious Objection.* 550 Washington Building, 15th and New York Ave. NW, Washington, DC 20005.

North Atlantic Network. A network of peace groups in countries facing the North Atlantic, Norwegian, and Baltic Seas. It is committed to facilitating a greater understanding of the region's rapidly expanding naval arms race. It coordinates international days of action to draw attention to the dangers of war at sea. It conducts conferences and provides educational resources. 853 Broadway, Room 418, New York, NY 10003.

Nuclear Weapons Freeze Campaign. A national organization comprised of local groups committed to a bilateral nuclear weapons freeze. It provides resources on nuclear arms control. 220 I St., Suite 130, Washington, DC 20002.

Nukewatch. A national project coordinatig nonviolent vigils and helping raise public awareness about the transportation of nuclear warheads and components by truck over U.S. roads and highways. (Eighty percent of all nuclear warheads are transported by truck). 315 West Gorman St., Madison, WI 53703.

Pacific Concerns Resource Center. Network center for Nuclear Free and Independent Pacific movement. P.O. Box 27692, Honolulu, HI 96827.

Peacework Alternatives. A group promoting discussion of the ethical questions of employment in weapons work and providing a network of services (i.e., counseling, workshops, finding nondefense jobs) for defense workers considering leaving their jobs for conscience reasons. 3940 Poplar Level Rd., Louisville, KY 40213.

Physicians for Social Responsibility (PSR). A group of health and medical professionals who provide information about the health hazards of nuclear weaponry and nuclear power. Box 295, Cambridge, MA 02236.

Prolifers for Survival. A network of women and men committed to nonviolence who support alternatives to nuclear arms and abortion. P.O. Box 3316, Chapel Hill, NC 27515.

Promoting Enduring Peace. An educational organization that offers free reprints of articles on peace and disarmament on a quarterly basis. Box 5103, Woodmont, CT 06460.

Religious Task Force. An interfaith group affiliated with MFS organizing primarily in the religious community for peace and disarmament. It organized the "Children of War" tour in 1985 and distributes an array of resources to the religious community on disarmament. 85 South Oxford St., Brooklyn, NY 11217.

Riverside Church Disarmament Program. An organization based at Riverside Church providing speakers and resources on Christian peacemaking and disarmament. It published *Peace in Search of Makers* and publishes a newsletter. 490 Riverside Dr., New York, NY 10027.

Sojourners Community. An evangelical and ecumenical Christian community that through its Peace Ministry offers resources and help to those who are raising peace issues as central to the church's life. It publishes a monthly magazine and distributes books, audiovisual resources, and other materials on disarmament. P.O. Box 29272, Washington, DC 20017.

Students/Teachers Organization to Prevent Nuclear War (STOP). A group of high-school students and teachers involved in education and action for disarmament. Activities include attending nonviolent protests, seminars, and trips to the Soviet Union. It helps organize local groups. Box 232, Northfield, MA 01360.

Vietnam Veterans Against the War. An organization of Vietnam veterans, formed in 1967 to help end U.S. involvement in Indochina, which actively opposes U.S. and Soviet military intervention and increased military spending. It is an advocate for veterans rights. It coordinates veteran support groups, and it publishes the newsletter, *The Veteran*. P.O. Box 25592, Chicago, IL 60625.

War Resisters League (WRL). A pacifist group that opposes armaments, conscription, and war. It publishes *The Nonviolent Activist* ten times a year as well as an annual peace calendar and disseminates a variety of resources on disarmament and social justice including an excellant guide on war-tax resistance. It has regional chapters nationwide. 339 Lafayette St., New York, NY 10012.

Women's International League for Peace and Freedom (WILPF). An international women's organization working for disarmament and social justice and nonviolent solutions to domestic and international problems. It publishes a magazine, *Peace and Freedom*. 1213 Race St., Philadelphia, PA 19107.

World Peacemakers. A mission group of the Church of the Savior that seeks to establish local groups both in their own churches and across denominational lines. It publishes a variety of resources on the Christian response to the arms race. 2025 Massachusetts Ave. NW, Washington, DC 20009.

NOTE: For a complete listing of 5,700 peace and justice groups and other resources see: *Peace Resource Book—A Comprehensive Guide to Issues, Groups and Literature*, edited by Elizabeth Bernstein et al (Cambridge, MA: Ballinger, 1986). Also see *The Peace Catalog*, edited by Duane Sweeney (Press for Peace, 5621 Seaview Ave. NW, Seattle, WA 98107; 1984).

Local Groups Involved in Nonviolent Resistance Actions

The following is a partial list of groups in the United States and Canada involved in organizing a variety of nonviolent resistance actions at nuclear weapons facilities, military bases, companies involved in nuclear weapons production, federal buildings, and other sites. For further information about other nonviolent resistance groups in your area contact: ALC, MFS, FOR, WRL (see preceding list) and the "Nuclear Resister," P.O. Box 43383, Tucson, AZ 85733.

Act for Disarmament Coalition, 139 Robert St., Toronto, Ontario, M5S 2KG, Canada
Ailanthus Community, c/o Haley House, 23 Dartmouth St., Cambridge, MA 02116
American Peace Test, Box 26725, Las Vegas, NV 89126
Ann Arbor Peace Community, 2122 Geddes, Ann Arbor, MI 48104
Bemidji Friends for a Nonviolent World, 1517 American Ave., Bemidji, MN 56601
Brandywine Peace Community, Box 81, Swarthmore, PA 19081
Brattleboro Atlantic Life Community, 80 Birge St., Brattleboro, VT 05301

Casa Maria, 401 E. 26th St., Tucson, AZ 85713

Catholic Action–Hawaii, 1918 University Ave., Honolulu, HI 96822

Chrysalis, 70 Adams Street, Burlington, VT 05401

Citizens for Alternatives to Trident and ELF, Box 364, Webster, WI 54893

Community for Creative Nonviolence, 1345 Euclid St. NW, Washington, DC 20009

Coalition for a Nuclear Free Harbor, 135 W. 4th St., New York, NY 10012

Coalition to Stop Trident, Box 411, New Haven, CT 06502

Chicago Life Community, 1020 S. Wabash St., Room 401, Chicago, IL 60605

Covenant for Peace, Box 1831, East Lansing, MI 48823

Cruise Missile Conversion Project, 730 Bathurst St., Toronto, Ontario M5S 2R4 Canada

Detroit Peace Community, c/o Day House, 2640 Trumbull St., Detroit, MI 48216

Disarm Now Action Group, 407 Dearborn #370, Chicago, IL 60605

Faith and Resistance Retreat, c/o Catholics for Justice, 3125 Chestnut, Kansas City, MO 64128

First Strike Prevention Project, P.O. Box 1960, San Jose, CA 95109

Florida Coalition for Peace and Justice, P.O. Box 2486, Orlando, FL 32802

Greenfields Community, 4216 Grant, Omaha, NE 68111

Ground Zero Center for Nonviolent Action, 16159 Clear Creek Rd. NW, Poulsbo, WA 98370

Groundwork for a Just World, 11224 Kercheval, Detroit, MI 48214

Honeywell Project, 1519 E. Franklin Ave., Minneapolis, MN 55404

Immanuel House, 2130 Burlington Ave. N, St. Petersburg, FL 33713

Jeremiah House, 2016 W. Moore St., Richmond, VA 23220

Jonah House, 1933 Park Ave., Baltimore, MD 21217

Kairos Community, 225 Lafayette St., Suite 207, New York, NY 10012

Knolls Action Project, 221 Central Ave., Albany, NY 12206

Livermore Action Group, 3126 Shattuck Ave., Berkeley, CA 94705

Long Island Catholic Peace Fellowship, 34 Jamaica Ave., Wyandanch, NY 11798

Los Angeles Catholic Worker, 632 N. Brittania St., Los Angeles, CA 90033

Nevada Desert Experience (NDE), P.O. Box 4487, Las Vegas, NV 89127-0487

New Hampshire Seacoast Clamshell, Box 734, Concord, NH 03301

Pax Christi Syracuse, 208 Slocum Ave., Syracuse, NY 13202

Peace House, 431 S. Weber, Colorado Springs, CO 80903

Peace Witness at GTE, c/o 136 Austin St., Worcester, MA 06109

Peacemakers of the Tri-Counties, c/o 126 N. Weadock, Saginaw, MI 48607

Resource Center for Nonviolence, P.O. Box 2524, Santa Cruz, CA 95063

Rhode Island Mobilization for Survival, Box 2534, Providence, RI 02906

River City Nonviolent Resistance Campaign, c/o Thomas Merton Center, 5125 Pennsylvania Ave., Pittsburgh, PA 15224

Rocky Mountain Peace Center, 1520 Euclid, Boulder, CO 80302
Save All Living Things, Box 810, Great Falls, MT 59403
San Jose Peace Center, 484 E. San Fernando, San Jose, CA
Silence One Silo, Box 9203, Missoula, MT 59807
Strategies and Action for Conversion, P.O. Box 283, Omaha, NE 68101
Witness for Peace at AVCO, Box 736, Wilmington, MA 01887
Witness for Disarmament, P.O. Box 181, New Haven, CT 06501
Women Rising in Resistance, P.O. Box 2096, Station A, Champaign, IL 61820
Women's Peace Encampment for a Future of Peace and Justice, 5440 Rt. 96, Romulus, NY 14541
Women's Pentagon Action Group, 339 Lafayette St., New York, NY 10012
Women of Faith, P.O. Box 14785, Hartford, CT 06114
Vandenburg Action Coalition, 273 Frederick St., San Francisco, CA 94117

NOTE: For information about nuclear weapons facilities in your area see William Arkin and Richard W. Fieldhouse, *Nuclear Battlefields* (Cambridge, Mass.: Balinger, 1985) and contact National Action-Research on the Military Industrial Complex (NARMIC), 1501 Cherry St., Philadelphia, PA 19102.

Denominational and Religious Peace and Justice Groups

Baptist

Peace Concerns Program, American Baptist Church, P.O. Box 851, Valley Forge, PA 19482-0851
Baptist Peace Fellowship, 222 East Lake Dr., Decatur, GA 30030

Brethren

Brethren Peace Fellowship, Box 455, New Windsor, MD 21776

Buddhist

Buddhist Peace Fellowship, c/o Fellowship of Reconciliation, Box 271, Nyack, NY 10960
Monks and Nuns of Nipponzan Myohoji, New England Sangha, 100 Cave Hill Road, Leverett, MA 01504

Catholic

Catholic Peace Fellowship, 339 Lafayette St., New York, NY 10012
Pax Christi USA, 348 East Tenth St., Erie, PA 16503
U.S. Catholic Conference, Office of International Justice and Peace, 1312 Massachusetts Ave. NW, Washington, DC 20005
(U.S. Catholic Bishops Pastoral Letter on War and Peace, The Challenge of Peace: God's Promise and Our Response available from the above address)

Disciples of Christ

Shalom Congregation Program, Christian Church (Disciples of Christ) 222 S. Downet St., Box 1986, Indianapolis, IN 46206

Episcopal

Episcopal Church Center, Public Issues Office, 815 Second Ave., New York, NY 10017

Episcopal Peace Fellowship, Hearst Hall, Wisconsin Ave. & Woodley Rd. NW, Washington, DC 20016

Evangelicals for Social Action, 712 G St. SE, Washington, DC 20003

Jewish

Jewish Peace Fellowship, Box 271, Nyack, NY 10960

New Jewish Agenda, 14a Church St., Suite 2 N, New York, NY 10007

The Shalom Center, Church Road & Greenwood Ave., Wyncote, PA 19095

Lutheran

American Lutheran Church, Office of Church and Society, 422 South Fifth St., Minneapolis, MN 55414

Lutheran Peace Fellowship, 2481 Como Ave. West, St. Paul, MN 55108

Methodist

General Board of Church and Society, The United Methodist Church Department of Peace and World Order, 100 Maryland Ave. NE Washington, DC 20002-5664

(Methodist Bishops Pastoral Letter "In Defense of Creation: The Nuclear Crisis and a Just Peace" Available from: Graded Press, 201 Eighth Ave. S., P.O. Box 801, Nashville, TN 37202)

United Methodist Peace Fellowship, 5123 Truman Rd., Kansas City, MO 64127

Presbyterian

Presbyterian Peacemaking Program, 475 Riverside Dr., Room 1101, New york, NY 10115

United Presbyterian Peace Fellowship, Box 271, Nyack, NY 10960

Reformed Church

Reformed Church in America, Office of Social Witness, 475 Riverside Dr. Room 1822, New York 10115

Reformed Peace Fellowship, 31 Shull Dr., Newark, DE 19177

Unitarian Universalist Peace Network, 5808 Green St., Philadelphia, PA 19144

United Church of Christ, Office for Church in Society, 110 Maryland Ave. NE, Washington, DC 20002

Groups Involved in Nonviolent Action Against U.S. Military Policy in Central America

Inter-Religious Task Force on Central America. A New York based interfaith group involved in organizing the religious community to oppose U.S. military policy in Central America. It publishes a newsletter and distributes an array of resources on Central America. 475 Riverside Dr., Room 563, New York, N.Y. 10115.

Pledge of Resistance. Begun in 1983 by a group of Christian peacemakers opposed to U.S. policy in Nicaragua, a network of over seventy-thousand people across the United States who have pledged to engage in acts of non-violent resistance if the United States invades, bombs, sends combat troops, or otherwise significantly escalates its intervention in Nicaragua or El Salvador. Many local groups have already organized local nonviolent actions to protest U.S. military policy in Central America. Contact National Resource Center of the Pledge of Resistance, P.O. Box 53411-3411, Washington, DC 20009-3411.

Sanctuary Movement. Begun in 1981, an interfaith network of over two-hundred churches and synagogues who, in defiance of U.S. immigration laws, have publicly stated their intention to shelter and transport "illegal" Central American refugees—mostly from El Salvador and Guatemala—who have fled their countries because their lives are endangered. For information about sanctuary and the legal status of refugees and sanctuary workers who have been indicted contact Chicago Religious Task Force on Central America, 407 S. Dearborn St., Room 370, Chicago, IL 60605.

Witness for Peace. An ecumenical network of faith communities throughout the United States who, over the last four years, have organized ongoing nonviolent vigils in war zones throughout Nicaragua in prayerful solidarity with the Nicaraguan people who are opposed to the U.S.-backed *contras'* attempt to overthrow the existing government. For further information contact Witness for Peace, Box 29241, Washington, DC 20017.

Groups Involved in Nonviolent Action in Latin America

Servicio Paz y Justicia (SERPAJ)—Service of Peace and Justice. An ecumenical organization based in Argentina working for the promotion and support of nonviolent movements for liberation in Latin America. For more information contact SERPAJ, Casa De La Paz, Mexico 479, 1097 Buenos Aires, Argentina.

Groups Involved in Nonviolent Resistance to Apartheid

For information concerning the nonviolent campaign in the United States to end all U.S. support for the racist South African government and abolish apartheid contact Free South Africa Movement, c/o TransAfrica, 548 8th St. SE, Washington, DC 20003.

Plowshares Disarmament Support Groups

For more information concerning ongoing Plowshares disarmament support activities contact:

Griffiss Plowshares, 106 Maywood Dr., Syracuse, NY 13205

Isaiah Peace Ministry, 66 Edgewood Ave., New Haven, CT 06511

Jonah House, 1933 Park Ave., Baltimore, MD 21217

New York Plowshares, 225 Lafayette St., Suite 207, New York, NY 10012

Richard Miller-Pantex Disarmament Action, c/o The Kindred Community, 1337 6th Ave., Des Moines, IA 50314

Pershing Plowshares Support Committee, P.O. Box 585, Orlando, FL 32802

Silo Plowshares Support Group, 5219 Lydia, Kansas City, MO 64110

Silo Pruning Hooks/Woodson Family Support Group, Gaudete Peace and Justice Center, 634 Spruce St., Madison, WI 53715

Trident II Plowshares/Pruning Hooks Support Group, Box 3291, Wayland Square, Providence, RI 02906

Witness for Peace at AVCO, Box 736, Wilmington, MA 01887

SELECTED BIBLIOGRAPHY

On Nuclear Disarmament, Nonviolence, Christian Pacificism, and Spirituality and Resistance

Aukerman, Dale. *Darkening Valley: A Biblical Perspective on Nuclear War*. New York: Winston/Seabury, 1981.

Bainton, Roland H. *Christian Attitudes Towards War and Peace*. Nashville, TN: Abingdon, 1960.

Berrigan, Daniel. *Uncommon Prayer*. New York: Winston/Seabury, 1978.

————. *Ten Commandments for the Long Haul*. Nashville, TN: Abingdon, 1981.

————. *The Nightmare of God*. Portland, OR: Sunburst, 1983.

Berrigan, Daniel, ed. *For Swords into Plowshares, The Hammer Has To Fall*. Plowshares Press, 139 Raritan Ave., Highland Park, NJ 08904, 1984.

Berrigan, Philip. *Of Beasts and Other Beastly Images: Essays Under the Bomb*. Portland, OR: Sunburst, 1978.

————. *Widen the Prison Gates*. New York: Simon and Schuster, 1973.

Bondurant, Joan V. *Conquest of Violence*. Berkeley: University of California Press, 1958.

Brandywine Peace Community. *Of the Heart and the Bread* (peace poetry). P.O. Box 81, Swarthmore, PA 19081.

Brown, Dale W., ed. *What About The Russians? A Christian Approach to U.S.–Soviet Conflict*. Elgin, IL: Brethern Press, 1984.

Caldicot, Helen. *Nuclear Madness: What You Can Do*. Brookline, MA: Autumn, 1978.

Cooney, Robert, and Helen Michalowski, eds. *The Power of the People: Active Nonviolence in the U.S*. Philadelphia, PA: New Society Publishers, 1986.

Del Vasto, Lanza. *Warriors of Peace*. New York: Knopf, 1974.

Deming, Barbara. *Prison Notes*. Boston: Beacon, 1966.

————. *We Cannot Live Without Our Lives*. New York: Grossman Publishers, 1974.

Dietrich, Jeff. *Reluctant Resister*. Greensboro, NC: Unicorn Press, 1983.

Donaghy, John. *Peacemaking and the Community of Faith*. FOR Covenant Peacemaking Program, Box 271, Nyack, NY 10960.

Douglass, James W. *The Non-Violent Cross: A Theology of Revolution and Peace*. New York: Macmillan, 1969.

————. *Resistance and Contemplation: The Way of Liberation*. New York: Dell, 1972.

————. *Lightning East to West*. New York: Crossroad, 1983.

Eagan, John P. *Baptism of Resistance, Blood and Celebration*. Mystic, CT: Twenty-Third Publications, 1983.

Ebner, Dan R., ed. *Peacemaking and Your Community: A Handbook for Local Organizers*. Fellowship of Reconciliation, Box 271, Nyack, NY 10960, 1984.

Ellsberg, Robert, ed. *By Little and by Little: The Selected Writings of Dorothy Day*. New York: Knopf, 1983.

Esquivel, Adolfo Pérez. *Christ in a Poncho: Witnesses to the Nonviolent Struggle in Latin America*. Maryknoll, NY: Orbis, 1983.

Farren, Pat, ed. *What Will It Take to Prevent Nuclear War?* Cambridge: Schenkman, 1983.

Ferguson, John. *The Politics of Love—The New Testament and Non-Violent Revolution*. Greenwood, SC: Attic Press, 1976.

Gandhi, Mohandas K. *Non-Violent Resistance*. New York: Schocken, 1967.

Grannis, J. Christopher, Arthur J. Laffin, and Elin Schade. *The Risk of the Cross: Christian Discipleship in the Nuclear Age*. New York: Winston/Seabury, 1981.

Graybill, Beth, Marilyn McDonald, and Bill Price. *Building Christian Community: Pursuing Peace with Justice*. World Peacemakers, 2025 Massachusetts Ave. NW, Washington, DC 20036.

Gregg, Richard B. *The Power of Nonviolence*. Nyack, NY: Fellowship Publications, 1959.

Hentoff, Nat, ed. *The Essays of A. J. Muste*. New York: Simon and Schuster, 1967.

King, Martin Luther, Jr. *Why We Can't Wait*. New York: Harper & Row, 1963.

————. *Where Do We Go From Here?* New York: Harper & Row, 1967.

————. *Strength to Love*. Philadelphia: Fortress, 1982.

Knopp, Fay, et al. *Instead of Prisons*. Brooklyn, NY: Faculty Press, 1976.

Kownacki, Mary Lou, ed. *A Race to Nowhere: An Arms Race Primer for Catholics*. Chicago: Pax Christi, 1980.

Lynd, Staughton, ed. *Nonviolence in America: A Documentary History*. New York: Bobbs-Merrill, 1966.

McAllister, Pam. *Reweaving the Web of Life: Feminism and Nonviolence*. Philadelphia: New Society, 1982.

McSorley, Richard. *Kill For Peace?* Washington, DC: Center for Peace Studies, Georgetown University, 1978.

———. *New Testament Basis of Peacemaking*. Washington, DC: Center for Peace Studies, Georgetown University, 1978.

McGinnis, James and Kathleen. *Parenting for Peace and Justice*. Maryknoll, NY: Orbis, 1981.

Merton, Thomas. *Faith and Violence*. Notre Dame, IN: University of Notre Dame Press, 1968.

———. *Gandhi on Non-Violence*. New York: New Directions, 1965.

Priestley, Denise. *Bringing Forth in Hope: Being Creative in a Nuclear Age*. New York: Paulist, 1983.

Rockman, Jane, ed. *Peace in Search of Makers: Riverside Church Reverse the Arms Race Convocation*. Valley Forge, PA: Judson, 1979.

Sharp, Gene. *Making Europe Unconquerable: The Potential of Civilian-based Deterrence and Defense*. Cambridge, MA: Ballinger, 1985.

———. *National Security Through Civilian-Based Defense*. Omaha, NE: Association for Transarmament Studies, 1985.

———. *The Politics of Nonviolent Action*. Boston: Porter Sargent, 1973.

Shelly, Maynard. *New Call for Peacemakers: A New Call to Peacemaking Study Guide*. Newton, KS: Faith and Life, 1979.

Sölle, Dorothee. *Of War and Love*. Maryknoll, NY: Orbis, 1981.

Stringfellow, William. *An Ethic for Christians and Other Aliens in a Strange Land*. Waco, TX: Word, 1973.

———. *Conscience and Obedience*. Waco, TX: Word, 1977.

———. *Politics of Spirituality*. Philadelphia: Westminster Press, 1984.

Taylor, Richard, and Ronald Sider. *Nuclear Holocaust and Christian Hope*. Downers Grove, IL: Intervarsity, 1982.

Thompson, E. P. *Protest and Survive*. New York: Monthly Review Press, 1981.

Wallis, Jim, ed. *Waging Peace*. New York: Harper & Row, 1982.

———. *Peacemakers*. San Francisco: Harper & Row, 1983.

———. *Rise of Christian Conscience*. San Francisco, Harper & Row, 1987.

Weber, David, R., ed. *Civil Disobedience in America: A Documentary History*. Ithaca, NY: Cornell University Press, 1978.

Welsher, Karl, ed. *Violence Ends Where Love Begins*. Tolstoi House Community, P.O. Box 102, Lake Worth, FL 33460.

Yoder, John H. *The Politics of Jesus*. Grand Rapids, MI: Eerdmans, 1972.

Zahn, Gordon. *In Solitary Witness*. Boston: Beacon, 1964.

———. *In Solitary Witness*. Templegate, 1986 (new edition).

On the Politics, History, and Consequences of Nuclear Weapons and the Nuclear Arms Race

Adams, Gordon. *The Politics of Defense Contracting: The Iron Triangle*. New Brunswick, NJ: Transaction, 1982.

Aldridge, Robert J. *The Counterforce Syndrome: A Guide to U.S. Nuclear Weapons and Strategic Doctrine*. Washington, DC: Transnational Institute, 1978.

————. *First Strike*. Boston: South End, 1983.

Alperowitz, Gar. *Atomic Diplomacy*. New York: Viking/Penguin, 1985.

Arkin, William, and Richard W. Fieldhouse. *Nuclear Battlefields*. Cambridge, MA: Ballinger, 1985.

Arkin, William, and Peter Pringle. *S.I.O.P.—The Secret U.S. Plan for Nuclear War*. New York: Norton, 1983.

Bamford, James. *The Puzzle Palace—A Report on the National Security Agency, America's Most Secret Agency*. Boston: Houghton Mifflin, 1982.

Barnet, Richard. *Roots of War*. Baltimore: Penguin, 1971.

————. *The Giants: Russia and America*. New York: Simon and Schuster, 1977.

Bertell, Rosalie. *No Immediate Danger: Prognosis for a Radioactive Future*. London: Women's Press, 1985.

Boston Study Group. *The Price of Defense*. New York: Times Books, 1979.

Caldicott, Helen. *Missile Envy: The Arms Race and Nuclear War*. New York: Morrow, 1984.

Cloud, Kate, et al. *Watermelons Not War: A Support Book for Parenting in the Nuclear Age*. Philadelphia: New Society, 1984.

Erhlich, Paul R., Carl Sagan, et al. *The Cold and the Dark: The World After Nuclear War*. New York: Norton, 1984.

Faculty of Massachusetts Institute of Technology, eds. *The Nuclear Almanac*. Reading, MA: Addison-Wesley, 1984.

Gerson, Joseph, ed., *The Deadly Connection: Nuclear War and U.S. Intervention*. Philadelphia: New Society, 1986.

Green, Mark and Gail MacColl, *Ronald Reagan's Reign of Error*. New York: Pantheon, 1983.

Gyorgy, Anna, et al. *No Nukes: Everyone's Guide to Nuclear Power*. Boston: South End, 1979.

Herken, Gregg. *The Winning Weapon—The Atomic Bomb in the Cold War 1945–1950*. New York: Vintage, 1982.

————. *Counsels of War*. New York: Knopf, 1985.

Hersey, John. *Hiroshima*. New York: Knopf, 1946.

Kennan, George F. *The Nuclear Delusion*. New York: Pantheon, 1976.

Lens, Sidney. *The Day Before Doomsday: An Anatomy of the Nuclear Arms Race*. Boston: Beacon, 1977.

————. *The Bomb*. New York: Dutton, 1982.

Lifton, Robert J. *Death in Life—Survivors of Hiroshima*. New York: Simon and Schuster, 1967.

Lifton, Robert J., and Richard Falk. *Indefensible Weapons: The Political and Psychological Case Against Nuclearism*. New York: Basic Books, 1982.

Loeb, Paul. *Nuclear Culture*. Philadelphia: New Society, 1986.

Macy, Joanna Rogers. *Despair and Personal Power in the Nuclear Age*. Philadelphia: New Society, 1983.

Melman, Seymour. *The Permanent War Economy*. New York: Simon and Schuster, 1974.

Sampson, Anthony. *The Arms Bazaar: From Lebanon to Lockheed*. New York: Bantam, 1973.

Scheer, Robert. *With Enough Shovels: Reagan, Bush and Nuclear War*. New York: Random House, 1982.

Schell, Jonathan. *The Fate of the Earth*. New York: Knopf, 1981.

Sivard, Ruth Leger. *World Military and Social Expenditures 1985*. World Priorities, Box 25140, Washington, DC 20007.

Spector, Leonard S. *Nuclear Proliferation Today*. New York: Random House, 1984.

Wasserman, Harvey, Norman Solomon, et al. *Killing Our Own—The Disaster of America's Experience With Atomic Radiation*. New York: Delta, 1982.

On U.S. Foreign Policy, Central America, and Liberation Theology

Barnet, Richard. *Intervention and Revolution*. New York: World, 1968.

Berrigan, Daniel. *Steadfastness of the Saints—A Journal of Peace and War in Central and North America*. Maryknoll, NY: Orbis, 1985.

Boesak, Allan. *Black and Reformed*. Maryknoll, NY: Orbis, 1984.

Boff, Leonardo. *Ecclesiogenesis: The Base Communities Reinvent the Church*. Maryknoll, NY: Orbis, 1986.

Bonner, Robert. *Weakness and Deceit: U.S. Policy and El Salvador*. New York: Times Books, 1984.

Brockman, James R. *The Word Remains: A Life Of Oscar Romero*. Maryknoll, NY: Orbis, 1982.

Brody, Reed. *Contra Terror in Nicaragua*. Boston: South End, 1986.

Burgos, Elizabeth, ed. *I, Rigoberta Menchu: Indian Women in Guatemala*. New York: Schocken, 1983.

Cabestrero, Teófilo. *Blood of the Innocent: Victims of the Contras' War in Nicaragua*. Maryknoll, NY: Orbis, 1986.

Clements, Charles, M.D. *Witness to War: An American Doctor in El Salvador*. New York: Bantam, 1984.

Chomsky, Noam, et al. *The Washington Connection and Third World Fascism*. Boston: South End, 1979.

Chomsky, Noam. *Turning the Tide*. Boston: South End, 1985.

Combelin, José. *The Church and the National Security State*. Maryknoll, NY: Orbis, 1979.

Cone, James H. *A Black Theology of Liberation*. 2d ed. Maryknoll, NY: Orbis, 1986.

Dilling, Yvonne, with Ingrid Rogers. *In Search of Refuge*. Scottsdale, PA: Herald, 1984.

Golden, Renny, and Michael McConnell. *Sanctuary: The New Underground Railroad*. Maryknoll, NY: Orbis, 1986.

Gutierrez, Gustavo. *A Theology of Liberation*. Maryknoll, NY: Orbis, 1974.

———. *We Drink from Our Own Wells*. Maryknoll, NY: Orbis, 1984.

Harding, Vincent. *There Is a River: The Black Struggle for Freedom in America*. New York: Vintage, 1981.

Hollyday, Joyce, ed. *Crucible of Hope: A Study Guide for Churches on Central America*. Sojourners Book Service, Box 29272, Washington, DC 20017; 1984.

LaFeber, Walter. *Inevitable Revolutions*. New York: Norton, 1983.

Lernoux, Penny. *Cry of the People: The Struggle for Human Rights in Latin America—The Catholic Church in Conflict with U.S. Policy*. New York: Penguin, 1982.

MacEoin, Gary, ed. *Sanctuary*. San Francisco: Harper & Row, 1985.

Nouwen, Henri. *Love in a Fearful Land: A Guatemalan Story*. Notre Dame, IN: Ave Maria, 1985.

Schlesinger, Stephen, and Stephen Kinser. *Bitter Fruit: The Untold Story of the American Coup in Guatemala*. New York: Anchor Press/Doubleday, 1982.

Tutu, Desmond. *Hope and Suffering: Sermons and Speeches*. Grand Rapids, MI: Eerdmans, 1984.

Zinn, Howard. *A People's History of the United States*. New York: Harper Colophon, 1980.

———. *The Twentieth Century*. New York: Harper Colophon, 1985.

PERIODICALS

Articles on the arms race, nuclear disarmament, U.S. intervention policy, and nonviolent resistance can be found in the following publications:

The Alert-Focus on Central America. 19 W. 21 St., 2nd floor, New York, NY 10010.

Baptist Peacemaker. Deer Park Church, 1733 Bardstown Rd., Louisville, KY 40205.

The Bulletin of the Atomic Scientists. 1020-24 E. 58th St., Chicago, IL 60637.

Catholic Agitator. Los Angeles Catholic Worker, 632 N. Britania St., Los Angeles, CA 90033.

CCCO News Notes. Central Committee for Conscientious Objectors, 2208 South St. Philadelphia, PA 19146.

Catholic Worker. 36 E. First St., New York, NY 10003.

Christian Century. 407 S. Dearborn St., Chicago, IL 60605.

Christianity and Crisis. 537 W. 121st St., New York, NY 10027.

Fellowship. Fellowship of Reconciliation, Box 271, Nyack, NY 10960.

Ground Zero. 16159 Clear Creek Rd. NW, Poulsbo, WA 98370.

The Mobilizer. Mobilization for Survival, 853 Broadway, Room 418, New York, NY 10003.

Mother Jones. 1663 Mission St., San Francisco, CA 94103.

The Nation. 72 Fifth Ave., New York, NY 10011.

National Catholic Reporter. P.O. Box 41928, Kansas City, MO 64141.

The New People. The Thomas Merton Center, 5125 Pennsylvania Ave., Pittsburgh, PA 15224.

Nonviolent Activist. War Resisters League, 339 Lafayette St., New York, NY 10012.

Nuclear Resister. P.O. Box 43383, Tucson, AZ 85733.

Nuclear Times. 1755 Massachusetts Ave., Fifth Floor, Washington, DC 20036

Peacework. American Friends Service Committee, 2161 Massachusetts Ave., Cambridge, MA 02140.

Plowshares Newsletter. Pershing Plowshares Support Committee, P.O. Box 585, Orlando, FL 32802.

The Progressive. 408 West Gorham St., Madison, WI 53703.

Reconciliation International. International Fellowship of Reconciliation, Hof Van Sonoy 15-17, 1811 LD, Alkmaar, the Netherlands.

Sojourners. Sojourners Community, Box 29272, Washington, DC 20017.

Weapons Facilities Network Bulletin. Mobilization for Survival, 853 Broadway, Room 418, New York, NY 10003.

Year One. Jonah House, 1933 Park Ave., Baltimore, MD 21217.

AUDIOVISUAL RESOURCES

The films and slide shows listed below are excellent educational resources on the nuclear threat, disarmament, Central America, and nonviolent resistance. For a complete listing of other audiovisual resources contact the University of Michigan Media Resource Center, 400 Fourth St., Ann Arbor, MI 48103 (published *1984 National Directory of Audiovisual Resources on Nuclear War and the Arms Race*) and the War Resisters League, 339 Lafayette St., New York, NY 10012 (published *1987 Peace Calendar* which lists over 150 films with scenes of peace and justice and addresses of 112 distributors).

"America's in Transition." A 29-minute film powerfully depicting U.S. involvement in Latin America during this century. Available from Office of Community Development Program Agency, Room 1254, 475 Riverside Dr., New York, NY 10115 (other audiovisual resources on Central America are also available from this organization).

"The Arms Race Within." An outstanding 60-minute documentary about the Agape Communities' nonviolent campaign to stop the transport of nuclear weapons by the "nuclear train." Available from Idanha Films, Inc., 6027 La Vista Dr., Dallas, TX 75206.

"Be Not Afraid." A superb 26-minute film documenting the events of the Peace Pentecost witness in 1983 sponsored by Sojourners from the worship service of 2500 people to the civil disobedience action at the Capitol Rotunda and the arrests of 242 people. Available from Sojourners, Box 29272, Washington, DC 20017.

"Choice or Chance?" An excellent slide show on the draft, registration, and military recruitment. Available from Registration/Draft Media Project of the American Friends Service Committee, 2160 Lake St., San Francisco, CA 94121.

"The Day After Trinity: J. Robert Oppenheimer and the Atomic Bomb." An 88-minute film profiling J. Robert Oppenheimer, the developer of the first nuclear weapons and examining how he became the architect of the secret Manhattan Project. It includes interviews with his family, friends, and colleagues. Available from Pyramid Films, P.O. Box 1048, Santa Monica, CA 90406.

"Every Heart Beats True: Christian Perspectives on Military Service." A 20-

minute film strip examining the teachings of Jesus, the peace witness of early Christians, the nature of military service today, and the response of contemporary Christians. Available from Packard Manse Media Project, Box 450, Staughton, MA 02072.

"For Life"- A compelling 29-minute slide show which traces the evolution of the nuclear crisis and discusses how people of faith can stop the nuclear arms race. Available from Sojourners, Box 29272, Washington, DC 20017.

"Gods of Metal." An exceptional 28-minute film about the faith, economic, social, and human cost of the arms race presented from a Christian perspective. Available from Maryknoll Films, Maryknoll, NY 10545.

"Healing the Wounds." A 30-minute slide show graphically depicting the tremendous repression in Guatemala, the life of the poor and sick, and the attempts of health care workers who have risked their lives to meet their needs. Available from Guatemala Health Rights Support Project, 1747 Connecticut Ave. NW, Washington, DC 20009.

"Hiroshima," "Nagasaki." Films depicting the 1945 atomic destruction of these two Japanese cities. They include live footage of these cities immediately after the bombing. Available from Wilmington College, Wilmington, OH 45177.

"In the King of Prussia." A 92-minute film dramatically reenacting the trial of Plowshares Eight who were convicted for their disarmament action at GE's King of Prussia, Pennsylvania, plant in September 1980. The defendants play themselves and Martin Sheen plays the judge. For further information about obtaining this film contact: Jonah House, 1933 Park Ave., Baltimore, MD 21217 or Emile DeAntonio, Box 1567, New York, NY 10017.

"The New Underground Railroad." A 30-minute film tracing the journey of a family in El Salvador to sanctuary in the United States and documenting the process of a congregation in Madison, Wisconsin, deciding to declare itself a sanctuary. Available from Audiovisual Center, Indiana University, Bloomington, IN 47405.

"The Trial of the AVCO Plowshares." A 75-minute color video documentary about the jury trial of the AVCO Plowshares who were convicted of wanton destruction and trespass as a result of their disarmament action at the AVCO Systems Division in Wilmington, Massachusetts on July 14, 1983. This documentary contains live footage of the trial proceedings including the testimony of defendants and expert witnesses such as Daniel Ellsberg, Howard Zinn, Retired Admiral Gene LaRocque, and Dr. Richard Falk. Available on $\frac{1}{2}$ inch VHS or Beta and $\frac{3}{4}$ inch from Global Village, 454 Broome St., New York, 10013.

"Paul Jacobs and the Nuclear Gang." A film about how civilians and soldiers were exposed to the atomic tests of the 1950s with a particular focus on Paul Jacobs, a journalist, who died from leukemia in 1978. Available from Donnelly/Colt, Box 188, Hampton, CT 06247.

"War Without Winners II." A 28-minute film showing how people think and feel about the nuclear threat both in the United States and the Soviet Union. It also includes interviews with military experts of the Reagan administration and former military personnel advocating disarmament. Available from Films Inc./PMI, 8214 N. Central Pkwy., Skokie, IL 60076.

"What Soviet Children Are Saying About Nuclear War." A 22-minute film in which Soviet young people are interviewed by American doctors about their awareness of the nuclear threat, their fears of nuclear war, and their hopes for peace. Available from Educational Film and Video Project, 1725 Seabright Ave., Santa Cruz, CA 95062.